PRAISE FOR *THEY SAY*

"*They Say* is a down-to-Earth, no shame, guilt-free guide for new and expecting parents! As a mom of three, I could relate to this all too well, and love her approach to parenting. Lauren accurately expresses many of the common emotions and frustrations of being a new parent. She makes you feel like you're not alone in this parenting journey, and reminds you that though we all make mistakes and all feel guilt, we're all doing the best we can."
   -**Stefanie Eadie**, fashion and lifestyle blogger, *According to Blaire*, www.accordingtoblaire.com

"Lauren Jumrukovski shares her own honest journey through early motherhood, and reminds all moms to trust their intuitions while raising tiny humans. Relatable and heartfelt, *They Say* will leave readers with a reassuring message—*Mama knows best!*"
   -**Kristin Helms**, author of *From Boardroom to Baby: A Roadmap for Career Women Transitioning to Stay-at-Home Moms*

"From bringing a newborn home from the hospital to feeding, potty-training, disciplining, venturing out of the house, housework, relationships, recharging as an individual, and much more, Lauren writes openly and honestly about her experiences as a mom. While Lauren shares personal experiences as well as tips and strategies that worked for her family, she is quick to point out that what worked for her might not be what works for others. Lauren's anti-guilt approach to parenting is refreshing and reassuring. From the advice she received from well-intended family, friends, acquaintances, and even strangers, to the challenges, successes, and amusing anecdotes she never dreamed of before motherhood, *They Say* encourages new parents to trust their instincts and do what works best for the parent and child."

   -*Sharon Neeley*, child care director

"As a new mother, this book is so refreshing! The 'they says' of this world constantly surround new parents, and it's often hard to know who to listen to or what advice to heed. *They Say* reminds parents that we are exactly who our children need. Lauren provides her honest thoughts and raw emotions she faces as a parent, all while offering practical tips for addressing the challenging moments. Above all, she reminds parents to confidently listen to our God-given intuition and to stand firmly in the joys and decisions of parenting, free of guilt and comparison. Not only has this book helped me keep a sound mind as I navigate the adjustments of becoming a parent, but it's also reminded me to see the beauty in both the good and the hard parts of raising a child."

   -*Callie Simmers*, licensed in K-12 special education and K-6 elementary education

"In *They Say,* Lauren writes to parents all over the globe, succeeding at promoting a culture of respect and tolerance when it comes to parenting, and encouraging new parents to follow their instincts."

   -Maria Rooney, former elementary school teacher and current pre-K teacher

"Lauren Jumrukovski does a fantastic job of normalizing intense emotions all parents face, and encourages parents to persevere and let go of the 'mommy guilt.' *They Say* focuses on trusting yourself as a parent and doing what you think is best for your family. It reminds us all to focus on the present and accept the impossibility of perfection. This book offers insightful tips from breastfeeding, to potty-training, to the transition from having one child to having multiple, and so much more!"

   -Erin Austin, Licensed Clinical Social Worker (LCSW), Early Intervention Professional (EIP)

"*They Say* is a real-life journey through the many joys and struggles of parenting. It's full of great ideas and common sense approaches to keep your new baby happy and healthy, while still keeping in mind your needs as a new parent. Filled with amusing and heartwarming stories from her own experiences, Lauren has gone far beyond your average parenting book."

   -Christy Sandefur, registered nurse

www.mascotbooks.com

They Say

Although the author and publisher have made every effort to ensure that the information in this book was correct at press time, the author and publisher do not assume and hereby disclaim any liability to any party for any loss, damage, or disruption caused by errors or omissions, whether such errors or omissions result from negligence, accident, or any other cause.

This book is not intended as a substitute for the medical advice of physicians. The reader should regularly consult a physician in matters relating to his/her health as well as the health of his/her children, and particularly with respect to any symptoms that may require diagnosis or medical attention.

Author photograph on page 307 by Kristie Bradley Photography

For more information, please contact:
Mascot Books
620 Herndon Parkway #320
Herndon, VA 20170
info@mascotbooks.com

Icons from Made by Made
the Noun Project

Library of Congress Control Number: 2019902177

CPSIA Code: PRFRE0519A
ISBN-13: 978-1-64307-111-4

Printed in Canada

For Renee, the very best kind of mom and friend. On Earth, she was an angel among us. She left us far too soon, but her love lives on in those she touched.

CONTENTS

PREFACE

A poem I wrote to my husband when our second child was seven months old:

Remember When...

Remember when we used to stay up late? Even until 1:00 a.m. plus, and then sleep in the following morning?

Remember when we used to wake up in the morning and relax in bed watching cooking shows (of all things) until whenever?

Remember when we would run to the store to get the ingredients for any recipe at the drop of a hat, and it took no time at all?

Remember when I went to the grocery store instead of you always having to go?

...when our grocery bill was substantially less because it didn't include diapers, formula, or baby food?

Remember when Daisy (our dog) was our baby?

Remember when we could watch hours of TV or movies

from the moment we returned home from work until we went to sleep if we wanted, all while snuggled up on the couch?

...when we used to eat dinners in front of the TV and take our time?

...when we could watch an entire show or movie without falling asleep?

Remember when we used to workout, sometimes even together?

...when we used to go out and party? Or even leave the house at all?

...when we used to dress up for Halloween?

Remember when our house was clean?

...when people would drop by and we wouldn't need to rush around throwing the mess into closets before opening the door?

Remember when we could go to the dentist or doctor anytime without a babysitter?

Remember when we could pack light?

Remember when we vacationed, just the two of us...Vegas?

...when we could shower (and heck, even use the bathroom) anytime we wanted to for as long as we wanted?

...when our dinners didn't always include a fruit?

...when our conversations each day didn't include the words "poop," "mess," or "potty?"

...when our medicine cabinet wasn't overflowing with children's medications?

Remember when we didn't sleep with the ever-present sound of baby monitors?

Silence—what's that?

Remember when we could make an eight to ten hour trip to New York easy, and even enjoy it while talking?

...or when we used to talk, period?

Remember when we traveled without a diaper bag?

Remember when we felt rested?

...when laundry was quick?

...when we could always brush our teeth in the morning and get ready?

Remember when we had a sports car?

Remember when I didn't say, "I'm worried about..." daily?

...when life didn't revolve around naps?

Oh, but don't you love it when...

When the kids smile? Especially when it is purposely at you?

When they speak in their sweet little voices?

When our daughter says, "CJ just gave me a little kiss?"

When our kids hug each other?

When our daughter calls out, "Mommy" or "Daddy" when she wakes up?

...and seeing that sweet little smile when we go get her?

When we are sad and the kids tell us everything is going to be okay and give us a big hug?

When they say something so polite and you think, *Wow, I must have done something right?*

When we watch our sweet babies sleep?

When they learn...

To walk

To crawl

To stand

To say their first word (and every other word thereafter)

To sing

To dance

To jump

To run

To feed themselves

When you feel so proud because our kids did something amazing?

When you smell that sweet baby smell?

When our daughter tells us, "You are the sweetest Mommy and Daddy in the whole world?"

When we get to celebrate our birthdays as a family?

When we go to special places and vacations together as a family?

When we get to enjoy holidays as a family and see the joy on the kids' faces?

When our children were born. Oh, the love you feel in that moment when you first see those sweet faces and hold them for the first time?

...and the love every moment after?

When we wonder, *What did I do so right in my life to be blessed with such amazing children?*

When we fall in love all over again seeing each other interact with the children?

When we get to kiss those sweet rolls and chubby cheeks?

When our daughter rubs our back or when our son hugs us tight?

When we watch our children interact with their grandparents?

When our daughter says, "I love you Mommy; I love you Daddy; I love you CJ?"

When we watch our kids play together?

When they hold our hands with those tiny little fingers?

When our daughter runs to us when we come home or when our son's eyes light up and he kicks those chubby legs?

When our daughter "reads" a book she has somehow memorized?

When we get to snuggle with one of the kids, or better yet, both at the same time?

When we hear the children laugh? Oh, it is the best sound in the world.

When the kids fall asleep on us?

When we get to watch a kids movie or show, cuddled up on the couch as a family?

When we can teach the kids something new?

When they ride on our backs?

When we watch them enjoy gifts, toys, the pool—anything?

When we think about all the amazing times, experiences, trips, and firsts to come?

"They say" parenting is hard. When you have a child, things are definitely going to change. Things are definitely going to be challenging—impossible even—but for me, it has all been worth it. At the end of the day, I prefer the second list, and I wouldn't trade our new life for anything.

INTRODUCTION

*The Ordinary Mom...Psst...You're Actually Extraordinary
(Worries, Mistakes, and All)*

I am just an ordinary mom. Sure, I received a Bachelor's of Science degree and a Master of Education degree, but I don't have a special background in parenting. I'm someone who has made mistakes, but has done some pretty great things too, and so will you.

If you are a parent—and that includes those of you who are expecting—you have already heard many pieces of advice. You will hear the term "they say" quite a bit throughout this book. I have received information about parenting from family, friends, the internet, television...the list goes on and on. In today's world, you have the internet at your fingertips. Literally, you click a button on your phone, and *voila:* you can search for any answers you need. When today's mom has a problem or an issue going on with their child, I'll bet the first thing most of us do is grab the phone and search for answers. When we do this, we are flooded with information. It may be information which makes us feel like we did the wrong thing based on what we have already tried, or it might make us feel like we did exactly the right thing...well, that is until we open the next article to find the exact opposite answer. Thus, there we are, once again feeling like we did the wrong thing. Well, one thing is for sure, if you research enough, the internet will always succeed at making you feel bad, no matter what you chose to do in any given situation. I feel like I am always feeling guilty about something (mommy guilt is a real thing) and almost everything I read ends up making me feel bad. Before having easy access to the internet, I believe parents relied on their doctor, maybe a book or two, and their own intuition to inform them if they were doing the right thing or maybe to try something different. Nowadays, there is nothing which makes us question that intuition more than social media and the internet. There are so many rules and opinions, it is impossible to know what is best.

Parenting can be scary. I started chatting with a lady on a flight once about parenting. She was a social worker who worked with children and parents. I will never forget when she said, "The truth is, parents are the only thing between infants and death." This may seem extreme when you first hear it, but we really do have a huge responsibility to take care of our babies. They have no ability to take care of themselves. We have to feed them, clothe them, and help them fall asleep. All of these things are essential to their well-being. Along these lines, my dad once said, "Just one second here, or a couple inches there, could be catastrophe." It's true! So, we don't need the internet to make us feel any worse. We already have enough on which to focus.

The internet makes us question ourselves as parents, and makes us question if we are doing the right things to raise our children. It is not only the internet. Sometimes, even when we speak with other parents, friends even, we can feel judged or we might immediately start comparing ourselves with how they parent, which can also make us feel less than great. I have found that I compare myself to others way too often. Did I breastfeed long enough? Am I disciplining my children correctly? Is letting my child "cry it out" at night wrong? Is it wrong that I am a working mom? Is it wrong that I am now a stay-at-home mom? I feel like I am constantly wondering if I am doing the right thing for my kids. Over time, I have learned that just because people do things differently than you, it does not mean you are doing it wrong. Comparing ourselves to others almost always makes us feel like that is the case.

I believe there are two things which cause "mommy guilt" more than anything else. They are listening to what "they say," and comparing ourselves to others. This is why it is so important for today's parent to trust your gut, trust your pediatrician, and continue to believe that you are doing a great job as a parent, no matter what.

The internet and what "they say" can give us anxiety because it makes us think there is one right way to do things, but there is no "one right way." Let's take this expectation out of the equation so we don't constantly feel like failures and can start trusting our instincts.

Sometimes, you have to go with your gut and use your mommy intuition. You know what is best for your child and for your situation. We can't always believe what "they say." Take the advice that comes your way with a grain of salt. Try what makes sense, but in the end, do what works best for your baby and for you. After all, mom (or dad) knows best. The only thing "they say" which I believe to be 100 percent true is that parenting isn't easy. I don't believe parenting is black and white. It's a lot of grey and a lot of what works for you. Again, I am just an ordinary mom—no doctor, no psychologist, just a mom—but even though we might be ordinary, we really can be extraordinary moms. Parenting is not an easy job, but you will do great things. The fact you are even reading a parenting book, are looking for answers, or even just worrying means you care. This is what makes a great mom—a little bit of TLC: tender loving care.

I believe moms are supposed to look mature. I am a parent of three, but I look at myself many days and still feel like a teenager. Believe it or not, I was even asked when I interned in an elementary school if I was a student. Sometimes, I ask myself, *Am I really mature enough to be a parent? I am still young myself.* Yet, each day I take care of those babies and all in all they are doing great. There are some tough days. There may even be days where I start to wonder why I had children in the first place. You cannot possibly love every single moment of being a parent, and it is important to realize that this is okay. I especially recall a particular day where I felt pretty down about my parenting skills.

My youngest at the time, my son, had reflux. My toddler, my daughter, was in the throes of potty training at the time. I thought, *I can go out really quick with the kids and pick up my son's new antibiotic.* For some reason, the previous antibiotic caused his reflux to flare up big time. I called the pharmacy to check on the prescription. "Oh yes, we received the prescription, we will have it ready in ten minutes," they said. "They said." That's the key word. I get the kids all ready and load them into the van. I pull into the parking lot of the pharmacy and am about to go inside when my phone rings.

"Mrs. Jumrukovski, we actually do not have any more of the antibiotic here. You can go to another pharmacy."

I asked, "Which pharmacy and how long will it take?"

"Oh, it shouldn't take too long."

I asked, "Can you call them and make sure it is ready in ten minutes?"

Silence.

I continued, "I have a potty-training two-year-old in the car and a baby. As you can see, I am in quite a rush."

"Okay, we will call."

I arrive at the new pharmacy and see that the line is really long. My daughter is in the back saying, "Mommy, can I please have some chicken nuggets?" Yes, I have bribed her with chicken nuggets in the past and she remembers. I swear, they remember *everything.*

"Sure honey." I thought, *By the time I get back, the line won't be as long.* So, I venture on to the Wendy's. The drive-through is extremely backed up and not moving an inch, when my son begins to scream. This "reflux" scream is like nothing I have ever heard. I mean, it is so loud, they can probably hear it inside the restaurant. So, I say, "I am so sorry sweetie, we cannot get chicken nuggets today."

Wrong answer! We go from one crying child to two in the matter of two seconds flat.

I race back to the pharmacy. There is now one car there, but it is the same car as I saw in line before. I wait, and wait, and wait some more. My daughter is whining and my son is still making screaming sounds like those from a horror film. As a car blocks me in, I think, *Oh dear, I will never get out of here now. I am stuck.* The panic begins to set in. Finally, I cannot stand the screaming another second. I get out of the vehicle, open my son's van door and begin trying to calm him down. Nothing works. Now, the fumes are collecting between the building and the van door, my ankles are getting so hot they start to feel like they will burn, and here comes the worry: *Oh no, could my son be breathing this stuff in?* I shut the van door and get back into the driver's seat. I try singing, storytelling, and asking my daughter, "Lili, can you talk to your brother?" Nothing works.

At this point, ten minutes have gone by. I roll down the window in a panic and literally scream, "What is going on?!" I start banging my hands on the steering wheel. I am about to lose my mind. Another two minutes pass and the car in front of me leaves. I did not even see them get a prescription. Maybe they were scared of my screaming—oops. The young pharmacy tech with possibly no clue how it feels to be stuck in the car with two screaming children and no hope of escape asks, "How can I help you?" There was no "I apologize you had to wait for 15 minutes in the drive-through."

I let him have it. "Last name Jumrukovski, and the prescription better be ready because I have been sitting here blocked in for 15 minutes with two crying children." I say this as my son continues to scream in the backseat.

He races off to get the prescription and I somehow have it in hand within 30 seconds. Now, I have my prescription and am feeling quite bad for being so rude and crazy, and my son is still screaming. I realize it is about time for him to eat; he is probably hungry. I park in a parking spot, take him out of his seat, and nurse him. He eats and I hope he will be okay to make it home now. The entire time I am nursing him, I try to distract my daughter by playing a game of "I spy," all the while thinking, *Please, please do not say you need to go potty, or worse even, please do not have an accident.* I put my son back into his car seat and he began screaming again, but worse than before, if that is even possible. I try to remain calm as I listen to the screaming for the entire 20-minute ride home. We made it home luckily without incident...or accident. By this point, I still hadn't learned to simply take a small potty seat along in the car. This would have made the trip a lot less worrisome. More potty-training "fun" to come later.

As I tell my dad the story, he says, "When you turn on the news later, we will probably see the headline, 'Crazy and aggressive woman spotted in the pharmacy drive-through.'" I sure hope not, however, the way things have been going, I would not be surprised!

These moments may sound horrible, and in the moment may even feel horrible, but afterwards I usually get a good laugh. I hope you get a good laugh at some of these stories throughout this book. Crazy experiences like these have taught me a lot.

They have taught me to make sure to take a portable potty seat along on any trip. They have taught me how to unhook a car seat with just one hand. Okay, but in all seriousness, they have taught me not to sweat the small stuff. They have taught me not to take things so seriously. They have taught me that just because I have bad moments here or there, it does not make me a bad mom; we are all human. Most of all, experiences like these have taught me what it really means to be a mom. I never knew how much time I would spend sitting on a bathroom floor, while my child goes potty. I never knew I would cry so many tears over silly things. I never knew how much I would be able to give, but all the while still feel guilty because it never felt like enough. Even though I feel I waited my whole life to become a mom, I never knew how often I would feel like I was horrible at it. I never knew how much I would grow to appreciate a minivan. I never knew how many times I would ask, "Should I call the doctor?" I never knew the volume of ridiculous statements that would leave my mouth.

"Don't put that pea in your nose."

"Can you stop grabbing your wee-wee? You are going to scratch it."

"Is that poop or chocolate?"

"Don't eat out of the trash can!" (I said this to a 13-month-old.)

"Don't grab her butt."

"Why does our house smell like poop?"

"Pee-pee goes in the potty."

"Don't stand on the table."

"No, you cannot eat the single red goldfish you found under the couch from who-knows-when."

"Get your hands out of your pants."

I never knew how much time I would spend wondering if my child ate enough, drank enough, slept enough, got to play with me enough, or even if they pooped enough. I never knew I would spend so much of my day smelling butts and wondering, *Did he poop or just poot?* I never knew how often I would use the word "poop" in general. In fact, based on the number of times words are used, the autocorrect on my phone even seems to automatically change most of the words I type to the word "poop." The amount of times I have invited my friends to a "poop party" instead of a "pool party" is ridiculous. Oh, the life of a mom. Don't worry though—times like these have also taught me that in between the rough spots, there will be lots and lots of good stuff. Also, most importantly, I never knew just how remarkable being a mom could be.

Join me in my parenting journey throughout this book. You will see plenty of ups and downs, but also many of the things I have learned along the way. I hope some of these ideas can help you in your journey as much as they have helped me in mine. Go ahead, try anything that makes sense, but remember, you do what you think is best, Mama!

If you haven't had a chance to read the forward, "Remember When," there may be parts of this book, even in just the introduction, where you might wonder if I question my choice to become a parent. I ensure you, I don't question that choice. It is the best choice I ever made. Are there tough times? Oh yes. But I have realized you have to own the tough spots just as you would own the great ones. It's all part of being a parent—the good, the bad, and the ugly. Even the tough times help shape us into the great moms that we are and continue to grow into. So, as you have seen already, there will definitely be plenty of tough days ahead, but the love you have for a child is nothing short of amazing. It cannot be put into words. That love will change you in ways you never thought possible. So, buckle down and get ready for the true ride of your life.

NEWBORN

The Baby is Here! Now, What Do We Do with It?

"I have to take good care of this little egg
or the baby will pop right out." —*My daughter*

I remember freaking out when I noticed the milk expiration date was past my daughter's due date. That was quite a reality check. Getting ready to have a baby and then actually taking care of that newborn baby can be scary, but it is also nothing short of a miracle. A TV show was on in the background one day, and I heard one of the characters say, "Why don't we figure all this stuff out after the baby comes? You know, learn on the job?" Well, to an extent, this is going to be what happens. We spend so much time and effort preparing for a baby, but it is an experience you could never imagine perfectly before actually being in it. I don't think it is possible to prepare for everything that will happen once you have a baby. Even second-time parents have lots of surprises. Every child is so different. Try not to worry too much about what's to come or about how your life will change. Let's face it, your life is going to change, but you will figure it all out and everything will come together.

The Hospital

First, let's talk about the hospital. I often see posts on social media of new mothers in the hospital with cute outfits and full make up. This was not the case for me. I actually took my family hospital photos with my son in my nightgown with wet hair and no makeup. Nothing about it was glamorous, with my swollen face and my rigged underwear which felt like a big diaper. I am going to say it: When you are in the hospital, if you don't want to put makeup on, don't. Don't worry yourself about looking great. Enjoy the time you get to rest before all hell breaks loose when you get home. On the other hand, if you want one more chance to put on makeup without a screaming baby watching you, go ahead. I wouldn't judge you either way! If you decide not to worry about your hair or makeup, try to enjoy that rough look you have after having that beautiful baby. After all, you worked hard. You produced a beautiful life, which is nothing short of amazing.

There are some helpful items you may not think to bring with you to the hospital. Bring a hair dryer. They don't always have one. You are going to want to (may even be forced to, like me) shower and you will not want to walk around with sopping wet hair, trust me. Also, bring cotton swabs if you are a cotton swab user. "They say" you should never use these to clean the inside of your ears, but if you are a cotton swab user, I bet it's hard to go without them. It is like a slight addiction. Have you ever tried to stop using them? Yeah, it's not fun. You may also want to bring your nursing pillow to help you nurse comfortably, and maybe even a baby book for your newborn. If you ask the nurses, they will usually put the baby's footprints in the book for you.

Sorting Through Loads of Advice

When it comes to parenting, there is one thing which is for sure, and that is that you will get plenty of advice. It starts when you are pregnant. People may share helpful ideas—they may share scary stories which are told in hopes of making you feel better about the upcoming birth process, or they might comment about how large you look, or how pregnant you look. Don't feel like you have to listen to it all. When people comment about how "pregnant" or "large" you look, take it as a compliment. There won't be too many times in your life when you will look like this and when your body will actually be growing a beautiful baby. It is a miraculous thing and for that reason alone, you look astonishing.

In addition to the advice offered by strangers, friends, my mom, or other new moms, plenty of advice was passed on to me from my husband's culture. My husband is originally from a beautiful little place across the sea in Eastern Europe. This means that I get lots of advice—some I probably never would have received otherwise—from my husband's very, very, very large family. Picture the movie *My Big Fat Greek Wedding*. Yes, his family is similar to that. I will share some of these pieces of advice throughout the book—who knows, maybe you will find some useful ideas to try. One of the first pieces of advice I remember receiving was, "Do not clip the baby's nails until she is 40 days old." This has a religious significance. I don't know about your newborn, but our newborns had dangerously long nails the second they exited the birth canal. We had plenty of those mittens you put over baby's hands, however, those things just kept falling off and newborns always manage to scratch themselves even if you use them all the time and keep the nails nicely clipped. Your newborn will get a scratch even if you do the best job you can at protecting them from it. Don't feel bad, but as you might have guessed, we decided not to follow this piece of advice. No matter how important it was to some, it was important to my husband and me to minimize the scratches.

A second piece of advice I received was to use holy water with oils in the baby's bath for the first 40 days. I will admit, when the holy water was brought to me, I was a little nervous—okay, very nervous—about using these oils on my baby's extremely sensitive skin, which seems to break out at the touch of a finger. We decided to go ahead and use the holy water. My daughter was fine, and you know what, she was probably better off. These are just examples, but it is a fact that you will get plenty of advice. You must decide which advice to use and which advice to ignore. Don't feel bad about what you decide. In the end, it is your decision as parents. You know what's best for you and your baby.

I know I said not to listen to every piece of advice you receive, but I have one piece of advice which is pretty important. When you have a newborn baby, never tell your husband, "Honey, remind me in five minutes to [insert task here]." I have learned that this will never end well. I promise whatever you put in that blank is 100 percent likely to be forgotten. This is how I flooded our brand-new house.

I was soaking some clothes—which were most likely covered in poop or food—in our upstairs laundry room, in an attempt to prevent some stains (which is nearly impossible). I plugged the drain and let the water run into the huge slop sink. I told my husband, "I have to go get dinner started really quick. Remind me to turn off the sink in five minutes." Famous last words. Of course, with two children, things happen quickly and we began the usual daily routine of putting out fires, and I soon began nursing my son. About 45 minutes later, my husband heard water running. We both realized at that moment, *Oh no, the water is running in the laundry room.*

We learned the hard way that there was no hole in the sink to let the water drain should it start to overflow. Water was everywhere. The floor was flooded. It had seeped into my daughter's closet and into her room. My husband went into the garage and water was literally pouring like a waterfall out through the electrical socket in the ceiling. All I heard was his yelling, "Our new house is ruined! Do you know how much this is going to cost to fix? Our brand

-new home!" Thank goodness my husband builds homes for a living, because he knew exactly what to do. Well, I realized that eventually, but in the moment when he began pulling dry wall down from the ceiling and destroying our garage, I was worried. He pulled all of the insulation out so that the ceiling could dry. The next day, he rented two huge fans and started drying our daughter's closet and floor. Who knew one could rent huge fans? Not I. It all ended up working out just fine, and we got it all fixed. Thank goodness the sink was over the garage, which was where most of the water ended up.

In the moment, when the disaster was happening, it felt like I had hit rock bottom. Before this happened, and within the first three weeks home from the hospital, a water pipe burst under our house and our heat broke. The heat had to be fixed after I started smelling smoke and could not find the cause. One thing was breaking after the next. I thought to myself, *Could anything else go wrong?* Well, the truth is, yes, many other things could go wrong. There is a saying from my husband's language which literally translates to, "It's not a human head." It basically means that things could be going wrong with material objects—such as your car, your house, your material belongings—however, thankfully, you are in good health. In other words, it is a material loss, not a human loss. Thankfully, you and your family are still in good health. This is so true. Sometimes, something happens and we feel it is so big and so horrible and so bad, but it usually really isn't as bad as it seems. Now I laugh when I think of and when I tell this story. I now try to remember that when tough things happen, we have to stop and think and put it into perspective. I ask myself, "Is this really the worst thing ever?" or "Will this matter ten years from now?" No, probably not.

There is one more piece of advice I do offer many of my friends who are having a baby. I always say, "It is normal to worry, but try not to worry too much." I know, you are probably thinking right now, *Easier said than done,* but I would say that nearly 100 percent of the time, all of the things I worried about eventually worked out just fine. I always worried about things like:

What if my milk never comes in well?

What if the baby never wants to take this bottle?

What if rocking the baby to sleep becomes a sleep association and makes them unable to sleep through the night?

What if I wait too long to wean off the bottle and they never want to give it up?

What if the sippy cup transition doesn't go well?

What if my child never gets potty trained or just keeps having accidents?

What if every single transition doesn't go well?!

Yes, I worried about all of these things with my first baby. With my second, I worried somewhat less about these things, but the worry was still there. Then, it hit me: all of the time I spent worrying had been wasted. Every single one of these things worked out just fine in the end for both of my children. I learned that all of these "what if" questions were completely pointless. So back to my advice to you; try not to worry. Try not to think about or dwell on the little things. Eventually, you will get your answer, and more often than not it will all work out perfectly. To worry about it just takes more time away from enjoying your baby. When raising our babies, we must, as my daughter would say, "Follow the hoot." What does this mean? As she and I were taking a walk one day, we heard an owl hooting away. My daughter said, "That's an owl. All we have to do is follow the hoot, Mom, to find it." To her, it was just so simple. We follow the hoot and we find the owl. In the same way, we just have to follow our mommy intuition, do what we feel is right, and not question our every move. Eventually, if we do that, we will find the owl and more often than not, everything will work out for the best.

Baby's First Nights at Home

The first few nights home from the hospital are quite unpredictable and likely different for each baby. One thing these nights probably have in common, though, is that you will hit some of the highest highs and the lowest lows of your life during this period of time. I will never forget when my daughter cried all night for three nights straight. This was all after she was a perfect little angel at the hospital. At the hospital, I thought, *Man, I got this down.* I was wrong.

We made it home and her nights and days were completely reversed. She was nocturnal. She wanted to sleep all day long and stay awake and scream all night long. We could not figure out what was wrong. We were exhausted. Might I add, this was all after a 30-hour labor experience. Our daughter just barely fit through the birth canal when it was too late for a Cesarean section. It was challenging to say the least. We were completely exhausted having missed out on an entire night's sleep and after having undergone the most physically demanding experience in my life. No matter what your labor experience is, it is a difficult experience that makes you exhausted. Anyways, I finally called the pediatrician who recommended I speak with a lactation consultant.

The lactation consultant helped me figure out that my daughter wasn't getting enough milk. This, along with the help of my mother who rocked my daughter for four hours while my husband and I finally got a little shut eye, saved me. After the three-day mark, things did get a little easier, but it was not easy by any means. During this time, you really have to try hard to stay positive, soak up those baby snuggles, and take in the sweet baby facial expressions as much as possible to help keep you sane.

You will have plenty of worry. The baby will make groaning or gurgling sounds while sleeping. I felt the need to lean over every few minutes to make sure the baby was breathing okay, forget about having a sound sleep. It's frustrating, but you will get through this. Try to enjoy each stage as it is, as hard as that is. What helped me a little—especially with my second—was treating each day like it might be the last child I will have. I tried to enjoy each moment as much as possible and take it all in—sights and even smells. I would hold those sweet babies so close and just smell their hair, skin, and even their sweet milk breath. I may sound crazy, but I always wanted to remember those things. In the moment, it seems so impossible to forget, but forgetting is easier than one might think. I realized I just had to take it all in, even the tears and the painful moments.

The Emotional Side

Becoming a mom changes you. I am so much more emotional now. I don't remember crying during a movie even once when I was younger. I didn't even cry at *Titanic*. I am serious. I remember I even used to try to cry because I thought there must be something wrong with me. Now that I am a mom, I find myself boo-hooing at a simple episode of *Grey's Anatomy*. I cry at all the movies, even *The Secret Life of Pets* and *Finding Dory*. I remember reading something a while back about how a woman's brain actually changes when she has a baby. When the baby cries, women actually have a hormonal response; this is different from men. I feel it for sure. When my babies cry, especially in the middle of the night, I feel myself get flushed. I feel anxious and even panicked at times. I especially felt this way when my babies couldn't be comforted, no matter how hard I tried.

Something that really surprised me—and honestly, something that people don't really talk about—are the feelings of frustration, anger, and maybe even rage that you might feel at times toward your baby. I am a lover and I love my children so much—I kiss them and hug them way too often, and I feel the love right in my heart for them daily. I will be honest though, there were times when I felt flat-out rage. I can think of a few nights when I was completely exhausted, and the baby just kept crying. My son had horrible reflux and there were nights when he would not just cry but he would scream, literally kick at me hard, push me away, and even bite me multiple times when I was trying to nurse him or calm him down. This would go on for hours.

When my son was close to one year old, there was a night I was trying to give him milk in his sippy cup before bed and he would not take it. He was screaming and hitting the cup away. Maybe the milk was simply too cold for him, who knows? He was arching and pushing away from me, so much so that it was hard to keep him in my arms and my arms were numb like jelly from trying to hold him. The exhaustion and pain I felt in moments like these were so real, and I remember becoming so angry. I would be so angry in fact that I have even imagined myself just throwing the baby down on the floor and walking out. For the record, I never actually did. I only imagined it. Maybe I shouldn't make this public knowledge, but if I could help one person, it is worth it. Maybe those parents out there who have had similar thoughts might feel better, and if you are a parent who hasn't had these thoughts, then you can feel better too, because you are one step ahead of me.

Anger is a very real feeling that we as parents can and will experience. Yes, even towards those beautiful, squishy, sweet baby faces. In these angry moments, I would remain calm on the outside (although if I am being honest, there may have been a time or two when I screamed out), but I would hold it together. Once the baby was calm again, the guilt would hit me like a ton of bricks. I would think, *How could I have ever let that thought cross my mind?* I would think maybe I didn't even deserve to have a child, let alone two of them.

After all the fighting and screaming, they finally sleep. They are so adorable and peaceful when they sleep. As I look at them, I feel guilty over all the times I lost my patience throughout the day, but I am also reminded how lucky I am. Maybe this is the universe's way of reminding us why we did this in the first place. Maybe it helps keep us going and gets us through the following day.

So what do we do in the angry moments? First, I have learned, we have to stay strong and forgive ourselves; cut ourselves some slack. Then, one thing my husband and I started to do was the switch-off. I would get to the end of my rope and hand the baby off to him. Then, he would arrive at the end of his rope and hand the baby back off to me. This really helped because we could step away before we got to the point where that rage would set in. If not your husband, then pass the baby off to a parent, family member, or friend. Even just lay the baby down in the crib and take a little break. Yes, the baby will likely still cry, but it is okay to remove yourself for a moment and get yourself back together again.

I also think we need to realize we are not alone. We are in an emotional state, with no sleep and raging hormones. We are doing the best we can. I needed to realize that those thoughts I was having in rage against my baby were just thoughts brought on at a time of anger. I did not act on it and knew I never would. The truth is, everyone has negative thoughts sometimes. What really matters is how we act on those thoughts.

I remember praying one night, out loud, "Lord, please help me see love when I'm angry or frustrated." So, I started trying to do just that. I thought of a few moments when I was so proud, when I felt loved, or when I felt so much love for my kids and I stored these times in my brain. When I started to become frustrated, I would close my eyes, take a deep breath, and bring those memories and the feelings associated with them back to my mind.

Although there are many rough experiences we have related to sleep, some of them can be so wonderful. One such time for me is when my baby wouldn't sleep, but he kept saying "Mama" over and over again in his sweet voice and then kept trying to give kisses by opening his mouth wide on my cheek; or, when I was rocking my son to sleep for his nap one day and he had his hand right on my chest. I could literally feel the warmth in his sweet, little, chubby hand going straight into my heart. These are the moments I never want to forget. In these moments, I cannot help but laugh and my heart swells. These are times I try to bring back into my mind when I find myself frustrated or overwhelmed.

Although this helps, I think we also need to talk about how we are feeling, rather than keep it inside. I bet a lot more of us have these angry moments than we think because people just don't want to talk about them. I think the mommy guilt we feel can play a role in this, but it really is okay. I mean, we just went through a life-changing experience. Our world was literally turned upside down. We are now taking care of this beautiful being who is now the center of our world. We are getting little to no sleep. If we do get sleep, it is erratic at best. We are in emotional and even physical pain at times. Our bodies have just recovered from delivering a whole human into this world. Heck, it sometimes still hurts to even sit or laugh. Our hormones are completely out of whack. So, it is okay. Let's just get it out there and not feel ashamed.

We can talk to a friend or our partner. We may even want to talk to our doctor or even a mental health professional. Sometimes these feelings can be normal, but sometimes we could be experiencing postpartum depression or postpartum anxiety and we may never even know it ourselves. I know for a fact that worries, anxiety, and mommy guilt are all very normal, but sometimes it is hard to know if they aren't something more like depression, especially when paired with hormonal changes, lack of sleep, and feeling like a prisoner in our own home (the normal things that come with having a baby). It is hard to know how much of these feelings are normal "new mom anxieties" or if we are feeling some postpartum depression. The truth is, this probably varies from person to person. From what I understand, postpartum depression or anxiety is extremely common, so if you feel like you are struggling (or even if your spouse or a friend feels you are struggling), talking to your doctor to sort through some of these questions and feelings can really help. We need to look out for each other. Sometimes, the person experiencing the depression is the last person to realize it, and it takes trusting someone else's opinion to get the help we need. If you are concerned about postpartum depression, or even if it crosses your mind, bring it up because unfortunately, someone else may not think to. Know it is okay, and that you are not alone, even though it may feel that way.

Don't be afraid to ask for help in general and don't be afraid to specifically tell people what kind of help you need. You may not receive as many offers to help as you would think and the help you do receive may be offers to simply hold that sweet baby, for example. Well, you are exhausted and sore, and maybe you would prefer to sit and hold your baby, while someone else tidies up your house rather than the other way around. Maybe you would want nothing more than for someone to hold the baby while you take a real nap. Don't feel bad about being honest and specific about what you need. This is a time in your life when you could use the help more than ever before, so please take it.

Speaking of offers to help, I believe there is nothing worse than someone saying, "Do you want me to do the dishes?" You could even replace doing the dishes with any other annoying chore in the house. I mean, is this a rhetorical question? Do you want me to do the dishes? I feel like if you really wanted to do my dishes, you would just do them. Maybe it just makes the person feel better that they have offered, so I have always ended up saying, "No, I will do them," because I have felt bad saying yes. Usually the dishes continued to sit there too. I will be the first to tell you, when you have a newborn and someone asks you if you want them to do the dishes or any other chore whatsoever, please say yes and don't think twice about it. They may not actually want to do them, but it's going to make life so much easier for you, so be a little selfish and go with it. After all, you deserve to be a little selfish after doing the most unselfish thing possible, bringing a life into this world and putting that life even above your own.

I didn't expect how challenging those first few days bringing baby home would be, but I also didn't expect the magnitude of love which would come with it. I think there are four feelings which are the absolute best feelings in the entire world and I didn't even know they existed until I had my first baby: looking at your newborn baby for the first time, when your baby starts purposely reaching for your hand to hold to take you with them, when your baby first gives you a hug and a kiss, and when your baby first tells you they love you. If I could just replay these four things in my mind over and over again, I swear, nothing could bring me down. My two-year-old just began saying, "I love you whole world" all on his own. It is like they know exactly how to bring you back up when you are down.

CARING FOR YOUR
NEW BABY

You typically leave the hospital with two things: a baby brush and what I call a nose bulb. It seems surprising you leave the hospital with this ever-important miniature human being with so many needs, who you need to figure out how to care for, but you leave with only two "tools," a brush and a bulb. When the nurse first places that sweet baby in your arms, you can be overcome with love and emotion. Then, once you return to reality, fear can take over as you think, *Okay, what am I supposed to do now?* I mean, shouldn't there be a baby instruction manual or something? Everything has a warning label on it these days. Even my coffee says "Caution: Hot." Well, the baby doesn't come with a warning label, but most of the baby's stuff does, and this only freaks us new parents out more. At least the brush and nose bulb are very handy items if you know how to use them. Honestly, I am not sure the hospital even gave me directions. Eventually I discovered their importance after going to the pediatrician with a thousand different questions.

Hopefully your brush is a good one. When I left the hospital with my daughter, I left with a rectangular, weird-looking brush with no handle. The bristles seemed pretty sharp for a baby. With my son, I left the hospital with a very soft brush which actually looked like a baby brush. Thank goodness I had the one from my daughter. The strange-looking brush has been a lifesaver when it comes to cradle crap. Oops, did I say cradle crap? Well, I think this term is actually pretty appropriate for what's referred to as cradle cap. For one, it is a two-word tongue twister, but it also is like crap because, although it is normal and not dangerous, it looks gross. It looks as if it would feel uncomfortable, and sometimes it seems impossible to alleviate.

I used the plain infant brush for my son for a while. Soon, his cradle cap was out of control and I went looking for my daughter's brush. I will share a piece of advice: If you have a strange, rectangular brush, keep it forever. If you don't, you can find them online. The sharper bristles really help remove the cradle cap. When you are shampooing your baby's hair in the bath, rub the brush around their head in little circles. This on its own can somewhat scrape free some of that cradle cap. If the cradle cap gets out of control—like it did for my children—you can try rubbing some Vaseline in the scalp a little before bath time so it can really soak in, and then proceed to wash the baby's hair in the tub with shampoo and the brush massage. There is a good chance the Vaseline will still be there after you wash the hair, but that is alright, as it can help moisturize the scalp even after the bath. My mom told me this technique was what my grandmother used to always tell her to do. Yes, that sometimes wanted, sometimes unwanted advice I was telling you about earlier, but it really did help us. "They say" you can even use oils, like olive oil, to alleviate cradle cap. A friend recommended using coconut oil. I learned about this idea too late, so I have not tried it, but my friend swore by it.

The other "tool" you leave the hospital with is the amazing "nose bulb." It is another surprisingly helpful tool. My children had minor nasal congestion more often than not. They pretty much always had at least one booger in there. If you are like me, you cannot stand to see the booger there, and you will feel the need to remove it immediately. I even found myself using my pinky finger to try to scrape it out. I know, it's gross. You are probably either right there with me, or you think I am nuts. I have found the "nose bulb" to be quite effective in removing the random "boogie."

For a long time, there were moments when I would squeeze the little bulb, let it go, and the booger was still there, maybe even after ten tries. It was positively maddening! Then, my sister-in-law taught me how to use it correctly. She hadn't even had children, so I don't know how she came across this piece of information, but she might have just saved my life. In all seriousness though, you squeeze the bulb and then place it in the nose gently. You should kind of angle it, where it is not completely centered in the nose. The side can almost touch the side of the nose. Then, the key is to let the bulb open back up while you are pulling it out of the nose. Voilà, the boogie is free and Mommy can stop being a "picker" for a little while.

When your child is pretty stuffy, even as a tiny baby, you can use the nose bulb along with some saline spray or drops. You can find it at most stores. All you do is spray or drop a little into each nostril and then use the bulb to suck it back out with the snot. You can even add a little more saline after you use your bulb for good measure, if you like. I will add, "they say" you should use the nose bulb no more than twice a day when needed so you don't cause any distress to those cute little noses. The spray and bulb have been a lifesaver for us as there are really not many, if any, medications for congestion out there for the wee little ones. If you are like me, any congestion scares you at night when you have a little baby, and the saline and bulb went far with easing my mind.

Bathing Your Baby

When I thought about caring for my newborn, I knew I would need to bathe her, but this task just seemed super intimidating, maybe even scary. I wasn't quite sure yet how to hold such a tiny and delicate little baby. Sometimes, because I felt the baby was so delicate, it made me nervous when handling her. Being nervous is not the best thing to be when taking care of a baby. My husband always says, "I wish you could have seen how rough they were pulling her out during the delivery." This does put it into perspective for me and helps me realize, to be careful of course, but not to be overly nervous because she will be just fine.

Bath time was uncomfortable for me at first, for sure. Not only do you need to hold the baby (usually in an awkward position), but you are holding her in this position while wet, soapy, and slick. My godmother gave my daughter her first bath at home, and it was amazing watching her flipping the baby this way and that and washing that baby head to toe in what seemed like seconds. She was perfectly comfortable, and definitely not nervous. I, however, could not hold the baby that comfortably yet.

I had tried giving a bath in those hard, plastic infant bathtubs first, but my child would scream the entire time and I felt worried she would slip off the seat. I ended up using a bath sponge and it has since worked wonders for all of my children. You may have seen these bath sponges—they are sometimes shaped like a bear and many are yellow. They are large enough to lay your baby down on the sponge on their back. I lay my children down on the bath sponge and then carefully wash their body, rolling them slightly to the side to wash underneath their backs. I always start with the face first (with only water), then wash their bodies with soap, and then I wash their bottom last as I would call that the least clean area. I finish up by cleaning their hair (as to keep them warmer longer) by pouring the water on their head and soaping it up. I would lift their head up slightly to wash the back and rinse. My children stayed plenty warm on the sponge because I would keep pouring water on their bodies throughout the bath. Both of my children loved baths and found this very relaxing. Many times, they would actually fall asleep on that sponge while I bathed them. As a bonus, I never had to worry about them slipping out of my hands.

I always laid the bath sponge inside the bathtub. This helped with the eventual transition into the big tub. "They say" some children have a difficult time moving from the individual bathtub to the actual bathtub because the large bath tub with all the water can be new and scary. We never had this issue because we started there. Once my children learned to sit up, they just sat up in the bathtub on their bath sponge. I was less nervous because even if they happened to fall back when sitting, it was soft.

The sponge helps, but every parent has a bath time scare where the child accidentally slips. I have even heard of plenty of parents whose children have broken or knocked out teeth in the bath tub. If it happens to you, it is okay. It's an accident and no, it does not make you "the worst parent in the world." I felt like I was telling myself this daily with an infant. If you are loving and caring for that child, you are a good parent. Unfortunately, accidents happen. It is all in how we deal with them.

Eventually, we just stopped using the sponge. Thank goodness both children have always loved their baths. I like to think the bath sponge has helped with that, but who knows? If you find your child hating baths, go ahead and try different types of bath tubs and ideas. I have even seen a laundry hamper used in the bath tub. The child can sit inside it and the bath water comes in, but the smaller area could make them feel a little safer. You can even put plenty of toys around them for extra fun.

In case the bath itself wasn't enough to fret about in the beginning, I will never forget having to keep the newborn's belly button dry. I was so worried, I must have kept the water many inches away at first. My mom told that me doctors used to tell them to use rubbing alcohol on the belly button to help dry it up. Now, doctors tell us to keep the belly button cord completely dry. The way I see it, as with many things, it worked before when we were children, and keeping it dry seems to work now too. Over time, so many different child-rearing techniques have worked, so try not to worry too much. I even remember having to use a little bit of rubbing alcohol on all of my children's belly buttons—per the doctor's recommendation—right after the cord fell off because it got a little yucky.

On top of figuring out how to give a bath, you have to decide how often to give one. We had quite a few family members give us their opinion on this issue before the baby was born. Some said you need to make sure to give the baby a bath daily. Others said careful not to give too many baths so you don't dry out the baby's skin. This issue had come up so frequently you would think we were trying to make a decision about her post-secondary education. It was such a big deal, believe it or not, that it was actually the single question we asked the pediatrician at the hospital. We asked, "Should we bathe the baby daily or every other day?" I am sure he was quite surprised by our single question when he answered, "Either way is perfectly fine."

We ended up bathing our daughter every other day, or even every third day at times. As I had feared, both children have sensitive skin like me. For my son, we ended up bathing him nightly as he really enjoyed routines. It always helped him to relax in the bath at the end of the night before bed. On bath nights, he slept better, so you better believe he started getting a nightly bath. Over time I learned, for most things, you just go with what works.

Do not fear—baths become easier very quickly. Unfortunately though, the after-bath experience only becomes more difficult. As infants, they may stay calm, or they may even cry as you dress them, but at least they stay put. I found myself spinning a hanger around my finger to distract my nine-month-old after his bath one night while I tried to get his diaper and clothes on. I had exhausted all other options and he wouldn't stay still. I thought to myself, *A hanger? It has come to this?* Then, *Could he get hurt? Not likely if I'm careful...I have to get these clothes on.*

Visiting the Pediatrician

With a newborn, you will go see the doctor somewhat frequently in the beginning, especially if your child is having trouble gaining weight like mine did (more on that later). I would recommend you write down all your questions as they come up. One would think you would remember the questions when you got to the doctor's office, but most likely you will not. You may want to keep a little notebook handy to jot down the questions as they come up. At first, I found myself waiting until the night before the appointment and I was asking my husband, "Honey, what were those questions we wanted answered again?" Sometimes, we remembered all of the questions, but most of the time we didn't.

Even if I write down every single question, it is guaranteed I will forget to ask at least one. My husband always says, "Didn't you write that down?" Yes, I did write that down. Then I get home and wonder, *Should I call about it, or can it wait until the next visit a few months from now?* If this is you, just take a moment and read through your list. I promise the doctor will allow you to take a moment to review your questions. If you have a great pediatrician, many of times they will cover most of your questions before you even have to ask, which is quite helpful.

At one of my first doctor's appointments, as I was eagerly taking notes, the doctor added, "While you are at the store, be sure to pick up a yellow legal pad to write down all of your questions for next time. You know the thick one with all the lines?" I actually started writing this down on my list before

I realized what he was saying. Don't feel embarrassed if this happens to you. Parenting can be many things and one of those things is humorous. I think the underlying advice in his comment was that there's no need to take everything so seriously because everything is going to be okay. Babies are not as fragile as one may think.

The Soft Spot

Speaking of fragile, then there is the soft spot. I remember going into a panic when my daughter, who apparently has better aim than a professional marksman, threw a toy directly at my son's soft spot. I worried, *How sensitive is the soft spot?* I immediately began searching the internet. Of course, every horrible story in the book came up and I became more and more panicked as I compulsively read through them. "They say" the soft spot is very sensitive. Watch for swelling or for if it begins to become sunken. I remember thinking, *How do I even know what sunken looks like? What does it feel like normally? I don't even know.* I worried, but the baby seemed perfectly fine.

I called my pediatrician anyway. If ever in doubt, just call. He said, "You have two young children. If the baby hits his head only once a day, you are lucky." This made me feel so much better especially because the day before, while running to my closet to get a new shirt because mine was completely covered in spit up, I had accidentally hit my baby's head on the trim of the door as I walked through. I thought I could clear it, but somehow didn't. I felt like a horrible parent. I thought, *What good parent could actually hit their child's head into a door frame?*

I worried and cried so much and felt so horrible that later I actually decided to measure the door. I am serious. You can't make this stuff up. Turns out, the closet door is much smaller than the regular doors, so I concluded that I must have thought I had more room to walk through. Then, and only then, did I let myself off the hook for accidentally hitting my baby's head against the doorframe. The thing is, though, we all make mistakes. We are not perfect, and we don't have to be perfect to be a good parent. Perfection is impossible. The pediatrician helped me come to this realization. When in doubt, always call your pediatrician. The internet has a way of causing unnecessary alarm. You have to be very careful about what you choose to read and believe. My pediatrician always makes me feel better, not worse.

Teething

As parents, I don't think we can hear the word "teething" and not cringe. One thing I learned pretty quickly is that teething can start way before you actually see the teeth. It starts with drooling. "They say" with teething comes many additional symptoms, some of which do not make sense. Doctors say teething does not cause fevers or runny noses. Many times, when my children were teething, they had fevers, runny noses, and even diarrhea. Could it have been just viruses which happened to occur with the teething? Maybe so, but I am not ready to rule out the possibility it could simply be caused by the teething itself. One thing we all can probably agree upon, however, is teething is miserable for all involved.

"They say" don't give medicine to your baby unless it is necessary, but when my child was in teething pain and my pediatrician recommended pain relievers, I went with it. There are plenty of other options out there. There are natural remedies. You can freeze a wet washcloth and let them chew it. You can put frozen fruit in a mesh teething bag for chewing. My pediatrician recommended letting an older baby chew on frozen bagels—just be sure to watch them so they don't happen to bite a piece off and choke. When it comes to over-the-counter medicine, if the pediatrician okays it, give it or don't give it. I believe the bottom line is to simply do what you feel is best for your situation. No matter your decision, it does not make you any less of a mom. In fact, all of the above ideas help your child feel better, so all of the ideas make you a great parent.

Diaper Changes

I think diaper changing is a learned art form. I will never forget trying to put a diaper on my newborn baby in the hospital for the first time. I hoped the nurses wouldn't come in and catch me during a change because I knew they would think I was a complete idiot. They would change the baby in front of me in less than 30 seconds. I think it took me at least five minutes at first. My excuse is newborns are so delicate, I was so scared I would hurt them somehow.

Over time, as I mastered the diaper changing art, I learned a few things. I learned to always put a new diaper under the old one during the change. This way, the diaper is ready to use, it saves some time, and it keeps the area under the soiled diaper clean. Any mess simply goes onto the new diaper. I learned there will be no shortage of "blowouts." A blowout would be a simple and more politically correct way of saying poop is everywhere. It is up their back, in their hair, on every article of clothing they are wearing…you get the idea. I learned you can simply pull the onesie down off their feet instead of over the baby's head. The top of most onesies have little folds in them for this purpose. I learned that if you are reaching for ointment or wipes, fold the diaper up as if you are about to fasten it, just in case. Otherwise, you may end up with a shower, and I promise this is not the shower you have been dying for. This is especially important for boys. I have even heard of something like a "peepee teepee" out there to cover the boys during a change, but for me it worked well just to remember to fold the diaper up.

Skin Issues

You will likely come across plenty of skin issues with a newborn. I cannot tell you the number of times I found myself searching "baby rash." The images and results which come back are scary to say the least. Just know there will be plenty of normal skin issues when you have a newborn. If you notice a rash, don't be afraid to give your pediatrician a call or have them take a look. My son had eczema and a milk intolerance, so he had and still has plenty of rashes. Even without a milk intolerance, my daughter had plenty of rashes as well. My son's allergist recommended using soap in the bath only twice a week. Basically, we could give him a bath every night if we wanted to with water only. We would use a paraben, dye, fragrance, and formaldehyde-free soap. On the water bath nights, I still washed his hands and feet and possibly his bottom with soap, but that was about all. We followed up every bath with a matching paraben, dye, fragrance, and formaldehyde-free lotion. It may sound gross or strange to give so few baths, but this simple regiment worked wonders for our son's skin.

Many babies, especially the adorably chubby ones, will develop rashes in their skin folds, particularly in the neck fold. My daughter had a horrible rash in her neck fold. It turns out that the best way to handle this is to clean it and dry it well during the bath. We did not use soap each day in this area because soap can cause more irritation. At least every other day, we would simply clean it well with a wet washcloth, while always making sure to dry it completely. I will say drying this area is much easier said than done. I used to call it flossing because you literally had to floss her neck with a washcloth because her chubbiness made it almost impossible to get in there. "They say" do not use baby powder or cornstarch on a baby. From what I heard, it is very dangerous if they accidentally breathe it in. My pediatrician, however, told me cornstarch works, and it did. I am not a doctor so be sure to ask your pediatrician first, but if they are okay with it, I just carefully shook a little cornstarch on my fingers, far away from the baby and then dabbed a little right on her neck, making sure no dust went anywhere. This helped us because it kept the area nice and dry which led to healing.

Diaper rash is another tough skin rash you may deal with. If your baby has diaper rash, especially if it is bad, it is always good to ask your pediatrician for ideas. What is tough about diaper rash is because it is so common, there are so many creams and ointments and recommendations out there. It is hard to know what works well and what doesn't. One recommendation which was particularly interesting came from my husband's family. In my husband's culture, they are known to cure diaper rash—believe it or not—with coffee. Basically, you find some European coffee at a specialty store. The coffee is super fine, almost like a powder. A little coffee is mixed into some Vaseline and then applied to the diaper rash. Although my mother-in-law swears by it, this is one we didn't end up trying. On a side note, there will be a few references throughout this book about home remedies and cures which I never would have known about until I met my husband. I find it interesting to think about these ideas being from just one small country. Imagine how many different ways of doing things are out there. Around the world, child rearing can take on a totally different form, but just because it is different doesn't mean it is wrong. This is another reason why I feel we have to be careful about what "they say." I don't think there is only one "right way" of doing things.

Back to diaper rash. I will share some ideas of what we did try, but once again, I am no doctor, so be sure to consult a doctor before trying anything here. The white, creamy diaper ointments never worked as well for us. I always use the tried and true vitamin A & D diaper ointment. There were times when my son ended up with really liquid poo, courtesy of all our medications for his constant constipation. There were a few times when the poo would burn his bottom. I know, it sounds horrible. I never realized poo could do such a thing, but it can. My pediatrician recommended putting some liquid anti-acid on his bottom prior to applying the diaper ointment. This would prevent the skin from being burned again from any more poo and help it heal. It sure did work. Another life saver was a calamine-based ointment. You will usually find this in any of the pink-colored creamy ointments. There was a specific ointment which was originally given to me by the hospital when my son was there for his constipation, which was magic. It was basically calamine with some added ingredients like aloe and other helpful oils.

Now sometimes diaper rash is accompanied with more of a yeast rash. It sounds horrible, but don't worry if this happens. Your child's pediatrician can help you figure out if it is regular diaper rash or a yeast rash. Our pediatrician recommended an over-the-counter adult antifungal cream, to be applied just on the outside area. Again, I will say, I am not a doctor, so be sure to check with your child's pediatrician before applying any medications. So, diaper rash, although sometimes scary and annoying, is nothing to fear. Once you have a few creams on hand, you will be good to go.

As if there aren't already enough rashes to worry about, there are two rashes in particular I never knew existed. First, I did not realize a rash sometimes coincides with strep throat. Second, I never knew there was such a thing as an "exit rash." When a child has a high fever, they can develop a rash, sometimes over their entire body, as the fever exits. I learned of this when we took my daughter to the doctor for one such rash. The rash was literally covering her entire body and I was worried. Although scary-looking, it was no big deal at all and was gone within 24 hours. Even still, always ask your doctor if you are unsure about a developing rash as there are many other rashes out there. Some are not as easy to deal with, and it is also simple peace of mind.

Tummy Troubles

Then there is the gas. Babies seem to have more gas than a hot air balloon and boy does the gas cause a lot of pain. Infant gas relief drops became my best friend. "They say" there is no proof they even work. I have heard it may be a placebo effect where we assume they are going to work, so it seems things are getting better. Who knows for sure? For my children, I really believed they worked and noticed improvement, and whether this belief was true or false, I will take it. Also, never underestimate the bicycle. Sometimes I found simply moving my baby's legs by bending them gently up and down like a bicycle really got things moving.

Not only did gas cause pain for my children, but there was also constipation, especially for my son. Sometimes, it is super difficult to tell what the culprit is when tummy troubles are present. Our pediatrician helped us time and time again over tummy troubles and I will be forever grateful. Over time, we learned prune and pear juice worked great for constipation. Believe it or not, we learned apple juice can actually cause some children to become constipated. We were shocked to learn this was the case for my son. As soon as we stopped the apple juice and switched to pear, we noticed major improvements. Most importantly, however, when in doubt, call the pediatrician. As common as these issues are, they will have plenty of great ideas to try.

When to Visit the Doctor

Another huge question when it comes to babies is, when should I go to the doctor? How many visits to the doctor is too many? There is really no such thing as too many visits. You do what makes you feel comfortable. I feel like I may have topped the charts on visits to the doctor's office, but if it helps my son feel better or quiets my worrying mind, then for me, it is worth it. My son's reflux was quite bad. I had asked friends, "When will this go away?" I heard, "Our child's went away around three months, four months, five months." We passed five months and there was no sign of my son's reflux even ebbing. The GI (gastrointestinal) doctor said that for many babies, it goes away when they turn one year old. We passed the one-year mark, and it was still there. The reflux meant lots of doctor visits for us, because we never knew what exactly was causing my son's pain or tears.

There were so many doctor visits and there was so much medication. There were times where my daughter literally remained sick for months. At one point, I remember laughing with my husband when I said my name on the phone with the pharmacy because we call so much. The second I said our last name, they recognized it and didn't even need me to spell it and let me tell you, it is a difficult name to spell. They must think we are the sickest family ever.

I will never forget the night when my first child had her first fever. This is a really scary time for a parent. For me, I never really got over the "fear of the fever." I am sure I called the doctor's answering service way too often for my kids when they had the high nighttime fevers, just to make sure everything was okay. One of the unforgettable moments from this night was when I called my mother-in-law, who told me to put either soap or vinegar on the baby's feet under their socks. "They say" it will make the fever go away. This is one of those home remedies I did not try. I did what I felt was right, which was a lukewarm bath and some fever medication. Once again, you do what you feel is right, even if it means calling the doctor on-call yet again, or even if it means using soap.

When my daughter was around 18 months old, I noticed she kept trying to put things up her nose. Watch out for any food which is small and round. One night, my daughter succeeded in putting a pea up her nose. I held the other nostril and had her blow out of the one with the pea in it. She successfully blew the pea out. Later that night, I checked her nose to ensure there were no other peas and I thought I saw something. It looked like something was blocking her nose. I had my husband look. He thought I was crazy and just thought it was part of her nose. I decided to take my daughter into the doctor's office to have them check it out anyway. I thought about not taking her because I honestly figured they would think I was crazy, especially if there was nothing in there, but in the end, I felt it best to go with my gut. Good thing I did, because the doctor looked in her nose and said she did see something in there. It was round like a rock and she tried and tried to get it out. Another doctor came to take a look and agreed there was something way up in her nose. I was instructed by the doctors to take her to the emergency room immediately because it would need to come out. Before leaving, one of the doctors told me not to worry, that they see this all the time. The doctor told me that one time he had a patient who put half of a Barbie doll dress up into her nose. I truly don't think I can figure out how that worked, but I hope I don't ever have to find out.

We went on to the emergency room. There, they had my husband try something interesting. He was asked to blow into my daughter's mouth hard while we held the free side of her nose closed with our finger. The nurses told us this sometimes works, that they have even seen whole Legos fly out of the nose this way. Unfortunately, it didn't work for us. Finally, they put an instrument up her nose past the item, blew up a tiny balloon, and then slid the item out of her nose. This worked. Turns out, it was a huge orange seed. They were given oranges at daycare and it seemed they didn't remove the seeds first.

I learned a few things here. First, toddlers may enjoy putting small things into their nose, and not even putting something just a little way up their nose, but all the way up. Gross and scary! Second, I learned if you have any concerns with any child care provider, bring them up. I brought my concern up at my child's school and they decided to no longer provide large oranges which have seeds to my child's age group. Third, I remember worrying so much about why my daughter was putting things up her nose. I wondered if she would always do this, but she stopped. I learned sometimes we have to just say, "This too shall pass." When you are in the middle of a stage it may seem that it will last forever, but they are usually over before you know it. It may seem like forever, but when you look back, that period of time is usually so small. I found I worried so much over nothing. We have to try to just live in the moment sometimes rather than worrying about what is going to happen later. And most importantly, I learned if you feel like you should take your child to the doctor, do it. It never hurts, and don't ever feel bad about it either. You may think you seem crazy, but at least you are a good, caring parent.

I will never forget the night when we rushed my first baby to the emergency room. I heard my daughter whining and saw her rocking back and forth on the monitor. When I went to check on her, she had thrown up literally everywhere and she was shaking uncontrollably. I put her into the bath tub and started trying to clean the mess off of her face, her eyes, and her hair. It was seriously everywhere. She would not stop shaking. She also seemed to be breathing funny. We took her temperature and it was low. I told my husband we are going to the hospital and we rushed her there. I remember crying and thinking in the moment that I wasn't sure if she would make it. Turns out, she was fine. She was sick with the hand, foot, and mouth virus.

The doctor explained some children shake when they are scared. She said it was likely she just got really scared when she threw up and it woke her. They thought the thermometer had simply not worked well. I honestly felt stupid for being so dramatic at first, but the more I thought about it, I did not regret taking her. You just never know. I believe, if we feel as parents it is time to go to the doctor, go to the doctor and don't feel bad about it. Even, if you get that doctor who rushes you out because it is "only a virus," again, don't feel bad. It is your baby. Always do what you feel is right.

Make sure you have doctors you trust. There will be times—and plenty of them—when you will just need to trust the doctor. I have found my doctor is usually right. If you don't think you can get to the point of trusting them, you may want to consider choosing another.

Keeping Up with the Joneses

Last but not least, watch out for social media and comparisons to others. These things can give us a never-ending case of keeping up with the Joneses. I remember when I had my first baby, as if I didn't have enough to worry about trying to figure out how to raise a baby, everyone was talking about their baby learning sign language. I would even get asked, "Have you used sign language with your baby yet?" I felt like some even made it seem like learning sign language was a developmental milestone which all children must meet, like walking. I will put it out there, *I did not use sign language with my children.* For my friends who used it, their children could literally tell them they wanted more way before my children could tell me. I use the word "literally" because my children did tell me when they wanted more, but it was more figurative in nature, like screaming or crying, rather than a gentle motion of the hand. Trust me, my baby sure communicated, just in a different way. So be careful of what you hear. Watch for the difference between a preference and a milestone. Just because it seems everyone is doing something doesn't make it a milestone which must be met. If something is simply not for you, don't question it or feel bad about it even for a second. Do what works for you and your family.

SLEEPING, OR LACK THEREOF

I never knew how much internal rage I could feel at a person who is loud when my children are sleeping. Who knew how much I would desire to kick a loud person at naptime right out the door, or let's be honest, maybe even punch them in the face. I promise I would never actually do it, but I will admit the thought has crossed my mind before. I will never forget the time I heard a delivery truck pull up the driveway during my newborn's naptime. I tried to run downstairs so quickly I basically attempted to fly. Needless to say, I somehow missed a few stairs and proceeded to roll down the rest, hitting each one, until the mailperson rang the bell anyway. Oh, the fury! I guess I learned my lesson, well, somewhat.

Ever since my children were babies, I felt the need to check on them in the night. I would ask my husband, "Honey, do you think he is breathing? I can't see it on the monitor," or "His head seems so close to the bumpers," or "Honey, do you think he is still okay [since the last time I went in there, maybe five minutes ago]? Should I go check on him again?"

My husband usually responded with "If you feel like you need to check on him, go ahead."

Then, of course, I feel like I have to go check on him. Do other parents feel this way, or is this just me being paranoid?

I would go ahead and check on my son. He would be making some of his strange breathing sounds which he regularly made while sleeping at night. It is like the sound you hear between the sobs when a child is crying uncontrollably, almost like a hiccup or something, but he isn't actually crying. We never knew what it was exactly, but it went on for hours at a time. Of course it made me worry, so I wanted to make sure he was okay. I do have a video monitor, but no matter how much I stare at it, I can never see if he is breathing. I will not sleep unless I walk in there and check.

I hold my breath as I walk in. I tiptoe, tiptoe, and of course step on a toy, the one that makes crunching sounds. He makes a move. I drop to the floor ninja-warrior style to hide. I say a quick prayer, *Please don't let me wake him up, please don't let him see me.* I freeze, hold my breath, and wait. I close my eyes too, as if that does anything. It's like when my toddlers play hide and seek. You can see their entire bodies hiding behind the chair, but their eyes are closed and they think if they can't see us, we can't see them. If only that actually worked though. Well, this night-time scenario is a common occurrence in our house. On the way back out of the room, I swear every bone in my body cracks, and it is extremely loud. I mean, aren't I still young? Why are my bones cracking? I think becoming a mom has aged me in multiple ways.

Many days I find myself wondering, *When did babies' sleep become so anxiety-inducing?* There are nights when I find myself down on my knees praying for the baby to fall back asleep on his own. Who can bring you to your knees like a baby who will not sleep?

I was at dinner with my husband's coworkers one night. One coworker was pregnant, about to have her first child. We started talking about babies of course. One mentioned that right after having the baby, you will think, *I could never do this again.* You think about having another and may believe it would be crazy.

You may even cringe thinking about it, but she said there comes a time when that "baby fever" returns and you think, *Okay, I could do this again.* People always say "I forgot" when you ask for advice, but it really happens. It's like you forget the tough times, or many of them, and you remember the good.

During the dinner conversation, this friend also mentioned that you may find yourself becoming anxious around five or six, anticipating bedtime. I could not identify with her more. I always felt that way, but I had never really thought about it. It's like I would start thinking I may have another sleepless night. I remember hoping and praying this night may be better than the last. I think part or most of it may be because, as the parent of a newborn, you are utterly exhausted. Let's face it, my kids were always fussiest around this time. "They say" it is the "witching hour." This is a time I wanted "them" to be wrong, but my babies always ended up being super fussy in the evening. In addition to this, both of my babies always wanted to cluster feed right when I was ready to hit the sheets. You finally get the baby down, maybe wash your face, if you're lucky brush your teeth, lie down, and right after you fall asleep, the baby seems to wake for another feeding.

This got me thinking, *Is there something else to all of this anxiety surrounding sleep?* I was reading a novel and on a couple of occasions in the novel, the main character went to check on her baby. She said she would check the baby to see if she was dry and if so, let her sleep. As I read this, I thought, *Really? Would she actually wake this sleeping baby for a diaper change if she was wet?* I mean, I for sure would not wake a sleeping, wet baby. Sometimes, the character would just rock in the rocking chair and look out the window while she watched her baby sleep. I thought, *I would never do that either. The noise may wake the baby.* I wondered, *Was there ever a time when moms weren't so worried about their babies sleeping through the night? A time when they would do these things?* I certainly think it is possible, or maybe other moms do these things and it is just me who doesn't.

Nowadays, discussions and even many articles and advertisements saying "Contact us, your baby can sleep through the night" lead us to believe our children should sleep and if they aren't, many times we take it personally and think it must be something we are doing wrong. We might think, "What is it that I personally need to fix or change?" With a newborn, I am sure you get asked 1,000 times, "How is the baby sleeping?" and specifically, "Is she sleeping through the night?" Sometimes, when I answered that question, I felt like I needed to compare myself to how well friends' babies were sleeping. The truth is, however, every baby is different so it is to be expected they will have different ways of sleeping and needs for comfort.

To further illustrate this point, when my son was having issues with gasping during the night, we ended up needing to see a pulmonologist. As requested, I brought a few five-minute video clips of my son gasping for the doctor to view. He told us we would need to have a sleep study to be sure, but his assumption was the gasping wasn't dangerous. He went on to explain how newborns and infants sleep very lightly. They are unable to fall into a deep sleep at such a young age. They learn as they grow, and eventually, they begin moving into a deeper and deeper sleep. He explained that this is why young babies wake at night more frequently, and as they grow, the night waking naturally decreases. He said for our son, his reflux has likely been causing him discomfort at night, which in turn has kept him at a lighter sleeping level throughout the night. The pain or discomfort prevented him from getting into the deeper sleep patterns. He said this would not last forever, and believed once the reflux resolved, he would finally be able to learn to sleep deeply.

I found this really interesting, because if what he was saying is true, our babies are not supposed to sleep all night. Yes, we know, based on what "they say," babies are supposed to wake up in the night to get all of the feedings they need to grow, but this is another way of looking at it. Babies are just not programed to sleep through the night yet, whether hunger is present or not. As a mom, I found this pretty interesting.

So what do we do about the anxiety over sleep? I think we need to stop comparing ourselves to others and feeling anxious over having our children sleep through the night, and, heck, even stop comparing our first child's sleeping habits to our second's. I am guilty of these things. We need to start trusting our "mommy intuition" and doing what works for us. Who cares what "they say" really? I promise eventually, every person starts sleeping through the night. We need to realize that when we are trying our best and doing what we think is best for our children, we are already being great parents.

I will never forget the time I heard the phrase "cry it out." I was at a friend's house and a great friend and mom said, "I let my child cry it out at night. It was the best thing I ever did. It worked." I remember wondering, *What on earth is "cry it out?"* Since that time, I learned quickly what it meant. "They say" you should let your child cry it out, but "they say" you should never let your child cry it out too. It is so confusing.

I will admit I let both of my children "cry it out" at one point or another and it did work for us. I will not forget the morning after I gave it a try, an article popped up on social media telling me why it was so horrible to let a child "cry it out." I felt terrible. I felt like I failed as a mom and I asked myself, *How could I have let my child cry like that?* Well, it did work. Soon after this, I remember seeing another article which compared children who cried it out to those who never cried it out. I remember reading by the time the children in the study were five, both sets slept through the night and neither set had any sleeping issues or problems regardless of whether or not their parents used "cry it out" in the past.

This is the stance I take on parenting. You do what you feel is right for your child. Again, I will say, as parents, we know our children best. However you decide to help your child sleep is most likely going to be just fine. We are not hurting our children if we let them "cry it out" and we are not hurting our children if we do not let them "cry it out." So, we should simply do what we feel is best for our children.

Sleep Associations

Another word which honestly makes me cringe is "sleep associations." A sleep association is basically a crutch your child uses to fall asleep. Nowadays, there is a lot of talk about how rocking or nursing your child to sleep could become a sleep association and could, therefore, keep them from sleeping through the night successfully. The internet talks about sleep associations like they are the plague. It's not that I don't think the ideas surrounding sleep associations would work, it's just when I personally think about them, I feel like I am doing everything wrong.

You cannot get around hearing "them" say, "Let your child fall asleep on their own." I've heard, "Don't rock your child to sleep," or "Don't nurse your child to sleep." I have heard "them" say if you rock or nurse your child to sleep, they will wake up scared and unsure of where they are. When they fell asleep they were in your arms, and when they woke they were in a new place. Then, they will need you in order to go back to sleep again. This makes sense and is a good argument for teaching your children to fall asleep on their own, but on the other hand, I decided to nurse and rock my children to sleep and they have done great, sleep associations and all.

When my son's gasping continued, we needed to have a sleep study done to help determine the cause. Overnight at the sleep study, I learned that he woke up over 20 times and this was actually a very good night for him. There were only two times during the entire night when I actually noticed he woke because he moved a lot or sat up. Otherwise, he seemed to be sleeping peacefully. Bear with me now, I am no sleep technician, but this led me to believe children may wake up way more than we think at night. If this is true, it seems our children must already know a little about putting themselves back to sleep. If our children woke up even around ten times per night, they would be waking about every hour or so. If your child wakes up less than ten times a night, I would say there must be times in there when they wake and are somehow able to put themselves back to sleep, right? Again, I am no doctor, so I am just guessing here, but this supports my notion that doing what you feel is best for your child and your family is always best.

It seems to me the best argument for infant sleep is not to let them fall asleep on their own or even to rock them to sleep. It is simply to trust your gut and do what you feel is right. Unfortunately, there is no manual, but babies are supposed to be rocked and fed, right? If you are snuggling your baby and keeping them fed, no matter the timing, no matter if it is to put them to sleep or not, rest assured, a fed and loved baby is a happy baby and the bottom line is you are doing the right thing.

My father-in-law told me a story one day about how he would always watch the sheep and baby lambs right near his childhood home. He said he would watch the sheep go out into the fields during the day. The babies would stay behind. When the moms came back, the baby lambs would not just go to any sheep. They would literally jump over each other and race to find their mom to nurse or snuggle. He said the ones who couldn't find their mom would not go to another sheep. They would "baaa" continuously, where it almost sounded like crying. This just goes to show me how important that secure attachment is not only just for human babies, but for mammals in general. I believe forming that secure attachment with your child can almost be more important than anything else.

So nurse your child to sleep if you like. Rock your child to sleep if you like. Do what is natural for you and don't feel bad about it. Remember, you can form that secure attachment in so many ways. Therefore, we shouldn't allow ourselves to feel bad if we decide against rocking our children to sleep either, or really for any of the parenting choices we make when we have our child's best interests at heart. What matters most is not the way in which sleep is achieved, it is that our children do sleep, and even more importantly, that they are loved and cared for. The way we form that secure attachment is less about the parenting styles we choose, even less about what "they say" we should do, and more about simply meeting our children's needs (physical, emotional, and yes, even behavioral), all the while, showing our children love.

So, what did I decide when it came to bedtime for my children? Due to his reflux, I had to hold my son upright for 15 minutes after each time he ate, so I had no choice but to hold him until he fell asleep each night. Well before the 15 minutes were up, he was out like a light, so I simply laid him down asleep. I have even heard "them" say that if your child falls asleep while nursing, wake them up slightly before you lay them down so they can still put themselves to sleep. I couldn't imagine waking my children up before putting them down only to go back to sleep, so I chose not to. Maybe it would have been an easy thing to do, and maybe I should have done it. Maybe it would have made things easier down the road, but I chose not to because it just did not make sense to me. So far, everything is going pretty well with bedtime even though I had made that choice. This is even the case with my son who has apparently had some underlying issues with his sleeping, including frequent night wakings, all unbeknownst to us parents until after his sleep study.

Based on what "they say," it seems if you prefer to rock your child before bedtime or naptime, the best-case scenario would likely be to rock them until they are drowsy, then lay them down and let them fall asleep on their own. If this works for you, wonderful! You are well on your way to your child learning to put themselves to sleep. However, if it doesn't work for you, don't worry. Once again, every child is different and I believe you should do what you think is best for you and your child. After all, this never worked well for us. It just led to a lot of screaming and crying in my house.

Sleep Training

Remember, you do not have to choose one approach over another. Even if you choose to rock your child to sleep, you can still sleep train (or teach your children how to fall asleep) if you so choose. I chose to combine the two. For my daughter, I rocked her to sleep for a long time, but very slowly trained her to fall asleep on her own. I chose to simply rock her a little less and less over time until eventually, I was able to lay her down drowsy rather than asleep. In the end, I only rocked her while I read her a book and then I put her down in the crib and she fell asleep.

I also think it is possible to sleep train in the middle of the night even after rocking or nursing your child to sleep at the start of the night. My daughter started sleeping through the night at around six weeks old on her own. She had rough nights here or there, but we were lucky because she was a great sleeper. Even so, we went through stages along the way when she started consistently waking up in the middle of the night.

This first occurred when my daughter was around ten months old. The pediatrician informed us at her age and weight, she could safely make it through the night without needing to eat. We decided to try the "cry it out" method to sleep train. When she woke up in the middle of the night, we would give her a few minutes to see if she would fall back asleep on her own. If she didn't, we went in to check on her. We did not pick her up, unless she had a poopy diaper, for example. I just laid her back down, patted her back for a minute or so, and used words to comfort her before leaving. Sometimes, she would stand back up and cry, but I would still leave the room after comforting her. After leaving, we would come back at increasing intervals to check on her again. We came back again at the two-minute mark, then again after another five minutes passed, again after about seven minutes passed, then ten, fifteen, and so on. When we went into the room, we always used the same terminology. I would always say, "No, no, night night, it is time to sleep now," as I entered. Before I left, I would always say, "Night, night, I will see you in the morning." I think using the consistent language made a difference.

Well, it worked. It took a few nights. The first night was really hard, because the crying went on for a long time. It about killed me. I was probably crying worse than she was. I felt horrible, but we kept checking on her so she knew she was cared for. The second night, when she woke in the middle of the night, we did the same thing, but this time it took less than half the time. By the third night, she fell asleep within five minutes. From there, she was back to sleeping through the night. So, interestingly enough, the "cry it out" sleep training method worked for us even when we were still bottle feeding and rocking our daughter to sleep at the start of the night.

We also rocked our son to sleep for a very long time. There were plenty of nights when his reflux bothered him and woke him, but on most nights he slept through the night. Then, after he turned 18 months old, there were a few nights he wasn't able to get comfortable in our arms anymore. It seemed rocking him was almost keeping him awake, so one night I decided to just put him in the crib. He tried to put himself to sleep and then started crying after maybe ten minutes. I remember saying to my husband, "What am I supposed to do now? I feel like I never know what to do."

Well, I went with my gut. I did not want to go in there and rock him more because it just didn't seem to be working for him, so I decided to pat his back for about a minute, told him I loved him and "Night, night, I will see you in the morning," then left the room again. This time, he went right to sleep on his own. It was almost like he told us he was ready to fall asleep comfortably in his own bed.

In the few nights following, we did have to use the "cry it out" sleep training technique which we used for our daughter, but this time we used it at the beginning of the night. It took a few nights of checking on him at increasing intervals. For these three nights, it luckily did not take more than 15 minutes overall for him to fall asleep. Each night, the length of time decreased until the third night, when he started lying right down and going to sleep on his own. Then, he naturally started putting himself to sleep at naptime as well. It was glorious. From then on, even on the rare occasion when he woke up in the middle of the night, I would simply go into his room, lay him down, gently pat his back for less than a minute, and leave. He would put himself right back to sleep.

I would say that, for us, the rocking and nursing "crutch" never harmed us or our children's sleeping. Once we felt ready to sleep train, things still ended up working out just fine. Every child is different. I believe whatever decision you feel is best for your child is okay. It will likely end up working out in the end. Now, it may not be without challenges or issues, because there will likely be some bumps along the way, but in the end, everything is going to be all right. We will get through it.

I share these sleep stories with you because it is so easy to feel bad about the choices we make for our families. The truth is, however, there is no instruction manual. There is no single book which tells us what is right and what is not. There will be illnesses, teething, growth spurts, and plenty of the dreaded sleep regressions. While facing these battles, I always remember thinking, *Is this going to get better, or is this just our new reality forever?* Well, it always did pass, so try to remember when facing these issues, it will pass eventually. Hang in there and don't give up. Don't question your parenting abilities in the meantime either. You are doing a great job.

Helpful Sleep Tools

While there were plenty of issues along the way which made bedtime difficult, there are some things which made bedtime much easier. First, never underestimate the bedtime routine, even for a newborn. I believe a routine can go a long way in helping our children sleep well at night. If there is a reliable routine, they can easily recognize it is bedtime and it can help keep them calm and comfortable leading up to their sleep. A nice bedtime routine could include a warm bath, drying them off, maybe a little lotion massage, putting on the pajamas, a story, a bottle, prayers, maybe even a certain song you sing each night. I even try to use some of the same language before bed, like telling my kids how much I love them, for example. I have found low lighting during the bedtime routine can make quite a difference. Keeping the lights low or off even during middle of the night feedings can make a huge difference as well. Basically, babies can get to the point where they associate the bedtime routine with long, nighttime sleep.

Then, there is the swaddle. I believe the swaddle requires the motto, "If at first you don't succeed, try, try again." Some people will say their babies hate to be swaddled. I was the first to say exactly that for my daughter and I chose not to swaddle her at night. Then, I started trying those swaddles with Velcro, and she seemed to handle those better. Still, neither of my children seemed to like the swaddle when I first put it on. I kept trying, however, because "they say" babies like to be swaddled. Eventually, I realized although they both always fought me putting them on, once swaddled, they calmed down quickly, especially when nursed right away. When they were swaddled, they slept longer and better. When I did not swaddle them, they would wake themselves up frequently with their startle reflex. I would see them throw their arms up in the air and when the arms fell back down, they woke up. So, in the end, swaddling helped substantially. Every child is different, so I am sure there are babies out there who truly never benefit from the swaddle, however, based on my experience, I think it is always worth a very good swaddling effort before giving up.

Once I had my kids swaddled and sleeping well, I started immediately worrying about how I was going to transition them out of the swaddles. I remember wondering if I made the worst mistake getting them so used to the swaddle. I thought maybe my kids would still be swaddled when they went to kindergarten. I always seemed to find something to worry about. Well, they weren't. Just like it took some getting used to swaddling them in the first place, it took some getting used to removing the swaddle as well.

The wearable blanket was a nice transition for us. Around four months old, we tried to transition our children to the wearable blanket. With both of my kids, we failed at first. I saw that startle reflex waking them up, so I would wait another week or so and then try again. Eventually, it worked. For my daughter, another idea which worked was to swaddle her with one arm out and then both arms out before transitioning to the wearable blanket. For my son, I just had to give it a couple of weeks and eventually he transitioned over smoothly. All of my children were sleeping well in the new wearable blanket between four and five months old. As with every transition, I made sure I was only changing one thing at a time. If I made too many changes at once and they started waking up, I would never know what particular change caused the problem. Then, you have to go back to square one, or start guessing.

Another must-have item for us was a sound machine which played white noise all night. After our first child was born, a great friend of ours told us we had to try white noise. I thought, *What on earth is that?* I honestly doubted it would make any difference, but I thought, *Why not?* If there was a chance the sound machine could make a difference and increase the length of sleep even a tiny bit, it would be worth a try. After all, our friend swore by it. The first night I tried the sound machine my daughter slept over an hour longer than she usually did and that continued to increase. It was amazing. We stopped using the sound machine around age one. Slowly over time, we simply turned the sound down until it was eventually turned off completely. Thankfully, the transition was easy.

A safely and slightly inclined place to sleep (approved by the pediatrician) right next to our bed when our babies were small was a colossal life-saver for us. We used this for both children. We wanted them close to our bed when they were little and I think the slight incline really helped them for comfort. It especially helped my son because of his reflux. He needed to be more upright. We tried using the bassinet; I feel like we all buy these thinking our babies will sleep so perfectly in them, but the lying flat thing was just unacceptable to our babies. If you are like me, then you probably worry about how the transition is going to go from the inclined rocker to the crib almost as soon as you put them in. The worry was again pointless as the transition went fine for all of my babies around eight weeks old.

Another item which we couldn't live without are blackout curtains. We have these in all of our children's rooms. It doesn't make the room completely black, which I think is a good thing because then they would really be confused whether it was naptime or night, but it makes it dark so they can sleep in a little longer than when the sun first comes up. I believe it helps them take longer naps as well.

I believe there will come a time in every parent's life when their child begins waking during the night, even if they never have before. I hate to say it, but probably multiple times. Although my kids slept very nicely from the time they were quite young, they both went through periods when they started night waking. One thing my pediatrician suggested with my second child was to remove the nightlight from the room. This was a pretty interesting concept. He said once you get him to sleep, turn off the nightlight. He said when they wake up and see everything around them, they are more likely to get up. If the light is off, sometimes, they just drift back off to sleep. I think it all depends on the child. An older child may be scared if they are used to having the nightlight, but maybe if I had kept it dark since they were tiny babies, it wouldn't have bothered them. This is just something to think about or possibly consider.

I know there are plenty of people out there where nighttime can be a beast. Nighttime is the time when children are separated from us parents. It can be challenging and even scary for them at times. Sometimes, I almost feel guilty when I tell my daughter this is her bed, and I need to go sleep in my own bed, knowing that I have someone else sleeping there with me. Don't let it worry you too much if you notice some anxiety around bedtime. I came across a chart one day which I thought could be beneficial. I believe a consistent bedtime routine always helped my kids feel comfortable and sleep easier. The chart provides a way to check off, or even better, place a sticker next to each bedtime step. You could make one of these on your own by listing all of the things which are part of the bedtime routine; for example, take a bath, dry off, dry hair, brush teeth, go potty, put on pajamas, say prayers, read a bedtime story, turn off the lights, and then go to sleep. The child can mark off each one and the last step, "go to sleep," can be marked in the morning. Once they get a certain number of stickers, they can earn something small if you like. From my experience, children love stickers, so this can be a neat way to get children a little more interested in bedtime and maybe even make it fun.

I have even seen a little contraption which plays a song with a little light show for a certain number of minutes and when it ends, the child knows it is time to close their eyes and fall asleep. You could also use lights with timers. A light could turn off after five minutes or so, which signals it is time to close their eyes and sleep. There are even special lights out there for children who wake too early. You can set them to turn on at a certain time. You can teach your child to stay in their room to rest at least until the light comes on. Some children may benefit from swapping a dim nightlight out for a bright one, or even simply leaving a door open with the light on for a little extra light. As I always say, do what works for you and your child and whatever you do, don't worry. These little bumps are likely stages which will pass.

For my daughter, naptime was actually the beast. She resisted her naps way more than her nighttime sleep. One day, I told my three-year-old daughter to stay in her bed, close her eyes, and go to sleep. She responded, "If you say so, but when you leave, I am going to get out of bed." Just great! Even at naptimes, I found I needed to pick my battles.

I did just that; I picked my battles. I quickly found that the more I fought it, the worse it became. After I tried what felt like everything that "they" said I should try, I decided to let it be. I let her stay in her room and read. Turns out, it was simply a stage and eventually it worked itself out. It did take some time, I am not going to lie, but in the end she started napping pretty consistently again. Remember, especially for the little ones, naps can also involve sleep training.

If there is one thing you take away from this chapter, let it be that all children are different. When it comes to sleeping, there is no perfect answer or perfect one-size-fits-all plan. Do what you feel is right for your child and that, my dear, is the perfect answer.

BREASTFEEDING

I am not sure if I could have ever been fully prepared for breastfeeding. Before having my first, I knew breastfeeding was important to me, but I could never have predicted quite how difficult it could be. You hear stories about the challenges of breastfeeding, but none of them truly compared to my actual experience.

Almost as soon as you are pregnant, I bet you will start hearing about breastfeeding. I feel like we need to prepare ourselves somewhat for the pressure out there to breastfeed. Many things "they say" and many of the things I read had me feeling like feeding my baby formula would make me a failure. Based on all the "talk" and the information out there, I felt like breastfeeding was something I had to do, at all costs. I worried so much that I wouldn't be able to breastfeed my child.

Try not to worry too much about nursing during your pregnancy. Try not to buy in too much when "they say" if you don't end up nursing your child it will be the end of the world. Some women choose not to breastfeed. Some women try and try to breastfeed successfully and it just does not work for them. Some women choose to breastfeed and do it successfully. Of these women, some have no issues, while there are plenty who face multiple challenges trying to figure it all out. In the end and after having three children of my own, I believe all of these women are right. A happy baby is a fed baby and that goes for one who is consuming either breast milk or formula. Don't allow yourself to feel guilty if you choose not to breastfeed, if breastfeeding simply doesn't work for you, or even if you choose to breastfeed longer than the average person would expect. I don't think it is the place of the media to decide what is best for your child. I believe you, the parents, are the ones who will make the best choice for your family, for your situation, and for your child.

After all my worries, I ended up nursing my first two children successfully for a long time, although it was not without challenges. I faced plenty of those along the way. Some women have an undersupply of breast milk, while some have an oversupply. Either of these circumstances can be challenging to navigate. Some have just the right amount. If this is you, I am totally jealous. I did not expect to need to supplement breast milk with formula for my first child. Based on everything I had read and heard, I cried when I learned I needed to supplement. I felt so guilty or like something was wrong with me. I thought, *Why can't I produce enough milk for my baby?* Looking back, I now realize that I should never have felt guilty. I was doing what was best for my child. I was allowing my child to be happy and healthy by supplementing. I know now that it was the best thing I could have done for her.

At the hospital, I talked with nurses and even lactation consultants and they all told me I needed to nurse my baby every three hours. When the nurses took the baby at nights during my hospital stay, they would bring her back to me every three hours to nurse. I didn't know any different, so I just assumed you should nurse every three hours all night and day.

When we got home from the hospital, my daughter became a different child. She was really fussy, especially at night. She would not sleep. She wanted to be held all night long. It got to the point where, when I would try to nurse her at night, and even eventually during the day, she would no longer want to latch. I would have to try so hard to get her to latch on to eat. At times, we were both in tears. I had no idea what I was doing wrong.

Luckily, my pediatrician recommended I go see a lactation consultant. We scheduled an appointment for the very next day. There, the consultant watched me nurse. I know this sounds strange, but after having a baby a lot of that vanity goes away since pretty much everyone sees everything. My daughter was weighed before and after I nursed so we could see how much milk she was getting. Turns out, she was not getting anywhere close to the amount of milk she needed. We had been home almost a week at this point, and my little girl was not getting enough food. She had been screaming and crying all night because she was starving. I had no idea all the screaming could be because I wasn't producing enough milk for her. Mommy guilt hit me like a ton of bricks.

So what was the plan moving forward? First I learned to never underestimate the placement of the baby while nursing. Making sure the baby has a good latch with their mouth open wide is important. It is helpful to have the baby lay on their side completely horizontal. My curved nursing pillow was an essential. It allowed my baby to be positioned perfectly, nice and high near the breast, and I didn't need to worry about stacking pillows all around me.

Second, we tried a new schedule. I nursed every hour and a half to two hours throughout the day. After I nursed, I supplemented with formula. After supplementing with the formula, I pumped to encourage more milk production. Why the need to pump? "They say" if you don't use it you will lose it. So, if I simply supplemented with the formula, my body would not know it needed more milk than it was producing. The idea was, if I pumped after I nursed, it would tell my body it needed to produce more.

It sounds exhausting and it was. I felt like a cow. Almost the only thing I did was nurse, bottle feed, and then pump. Shortly thereafter, it was time to start all over again. To be more specific, if I nursed the baby from 8:00 to 8:30, I would then make a bottle and bottle feed from 8:30 to—let's say—8:40. Then, I would get the baby situated and the pump ready, pump, then clean it. By this time it was 9:15. Then, I would nurse again between 9:30 and 10:00. Literally, all I was doing was feeding. You know when "they say," sleep when baby sleeps? I always thought "they" were crazy. Who has time for that? Well, I definitely didn't have time for that then because when the baby slept, I spent a lot of that time pumping. At night, I got a break from the pumping. I would simply nurse and then supplement with the formula at each feeding. We continued to see the lactation consultant who monitored the milk my baby was getting. I was able to decrease the amount of formula I was supplementing over time. This went on until just after my first baby turned seven weeks old. Was it hell? Yes. Did it impact my mental health? It is likely. But, did it work? Yes.

These seven weeks were a struggle for me. I was exhausted and felt really down. There were plenty of times I felt like a complete failure. I almost gave up nursing multiple times, but I decided to push on. I am glad I did, because once I was able to stop supplementing, things became much easier, but getting there was not easy to say the least. At the time, talking with good friends about the struggles I was feeling pulled me through. Now, looking back, I believe if I had quit, it would have been just fine too. The important thing is my baby would have been getting all of the milk she needed either way. I never would have guessed at the time, but my third baby needed to be switched to formula at six weeks old and she is as happy and healthy as can be.

I hope this experience helps other moms out there. People don't always tell you just how difficult breastfeeding can be and there are not many people out there who will tell you it is completely fine should you need to supplement or formula feed only. Don't let the things "they say" make you question your decision when it comes to feeding your baby. From experience, I advise to be careful not to let these opinions prevent you from making sure your baby is getting all the food they need to be happy and healthy. I wish I had known that it would be okay to supplement with formula earlier so my sweet little baby wouldn't have been starving. I am not saying if you face one challenge breastfeeding to just give up. I myself made the choice to hang in there. I am simply saying we as moms should make the decision we feel is right for us and for our child. If that choice is to breastfeed no matter the challenges, then by all means hang in there. You can do it. However, if it is not working out and the negatives outweigh the positives for you and your child, then know it is okay. I don't think any mom should feel guilty no matter what it is they decide.

So, what did I learn from all this? The need to supplement did not make me a failure. Supplementing made me a great mom because I was making sure my daughter had everything she needed to be happy, to be comfortable, and to grow.

I think it is really easy to judge the decisions of other moms when it comes to breastfeeding, especially when they do the opposite of what we are doing. We all want to feel like we are making the best decision for our child, but I think we need to try to feel comfortable in the decisions we make for ourselves and our baby and support other moms for whatever decision they make, even if it is different. The key here is we want our babies to have the calories and nutrition they need to grow. Any mom who is doing just that is doing a great job, no matter how it is done.

If you are like me, and you didn't even realize your baby wasn't getting enough, don't allow yourself to feel bad. You were doing what you felt was right. You were feeding your child. No one can ever truly know why a child is fussing. We are not mind readers. If we are loving and caring for our children, we are doing a great job no matter what. Everyone is going to make mistakes. We are human. We have to recognize that those mistakes do not make us any less of a parent.

Breastfeeding Challenges

Undersupply and determining a feeding schedule were not the only challenges which came my way while nursing. First, while we are trying to figure out this whole breastfeeding thing, we can experience quite a bit of pain. As if the pain from the birth experience itself isn't enough, it can be extremely painful as the milk comes in. In the beginning, my breasts were so terribly sore. What helped me most were hot showers. Hang in there, because the pain subsides pretty quickly. In addition to the sore breasts, painful cramping in the abdomen while nursing is common as the uterus continues to contract and shrink.

Once the pain subsided, there were more "pains," just maybe not the physical kind. One challenge I faced was the way my milk "let down." What is a "let down?" This is when the milk starts flowing to the baby. I am sure it is different for everyone, but I could tell my milk was flowing as I would feel a strange sensation in my breast and my baby would start to noticeably gulp the milk. It seems the milk "let-down" can be different from woman to woman. The number of let-downs during a nursing session can vary as well as the amount of milk which comes with each. The sensations experienced during the let-down can also be different, based on my conversations with other moms. For me, I usually had a let-down every five minutes or so, or about three times during a 15-minute nursing session. It sounds good to have three let-downs during a session, but my challenge was, each time, the baby would get a good flow of milk for a very short time and then not much of anything as the baby waited for the next let-down. The same thing occurred whether I was nursing or pumping. When the milk flowed less, my babies had a tendency to get lazy and even fall asleep. In order to have another let-down, however, the baby had to keep sucking to tell my body they needed more.

I figured out a trick which I think helped my reluctant, sleepy eaters. From early on, when my babies would stop sucking, I would tap their leg or bottom area gently a few times until they would start sucking again. This worked because it would wake them up enough to remind them to continue drinking. The more I did this as I felt my let-down coming on, the more they associated the tap with the need to drink the milk that was coming. This also really paid off down the road. My babies got used to the patting and it became a learned behavior. When I would pat, they would suck or drink. This was a big help during our bottle and sippy cup transition, because I would simply tap their leg and they would automatically begin drinking again. This small thing was a life saver because both of my children were reluctant to drink out of a bottle or sippy cup, especially at first. Who knew such a simple act could be so beneficial.

Another challenge I faced while breastfeeding was biting. My son was a biter. It was not fun, and the pain, oh the pain! Based on things "they say" about biting, it seems my son was an early biter at only four months old. I remember thinking, *Of course this would happen to me.* I was staying home with my son, so I planned to try to nurse him for his first year. So, what did I do? Well, I stuck with it. I tried a lot of different strategies and tried to stay patient.

First, I tried ignoring it. This was tough because it seriously hurt. Sometimes, I would literally scream out in pain. I mean, it is a pretty sensitive area. There were times he even drew blood, so this led me to my next strategy, which was yelling. When he bit, I would yell out like I was in pain. I tried just yelling. I tried saying, "No, that hurts," very loudly. Sometimes, this would shock him enough to make him stop, but overall the biting continued. It tended to happen while he wasn't actively drinking, so I found I had to really focus on nursing (which was hard with my daughter running around at the same time), and anticipate when he slowed down. During those times, I had my pinky finger ready. If he started to bite down, I would sneak my pinky finger in, break the seal and pull him away from the breast. I had learned the hard way not to get so surprised that you just jerk them off…also a very painful experience. He didn't like me stopping the flow of milk so much, so this helped. Once I stopped, I would say, "No, that hurts," sternly. Then, I would put him back on again.

My lactation consultant I had used in the past told me to try to nurse him with no distractions. I remember thinking, *How am I going to do that with a two-year-old around?* She was right though. It was best when I could nurse him in a dim, quiet room with the television off. I used the television at times to distract my two-year-old, so this was hard. I even learned if I sat there and looked at my phone while he nursed, he would be more likely to bite me. In the end, the best thing I could do was just anticipate it coming, immediately unlatch him, and tell him no.

During this process, which seemed to go on forever, I learned my son's reflux seemed to make the biting worse. I think the pain of the reflux made him bite down or arch back and yank frequently. I found the more the reflux was under control, the better he did. His pediatrician helped me with this. If this happens to you, hang in there. It took some time, but it stopped eventually.

If these issues so far didn't seem like enough, I had another big issue. I had this strange condition where my breast milk had too much lipase in it. Something with the balance was off which caused the milk to start smelling and tasting horrible after just three days in the fridge and even after three days in the freezer. This meant it was difficult to save the breast milk for more than three days. If I did want to store breast milk, I would have to continue rotating it out frequently with new milk. Goodbye to the idea of saving breast milk in the freezer for up to six months. The longer it stayed in the freezer, the worse it got, so whenever I pumped, I would freeze the new milk and feed the baby the oldest milk I had saved to keep my store as fresh as possible.

This was especially maddening when I needed to build up a breast milk store to go back to work. The milk in the freezer would not be good and the milk in the fridge would only last three days. Basically, what I ended up doing was pumping as frequently as possible to build up enough fresh milk in the fridge. I would pump in the early morning before the first feeding as well as at night after the last. I finally saved up enough fresh milk in the fridge to last for my first day back. Then I would hope to pump enough milk at work for the following day. This was especially stressful, because the anxiety of needing to produce enough led to less milk. This was just one more thing which was exhausting.

Unfortunately, this issue meant there were times we were left with breast milk which was no longer drinkable. Although I was assured it was safe, my babies simply wouldn't take it. I would try to mix some of the older milk with new milk to dilute the taste as best I could.

At least this meant I found other valuable uses for breast milk. There is not much breast milk can't do. If my children got a scratch, I would de-thaw some breast milk and apply it to the cut over a couple of days. The scratches healed immediately and are miraculously gone in a day or two using breast milk. There aren't many ointments out there which are great to use on a young baby, so this was quite valuable. I even thawed breast milk to use on minor cuts for my sixteen-month-old well after I was finished nursing. It worked like a charm. I rubbed breast milk over baby acne or even skin rashes. It worked wonders. I would put a couple of drops into my babies' eyes when they had little green boogies or a clogged tear duct. Believe it or not, it really helped.

I swear you will not get through nursing without at least one power outage, especially if you have a nice breast milk store in the freezer. It must be a rite of passage or something. As if we new moms don't have enough to stress out about, right? If this happens to you, or if you have any other reason you need to dispose of breast milk, don't throw it out. Put it into the baby's bath. Yes, just pour it right in there and let them soak. It really can work wonders for their skin and it makes you feel a lot better than throwing out that liquid gold.

Another issue I faced was nipple soreness, especially in the early days. Breast milk and lanolin were lifesavers. I think lanolin may be one of the most important things to invest in when it comes to breastfeeding. After nursing, I always expressed a little breast milk and rubbed it over my nipple area, let it dry, and then applied the lanolin. This made things a lot more comfortable.

If these issues aren't enough to deal with, all the while, you have to remember which breast you fed on last. When you breastfeed, you can't always start with the same side or you will have some major lopsidedness going on as one breast might think it needs to produce more than the other. This seems easy enough, until you have physical and mental exhaustion. I swear there were times I couldn't even remember my name, so how on earth was I supposed to remember which side I nursed on last? I found a nursing bracelet which helped. It was one of those soft bracelets like a big rubber band. On one side it said "right" and on the other side it said "left." So basically, you just reverse or flip the bracelet as you start each feed and then when you were ready to feed again, you look at the bracelet and it will tell you which side to begin on, right or left. The bracelet also had a little square you could slide to tell you which time you nursed last too so you knew when to feed again. If you don't want to go out and purchase anything, you can simply put a hair tie on your wrist and switch it to the other wrist when finished nursing as well. There are even free apps which can be used to track breastfeeding. Every little trick helps.

Once you feel like you have everything down, don't be surprised if something unimaginable happens. For us it was the stomach bug. This might sound crazy, but nursing my son while I had a stomach bug was the single most difficult experience I have had in my life so far. Thank goodness it was short-lived. I came down with the stomach bug in the early evening. I thought, *Okay, I can get through nursing him two more times and put him to sleep and all will be okay.* That was not the case. I remember I nursed him and had to quickly unlatch him, hand him to someone, and race to the bathroom to be sick.

I tried to stay hydrated, but could keep nothing down. Because of the dehydration, my son wasn't able to get enough milk. This meant he woke up a few extra times during the night, thirsty. I didn't have enough frozen milk stored to get him through the night, either. I was worried the baby would catch it, but thank goodness he didn't. I learned that good handwashing is key and sometimes the antibodies passed through the breast milk can help them fight the illness. Well, it finally ended. It was absolutely horrible, but there was one positive thing I learned: If I could get through this, then I could do anything, and I mean *anything.* It gave me a new perspective about just want "hard" meant. I thought nursing was difficult, I thought parenting was difficult, but I learned it could always be worse.

Pumping

Pumping was difficult for me. My body wouldn't produce as much on the pump. My pediatrician told me this was normal as the baby is much more effective at getting the milk than a pump. He told me the baby was likely getting more than what

I could pump. So, why do it at all? Well first, babies need to eat so frequently, we would hardly be able to go anywhere alone without leaving pumped milk. Secondly, I learned the hard way it is important to introduce the baby to a bottle sooner rather than later. When I tried to wean from the breast, my babies downright refused bottles at first. This was stressful to say the least; so if you can manage introducing the bottle with pumped milk, I would definitely recommend it.

I call pumping a necessary evil. I did find a few things which helped make pumping a little easier, however. First, make sure the breast shield—the part which goes directly on the breast—fits correctly. I had no idea the size that comes with the pump may not work for everyone. When you are pumping, the nipple should not touch the sides of the shield. If it does, it may be helpful to order breast shields with a larger diameter.

When packing the pump bag to take with you, you may want to consider packing some breast pump cleaning wipes, to wipe the parts down after use. I liked to always have cotton swabs in my pump bag. After you pump or rinse out the pump parts, some water can remain in the breast shield valves. I found if the parts did not dry completely before the next use, the water droplets would get sucked into the tubing. I used a cotton swab to dry out all those hard to reach places before I pumped. Also be sure to have a cooler with ice packs to keep your pumped milk fresh. A tube of lanolin is another great thing to carry with you. "They say" bring along a photo of your baby as looking at the baby can help the milk let-down. This didn't work for me, but I hear it works for some. For me, strangely enough, thinking about water helped my milk let-down. I would close my eyes and imagine a warm shower. I have no clue why it worked, but maybe my weirdness will help someone else.

Other helpful items are plenty of milk storage bags or containers to store milk in the freezer. I loved the micro-steam bags because you can use those to sanitize your pump parts in the microwave. I personally found this much easier than boiling them. Perhaps the most important item of all would be the breast pads. You definitely want to avoid leakage during the day. Breast pads can save you some embarrassment. One thing I didn't realize about breast pads at first is there are so many options out there, some of which can irritate your skin. I found one particular kind which was very comfortable for me. My advice would be, don't stock up on boxes of breast pads until you find some you like. They even make washable breast pads you can simply throw in the wash.

Weaning from the Breast

Weaning your baby from the breast is another topic people don't talk much about. I thought it would be as simple as to just stop nursing my baby. Wrong. I learned weaning is much less painful if it is done slowly over time. If you just stop, the milk can build up and be very painful and you can even get clogged ducts, which I hear are horrendous. I weaned over the course of a couple of weeks. It was still very painful, but I do think the slow wean helped a great deal. Those who weaned even more slowly than me told me they felt much less pain than I did.

Once I was ready to wean, I simply dropped one feeding at a time, leaving the morning and nighttime feedings for last. The pain I felt was very similar to the pain when my milk was coming in, when my breasts were very engorged and swollen. Switching out cold cabbage leaves on my breasts all day helped immensely. I also used cold ice packs, and even frozen corn kernels wrapped in panty hose (courtesy of a great friend). Warm showers and massages were helpful. I would express a small amount when it was very painful, but not too much as I did not want my body to think I still needed the milk production. Slowly, but surely, the pain subsided.

Something else people don't always tell you about is the mental side of things. It was not just the physical pain I experienced, it was also emotional pain. I missed being able to nurse my babies, especially at first. I missed the closeness. I shed plenty of tears over it. My hormones also seemed to go crazy, so I was much more emotional as I went through the weaning process.

The goal of this chapter is not to scare anyone. The goal is to share that it is normal to experience challenges. It may take some time to work out all of the kinks. It is important to know these kinks are to be expected. I remember being pregnant and thinking breastfeeding would be natural and it would just happen without issue. Well, I am here to tell you, if issues arise it is normal and okay. Remember, a happy baby is a fed baby. This is what matters most, not the process it takes to get there or how you go about making it happen.

SAMPLE SCHEDULES AND TRANSITION TIPS FOR BABY'S FIRST YEAR

In the previous chapter, I shared how I left the hospital thinking I should simply nurse every three hours, but this did not work for me. My children gained weight better and my milk came in better when I was feeding my babies every hour and a half to two hours throughout the day. So, what are we moms supposed to do when it comes to feeding? Unfortunately, I don't think there is one easy answer. I think it depends on the child and mom. It depends on how much milk the mother produces. I was never a mom who had a never-ending milk supply. If anything, I produced less than I needed, but the feeding schedule we chose worked well for us. As I share samples of the schedules we used, don't forget that every baby is different. What worked for me may or may not work for you. The key is there is no manual, no schedule which is set in stone that works for any and all babies. Choose a schedule based on what works for you, based on what works for your baby, and based on the advice of your child's pediatrician.

Sample Feeding and Sleep Schedules

Month 1:

We nursed every one and a half to two hours during the day. In total, it was about nine to ten nursing sessions per day (over the 24-hour period). At first, I nursed every three hours throughout the night. I monitored the dirty diapers based on the hospital recommendations to ensure the baby was getting enough to eat. In the early days, both of my children slept and ate for most of the day and night, especially in the early parts of the first month. We mostly nursed then slept. There was a little waking time between the naps and the next feeding time. As my babies grew, I would let them be my guide. If they wanted to sleep longer between feedings at night, I let them as long as it was okay with the pediatrician and wasn't interfering with their weight gain.

Month 2:

We nursed every two hours throughout the day for a total of nine feedings a day. I really struggled, especially in the first couple of months, on whether I should wake my children when they were sleeping to eat or wait until they woke on their own. After all, they say, "Never wake a sleeping baby." Since I had to feed my babies every one and a half to two hours during the day, this proved quite challenging. I ended up leaning more towards waking them from naps during the day if they needed to eat, but letting them sleep at night. I didn't wake them from every nap, but I tried to do my best to work in the nine feedings throughout the day. I think this really helped my children sleep better at night. They got plenty of food during the day, which helped them go longer stretches at night. Naps were different than night time sleep as well. During the day, there would be some noise as they slept. They would sleep in a rocker or a swing with light coming in through the windows. At night, they would sleep in a dark room.

The last regular feeding for us was a late "dream feed." Sometimes, I would nurse around 9:00 p.m. and my babies would fall asleep afterward. I would hold them or lay them down, and even interact with them if they woke until about 11:00 when I would do one last nursing session before putting them to bed for the night. Sometimes, my babies wanted to cluster feed at this last feeding and I let them. They would be nice and full before bed and would sleep for a longer stretch of time. The later bedtime meant they were sleeping more of the hours when we were asleep.

Before having a baby, I assumed babies should all go to sleep early. This works for some, but it took some time for us to start putting our babies to bed early. Now as toddlers, my children go to sleep around 8:00. Over time and very slowly, we moved the bedtime earlier and earlier. An earlier bedtime became easier for us when I wasn't breastfeeding as frequently.

During the second month, my children were awake a lot more during the day. Their naptimes would vary greatly. Some days they would nap a lot and some days not as much. There wasn't a lot of consistency yet. In the early months, we would try to follow the schedule of eat, sleep, play, and repeat. Usually, my babies would fall asleep after a nursing session. When they woke, we would play and interact until they were hungry again. I think this schedule helped them get some energy out during the day as well as plenty of sleep, which in turn helped them sleep well at night.

Months 3 and 4:

During months three and four, I still nursed eight times a day during waking hours, about every two hours. We were lucky because during the third month, many nights, my children slept through the night. This meant night time feedings weren't needed, unless they happened to wake. When my children woke during the night, I always nursed them and put them right back to sleep. Remember, not all babies sleep through the night at this point. Some do not sleep through the night for a very long time and this is all normal and okay. Try not to compare or get discouraged by how long your baby sleeps, and let your baby be your guide. Every baby is different.

My daughter would wake up around 8:00 a.m., nurse, and go back to sleep until around 10:00 or 10:30. Then, she would take two or three naps during the day. We still kept both of our babies up pretty late at this point, until 10:30 or 11:00 at night for the "dream feed." The nap schedule at this time was pretty inconsistent. Naps still took place in a swing, rocker, or on my chest around this age. We started transitioning naps into the crib when they were around four months old. This worked out for both babies, slowly but surely.

During the fourth month, my milk had come in very well and after a long night's sleep, I would have too much in the morning. This caused my daughter to spit up, projectile style, after her first feeding of the day. I ended up needing to pump for a couple of minutes before the first feeding so the milk flow wouldn't be so strong. This worked well; no more projectile spit up, thank goodness.

This month included the bottle strike as well. My children hated bottles. They only wanted to nurse (more on this later).

Months 5 and 6:

During month five, I decreased the nursing sessions for my son to seven per day. By the time month six came to a close, we had introduced baby food for my daughter. We slowly introduced it earlier for my son (when he turned four months old) due to his issues with reflux. By the end of the sixth month, my son was nursing six times with three baby food meals and my daughter had switched to formula. She was given five six-ounce bottles per day with baby food in between.

As I was still breastfeeding, my son ate or drank every two hours or so. His schedule was (times are approximate as I learned babies can be quite unpredictable):

8:00 a.m. – Nurse
Nap
10:00 a.m. – Baby food and baby cereal
12:00 p.m. – Nurse
Nap
2:00 p.m. – Baby food and nurse
4:00 pm. – Nurse
Nap
5:30/6:00 p.m. – Baby food and cereal
7:30 p.m. – Nurse
9:30 p.m. – Nurse and bed

This schedule seems strange when I look at it now. You can really see why each baby is different. This schedule allowed me to nurse my son six times a day. It also allowed me to nurse him before his three naps and bedtime. As I mentioned earlier, "they say" you shouldn't nurse your child to sleep, however, I did. It worked for us. The naps you see here ranged from about 30 minutes to two hours in length. Naps were still pretty inconsistent, but they started to resemble some sort of a scheduled at this age. Both of my babies still nursed upon waking and went back to sleep for a morning nap. Around this time, my baby and toddler's nap schedules started to overlap a little and this was nothing short of amazing.

Month 7:
This is where the schedules really started to vary between my nursing baby and my formula-fed baby. I will share both schedules below.

My formula, bottle-fed daughter's schedule:
7:00 a.m. – Bottle
Nap
10:00 a.m. – Cereal and baby food
12:30 p.m. – Bottle
Nap (anywhere from one to two-and-a-half hours)
3:30 p.m. – Baby food
5:30/6:00 p.m. – Cereal and baby food
Nap (usually a short 30-minute nap)
9:00 p.m. – Bottle and bedtime

My breastfeeding son's schedule:
(This month, I nursed five times a day with three meals in between.)
6:00 a.m. – Nurse
Nap (depending on when he woke)
8:00 a.m. – Breakfast
10:00 a.m. – Nurse
Nap
12:30 p.m. – Lunch
2:30 p.m. – Nurse
Nap
4:30/5:00 p.m. – Dinner
6:30 p.m. – Nurse
9:00 p.m. – Nurse and bedtime

Due to his reflux, more frequent feedings of less volume worked best for my son.

Month 8:
My daughter's schedule remained the same as month seven. However, my son's schedule did change. We decreased nursing

sessions to four times a day with three meals in between. This would remain my son's schedule until his 11th month:

6:00 a.m. – Nurse
(Sometimes a nap here, depending on waking time)
9:00 a.m. – Breakfast
11:30 a.m. – Nurse
Nap
2:30 p.m. – Lunch
4:30 p.m. – Nurse
Nap
6:30 p.m. – Dinner
8:30 p.m. – Nurse and bedtime

Late afternoon naps were usually the short naps for my children. Eventually, the afternoon nap would no longer be required.

Month 9:
My son's schedule remained the same this month.

My daughter's new routine:
7:30 a.m. – Cereal and baby food
10:00 a.m. – Bottle
Nap (one to two hours)
1:00 p.m. – Baby food
3:30 p.m. – Bottle
Nap (one to two hours)
6:00/6:30 p.m. – Cereal and baby food
9:00 p.m. – Bottle

What accounted for the change in my daughter's schedule that month is that she no longer needed her early morning nap. We began our day with breakfast rather than the morning bottle.

Month 10:

My son's schedule remained the same, but this month, my daughter decided to become a picky eater. She didn't want to eat her baby food unless it was in a squeeze packet. She preferred to feed herself finger foods. Our pediatrician recommended a new schedule and it worked. We paired mid-day bottles with her meals, allowing her to eat first and finish with her bottle. The idea was she would be hungrier at each meal, thus more likely to eat her food. I think the new schedule helped with our transition to regular milk in the sippy cups because when my daughter turned one, we simply changed the formula to milk with each meal. Her new schedule was as follows:

8:30 a.m. – Breakfast, followed by bottle
10:00/10:30– 6 oz. bottle
Nap (45 minutes to two hours)
1:00/1:30 p.m. – Lunch and bottle
Nap (45 minutes to two hours)
5:30 p.m. – Dinner and bottle
8:30 p.m. – 8 oz. bottle and bedtime

Month 11:

My daughter's schedule remained the same, however, she started fighting and even skipping her afternoon naps.

For my son, we transitioned from breast milk to formula this month. We found a special formula that helped my son's reflux, more so than the breast milk. With this change, we also changed my son's feeding schedule to something similar to my daughter's schedule at this age. He also dropped his afternoon nap this month, which meant he was only needing one mid-day nap. His new schedule was as follows:

8:00 a.m. - Breakfast, followed by bottle
12:00 p.m. - Lunch, followed by bottle
Nap (two and a half to three hours)
4:00 p.m. - Dinner, followed by bottle
8:00 p.m. - Bottle and bedtime

Month 12:

My son's schedule remained the same this month. My daughter dropped her extra mid-morning bottle along with one nap. My children had the same schedule during their 12th month:

Breakfast with bottle/sippy cup
Lunch with bottle/sippy cup
Nap (two to three hours)
Dinner with bottle/sippy cup
Bottle/sippy cup before bed

There is so much information here, but I feel it is important because every baby and situation is different. Some babies have medical issues which interfere with feeding, such as my son. Babies are nursed for varying amounts of time, while some are bottle fed from day one. Nursing moms produce varying amounts of milk. Every baby and schedule is different, but as I have said before these are the schedules which worked for us. You can see just how different schedules can be even between siblings. You can see that nursing sessions or bottle feedings and naps are gradually dropped until eventually it evolves into a more regular feeding and nap schedule as they become toddlers.

In one of the novels I recently read, I remember one of the characters saying that time was just a human invention. I thought this was an interesting concept. I guess it is a human invention as humans originally told time by following the sun. The more I thought about this concept, I realized just how much we put into time today. Time is everything. Schedules for our children are everything. We wake up around this time, eat breakfast, lunch, and dinner around these times. We go to sleep at this time. I think a schedule can be quite valuable for children, but on the other hand, it can cause me a great deal of stress the second I veer away from it. I feel stressed if we stay out in the morning too late, because my baby might fall asleep in the car and we may miss a good naptime. I worry if we eat lunch too late, my baby might go down for a nap too late, and then he won't be able to go to bed as easily at night. In the end, I guess time is just a human invention. I believe there was a time when time didn't matter so much. Maybe people didn't feel so horrible for being late.

I am not trying to get too life-altering with this thought here, but I believe when planning out our routines, it is always nice to plan in some "flex" time. You never know when a neat opportunity or experience could present itself, and you want to take advantage of those opportunities to take some time to enjoy yourself. In these moments, you don't want to feel like you need to rush to move on to the next task at hand. These little unexpected moments can be the moments which bring us the most joy in life. I have learned that some of these moments could even be worth a missed nap, if you can believe it. I actually have to remind myself not to be so busy. Every day there are things we want to accomplish or check off our list. I feel like I always have a schedule in my mind. When I think about it this way, it sounds exhausting, and it truly is. This flex time can be a little extra time when we can just sit back, relax, and enjoy the moment. It can give our bodies and our minds a little break.

Feeding Challenges and Transitions

When I think about what "they say" about children and eating, it completely stresses me out. They say if the breast milk or bottle touches the baby's mouth, it must be used within one hour. After the hour, you must discard it. They say if you are feeding a baby with a spoon straight from the baby food jar, you cannot refrigerate and save the remainder. Only food which has not come in contact with that spoon should be saved (and for 24 hours or less). They say you should never heat up food more than once. They say you should never thaw and re-freeze items. They say breast milk only lasts for three days in the fridge. They say ground beef should be used within two days after store purchase. They say, they say, they say...the list goes on and on.

I find all the rules completely overwhelming. I am no food expert, so it is hard to keep track of what you actually can do these days. I always tried my best to follow all of the rules just in case, but I assume our parents think we are crazy. They didn't do any of these things or follow any of these rules. We turned out okay. It made me realize I need to stop worrying so much about every little thing. It is enough to drive a person insane. I think the best course of action is simply to do our best to follow the information we receive from the hospital, OB, and pediatrician. If there are questions, ask, and in the interim, try not to let it stress us out too much.

Breast to Bottle Transition

I found transitioning from the breast to bottle and then from bottle to sippy cup to be pretty anxiety inducing. I mean, at least for me, what transition is not anxiety inducing, but these two were huge. My kids had a lot of trouble with these transitions. I guess they didn't like change when it came to their eating habits.

I didn't produce enough milk for my daughter, so we supplemented formula at each feeding for a while after she was born. Once we no longer needed to supplement, we stopped the bottles all together and I exclusively nursed for a while. Once I started preparing to return to work from maternity leave, I tried a bottle thinking there should be no issue as she had so many bottles as an infant. Man was I wrong. She flat out refused it.

I tried everything. I tried different bottles and what felt like hundreds of different nipples. I tried having different people give her the bottle. I even tried leaving the house completely while someone else fed her. I tried putting her on the breast and then quickly switching her to the bottle nipple. I tried waiting until she was very sleepy and relaxed to start the bottle. I tried putting breast milk in the bottle. I tried putting formula in the bottle. I even tried putting her favorite thing, her vitamin D drops, into the bottle with the milk. I tried feeding her in different positions, even in different places, like a bouncy seat, for example. I found the most success (and by success I mean she took maybe a half an ounce) by walking her around bouncing her while she drank, being outside while I did this was especially helpful. But the thing that did it in the end was simply not giving up.

Everyone told me, don't give up; she will take it and she did after two full weeks of trying. I kept trying the bottles, and sure enough, the day before I went back to work, she drank some from a bottle. I had her in her bouncy seat and I tried this new, super expensive bottle nipple which looks extremely strange. It was supposed to look and feel just like a boob. She took about an ounce from this nipple and then I immediately put a regular nipple on the bottle and she took a couple more ounces. Later that day, she took an entire bottle from my sister in that same bouncy seat. I cannot even put into words the relief I felt when she took that bottle the night before I went back to work. I literally jumped up and down and did a happy dance. So, don't give up. It will happen. Keep thinking positive. They will take it if you are patient. Stick with it. Even if they don't end up taking it before you return to work, once you aren't there to feed them and once they get hungry enough, they are going to eat. These were words from our pediatrician. I know it sounds stressful, but hang in there.

We switched my son from breast milk to a special formula when he was around ten and a half months old. He already struggled with bottles in general, and the fact that he hated the taste of formula did not help. Once again, sticking with it did the trick. We tried different formulas (especially with the specialized formulas, different brands do taste different) and I kept offering bottles. I started mixing my breast milk with the formula and slowly decreased the amount of breast milk in the mixture. I bounced him around the house while he ate. It was the only way he would take it. My arms always felt like jelly at the end of a feeding, but eventually, he caught on and he started taking the bottles of formula just fine. So, once again, I say to just hang in there.

I know I am talking a lot about the liquid diet here, but for me, food-related transitions were worrisome to say the least. I found myself full of questions, especially when transitioning to milk. Is my baby drinking enough? Is my baby going to be hydrated enough based on the liquids he is taking in? Are my children getting enough calories, enough nutrients? My child loves his bottle—how is he going to do without it? The bottle is part of our bedtime routine. Will my child go to sleep without it? What if my child doesn't like the taste of milk? Try not to worry. As parents, we will likely find ourselves worrying about what is to come, but as we look back we will almost certainly find our worries were futile as it all works out in the end.

Bottle to Sippy Cup Transition

Switching from the bottle to the sippy cup was one of those nerve-racking transitions for me, so I tried to simply handle it like I had other successful transitions in the past. When facing a transition, I have found it beneficial to change only one thing at a time. What ended up working for us was to slowly change one bottle feeding to one sippy cup feeding, until we were down to all sippy cups. Even still, my children had a hard time transitioning to the sippy cup at all because they were switching from warm milk in the bottle to cold milk in the cup. So, I backtracked a bit and started heating their bottles a little less and less until they were room temperature. With the sippy cup, I started heating the milk to room temperature, and then slowly heated them less and less until it was completely cold.

I transitioned the middle of the day feedings first, just as I did when weaning from the breast, and saved the naptime and night time feedings for last. We tried many different sippy cups until we found ones which worked. We loved the sippy cup lid which looked and acted like a bottle nipple but was actually in the shape of a sippy cup lid. They screw onto the bottle, just like a regular nipple would. These worked wonders for us. It still resembled a bottle, and I could help them hold it like I would a bottle at first if needed. This was especially helpful when we first transitioned the naptime and night time bottles. Once we got used to the sippy spout, we switched to straw cups. My young toddlers found it easier to suck through the straw, likely because they didn't need to tip the cup and it was more like sucking on a bottle nipple.

Leaving the bedtime feeding for last meant my kids had a sippy cup of milk before bed for quite some time. For my daughter, we stopped offering the milk before bed around the time where we were thinking about potty training.

For my son, we removed the last cup of milk a lot sooner due to his reflux. The liquid was not helping him just before bed. This was a bit of a challenge because he loved his bedtime milk and it was part of his bedtime routine. One of our doctors suggested rather than simply stopping the milk, to give him less and less overtime. So, we decreased the amount by an ounce every few days at bedtime. Eventually, he was only taking an ounce. At that point, he stopped caring for it so much and we just took it away.

For us, slowly but surely we won the race, but I have heard

"them say" when it comes to transitions, a cold turkey approach is best. In this approach, basically you just remove all the bottles and only provide milk in the sippy cup from that point forward. I haven't tried this approach when it comes to feeding, but I bet it could work if you needed it to. There are always multiple paths to a destination. So, I will say it again: Do what works for your children and your situation. Every child and family is different. Use that mommy intuition.

Don't be surprised if once you make it through the bottle to sippy cup transition, you later find your children don't even like milk. My daughter wasn't a big fan of milk as a young toddler. It actually seems pretty common, I've found after talking with friends whose children don't love milk. For my daughter, what worked best was to stick with it because eventually, she drank more and more. Surprisingly, by the time she was four, it became her drink of choice. We couldn't even keep milk in the fridge it was gone so fast.

How important is drinking lots of milk anyway? I have heard "them say" that, when you think about it, it is strange that we are the only mammals who drink other mammal's milk. This is an interesting thought. I guess I will just use this idea to make me feel better. If anything, it tells me that we are all dealing with different situations and stressors, but in the end it is quite likely that our kids will be okay. One of my child's doctors told us too much milk can actually impact iron absorption. Sometimes, too much milk fills them to the point where they won't eat as much. So, once again, try to not worry yourself too much over the milk issue. Offer the nutrition as best you can and do what you feel is best for your child. When in doubt, always reach out to your pediatrician. Mine has a plethora of great ideas and always makes me feel better as it is usually not as big of an issue as I make it out to be. If they feel there is an issue, they can guide you to the appropriate professionals to help you out.

All things considered, it can be alarming when it comes time to decrease the amount of liquids our children are getting in their diet, because it is a huge change. I had to remind myself as food intake increases, so do the nutrients and calories they are taking in from that food. We can't expect our kids to take as much milk as they once took formula. They simply don't need as much. I will never forget my pediatrician saying, "Don't worry, children will eat. They will not let themselves starve. They will take the milk, the bottle, the formula, or the cup when they get hungry or thirsty enough, so do what you think is best and try not to worry in the meantime."

Baby Feeding Troubles

When you hear about picky eaters, one usually thinks toddlers, but there were times even feeding my babies was a struggle. First, starting baby food for the first time can be exciting, but I have learned it can also be challenging because they may even hate it at first. It is so different from a bottle, so it may take some getting used to. Don't give up; they will eat it eventually.

My son has always been a pretty good eater, but there were times he became uninterested in his baby food, especially certain types of vegetables. During these times, I would offer him at least two different kinds of baby food during the meal and alternate them. I might do a couple of bites of his favorite and then sneak in a bite of the one he wasn't into. Another idea which worked for us was giving him a second spoon. This usually distracted him a bit so I could sneak the bites in his mouth and make him a little more interested in eating. We even gave him a small toy to play with at his high chair while we fed him at times for a little distraction. Also, play around with the foods they are eating so they get some nice variety and you might find some new foods which spark their interest.

My daughter went through a stage at about nine months old

when all she seemed to want was squash, yogurt, or those baby food squeezable pouches. Anything we gave her in a pouch, she would eat. This became frustrating, but we realized she seemed to favor foods she could feed herself. Thus, we tried giving her squishy, small finger foods she could feed herself by using her hands. In between these bites, we snuck bites of baby food into her mouth. We also gave her the pouches since she seemed to like them. If you are struggling with this, you can even buy the reusable baby food pouches which you can fill with anything you like. I was so worried she wasn't eating enough and that it would last forever, but soon she was back to eating baby food again and she had a great taste for lots of finger foods.

I remember when my daughter was a young toddler, my pediatrician said to offer three items at each meal: two items you know she will eat, and one item she probably won't. He said if she doesn't eat it, continue to offer it again at other meals. Eventually, the child may eat it and actually enjoy it. This has worked really well for us. "They say" it takes multiple tries for a baby to begin liking a particular food, so try not to give up. Sometimes I find this true, and sometimes not, but if it helps a child to expand their appetite and enjoy new foods even a little, for me it is worth the try.

ALMOST OUTNUMBERED: FROM ONE CHILD TO TWO

Once you're getting used to one child, you may find yourself having a second. I remember being so busy with my first child that my second pregnancy flew by. I felt unprepared for the second baby and I was scared of what was to come. I wasn't sure if I would be able to manage two children at once, especially when they were just under two years apart. I wondered, *Could my heart possibly be big enough to love another child as much as I love my first?* Turns out, it is unbelievable how easily your heart can expand to love another child just as much. There is so much love, but it all fits in there just right. The love was the easy part. The challenge was learning to manage two children at once. It was such a big change and to be honest, I would not call it an easy change. To say it took some time for us to get adjusted to a new schedule would be an understatement, but we did get there. I promise you do adjust, no matter how hard it seems at first. Eventually, you will get into more of a routine and things will calm down. You will start getting used to it. I am not saying things will always be easy, but there will be plenty of good moments to make up for the rough ones.

You may have some extra tough days, and these days might make it pretty difficult to focus on those positives or good moments, but try, because it will be worth it. One day, I specifically recall, was a very busy day...

I wake the kids and start getting them ready for my daughter's first visit to the dentist. Of course, I just barely have enough time to feed both of the kids breakfast in the morning, so I don't feed myself. I dress both kids, but I am still in lounging clothes. I remember seeing a quote once about how a mom makes sure her kids look great when leaving the house only to look like a slob herself. That is definitely me, and I'm okay with it. I get my daughter on the potty, change my son's diaper, and we are about to head out and actually be on time! Wow, this never happens. That is, until my daughter reminds me we haven't brushed her teeth.

I tell her, "Don't worry, they will brush your teeth at the dentist."

This leads to tears, a fit, and a whining, "No, Mommy, we *have* to brush my teeth before we go to the dentist and make sure they are *clean*."

Oh, that face she is making as she gazes up at me with those big eyes. It gets me every time. Thus, I rush upstairs, put my son in the crib, and brush her teeth as fast as possible.

Then comes the, "Mommy, I *want* to do it."

I respond, "No, we are going to be late. Let Mommy do it."

Thank goodness, she accepts and lets me brush them. It is a miracle. Most days, I would have gotten more tears and a fit. We leave the house with an arrival time of only five minutes late. Not so bad right? Not really, but it was only because I had planned to leave the house in time to get there 15 minutes early. A note: With kids in tow, always plan to get everywhere at least 15 to 30 minutes early so you may actually arrive on time.

On the way to the dentist, I had received a call from the GI doctor's office because I left a message the day before about my son being constipated yet again, even though he was taking medicine three times a day to help. The nurse told me the doctor would like to do an X-ray today to see how much fecal matter my son had in his system. I added this to my list of things to do. As my son had been super fussy, I planned to take him to the doctor in the afternoon after naps—however, now we would be making a trip to the hospital to get an X-ray.

At the dentist's office, a really good friend of mine who is a dental hygienist cleans my daughter's teeth. I was a little unsure of how this might go. My son was with me and my husband wasn't there. Turns out, my daughter did perfectly. My friend was able to use all of her tools, clean her teeth, and even floss. My daughter sat there perfectly happy and my son was so good, just sitting there in my lap. When we left, my daughter actually said, "I love the dentist." Win!

I scarf down half a not-so-tasty breakfast bar and head over to swim lessons. Luckily, swim lessons went wonderfully! Both my daughter and son were on their best behavior. Another win! Wow, this is too good to be true!

I wanted to make sure my son was feeling okay before putting him through this inevitable wait time and X-ray, so we safely rush on over to the doctor and luckily make it there before the lunch cut-off. The doctor confirms my son is well, but he has a bruise on his gums from his molars which are coming in. He tells me the painful teething, the reflux, or the constipation could all be causing him to be fussy. He says he will let the GI doctor work through the GI issues, but that he can confirm my son is well with a bad case of teething.

On the way home from the doctor, I pick up some fast food including a kid's meal as a reward for my daughter for doing well at swim lessons. I know, mother of the year, right? I do bribe my children to behave and listen at their outside activities. Hey, whatever works, right? When we get home, I have to bring a million things inside: the toys to keep my son awake in the car so he will not fall asleep and then miss his nap, food, drinks, the diaper bag, the swimming suit and towel, the baby carrier, and both kids of course. I get everything inside and hurry to feed the children with the hopes of putting them down for their nap before their busy afternoons start. After all, it is starting to get late. When I say late, I mean like midday, but why does it feel like it is bedtime?

I give my daughter her food. I let my food sit and make my son his special lunch, soy and dairy free macaroni and cheese. I'm not sure what is in this stuff, but it looks healthy. As I make the special macaroni and cheese, I heat up some sweet potato to give my son while he waits for his main course. Of course, he eats this too quickly and then proceeds to scream for his macaroni and cheese, which for some reason is taking way longer than the recommended nine minutes to cook. I sit down and take two bites of my food as we wait. My daughter says, "Mommy, I need to go potty." I am so glad she tells me, but does it always have to be at the worst time ever? I put my burger down, take her to the bathroom, and go finish putting together the macaroni and cheese. My son continues to scream and my daughter joins in, yelling she is done going potty and that I need to come get her "right this second." Now, here is "modeling" behavior at its finest.

I yell back, "Honey, you need to be patient. I am putting together your brother's lunch. He is so hungry that he is screaming." Yeah right, patience, what's that?

I run and get my daughter as I blow, blow, blow, the scolding macaroni and cheese, for which my son continues to cry. Finally, I put the food on his plate and he is happy. I sit down and eat my freezing cold fast food. Yuck, but at least I am eating. At this point, I am already starting to become frustrated, but I try to keep calm and "let it go" as Elsa would say.

I start a show for my daughter as I get my son ready for his nap. He is covered in macaroni and cheese and it really stinks. I realize there is no cleaning this stuff off, even with wipes, so I put him into the bathtub. I take off his diaper and he has pooped. It's a normal poop, so I am wondering if I am supposed to still get this X-ray. As a mom, I swear my days have so many more questions than answers! My son proceeds to somehow pull the dirty diaper out from underneath him. Poop is now on his floor. Oh, great! I wipe him off and then start to wipe the floor. As I do this, my son runs over and squats beside his crib. I try to get him, but it's too late; he has already peed all over his floor. Fantastic! Now, I clean this up too.

Once in the bath, the soap falls off the side of the tub four times before I can make it stay put and my son is screaming because he wants to hold it. Finally, I get him all cleaned up and dressed. As I rock him to sleep he looks up at me and says, "Mama, I love you," pretty clearly for a 15-month-old. My heart just melts, and all the rushing and frustrations of the day go away. I lay him down in his crib and go clean up messy clothes, the extra cereal with milk I left on the counter this morning which has likely started to smell, the food and napkins all over the place, and my son's high chair. It's all good though because the loving I received has made my day all better.

Oh, but I am not out of the woods just yet. I run upstairs to grab my daughter's ballet leotard. Thank goodness my husband came home to take her to ballet while I take my son to get the X-ray. I am flipping through the stack of clothes which I laid flat but have yet to have a chance to fold, and I flip the top half of the clothes off of the back of the dryer. *Really, did that have to happen?* There is no way I can reach the clothes back there. I grab the hook which is used to pull down our attic, climb up on the top of the dryer, and start fishing for clothes. They come out dusty and need to be rewashed. Well, at least I figured out how much that area needs to be cleaned. My husband comes upstairs and laughs as he sees what I am doing while kneeling atop the washing machine. I had to laugh too. At some point, the daily craziness just becomes humorous. I quickly pack up my son's dinner which I had forgotten all about and rush out the door. In the car on the way to the hospital, I take a deep breath.

Sometimes with two, I swear I am just rushing, rushing from one thing to the next. At times, I feel like I can't think or even breathe, but at the end of this day, I look back and remember how proud I was when I saw my daughter actually swim. I mean really, it brings tears to my eyes because I am so very proud of her. It makes my heart so full. I remember how proud I felt when my daughter sat in the big dentist chair and smiled. I remember the hugs, the snuggles, and the "I love you's." Ladies and gentlemen, this is what life is all about. When in doubt, when things get tough, wait for it. Yes, wait for it. Wait for the positives. They will come, I promise, and those positives will be the things which continue to stay with you. And, they will help get you through life with two.

Adjusting to More Than One Child

As I transitioned from one to two, I remember feeling so much guilt because I couldn't give either child as much attention as I wanted. At first, I felt like I could not give my older child enough attention, because the baby needed so much time, and then slowly, as the baby was able to calm himself more, he was held less, and I felt the baby was not getting enough attention. At least, he was definitely not getting as much attention as my first born did as a baby. I remember wondering, *Is the substantially less attention going to impact him negatively?* I had to tell myself it probably wouldn't harm him. In actuality, maybe it ended up making him a bit more independent than his sister, which is not necessarily a bad thing. As a young toddler, my second born was able to entertain himself a lot longer than his sister ever could. I wonder if this had anything to do with the more independence he needed as an infant. I will say it again, during this stage, we have to do what works for our family and we have to believe as long as we are showing each child love and doing what works best, that won't harm anyone in the long run, and maybe it will even make things better.

I honestly think our true key to success was baby wearing. The baby wrap carrier was essential for us, especially when my second child was small. I would wrap that baby right up to my chest and he would sleep. I would use this time to make breakfast or lunch for my daughter or to do activities with her.

With a baby and a toddler, some (or lots) of jealousy is sure to take place. We tried to give our first born some one-on-one time each day, even if it was only ten or 15 minutes. When Daddy got home from work he could give her attention, but I also thought it was important for her to get some one-on-one attention from me since I was always with the baby. Also, finding someone to watch the baby so my husband and I could spend some time with our first born like we used to as three was really beneficial. I think the shock of no longer having the time together as three could be tough for any toddler. Still having moments with the three of us from time to time really seemed to make a difference in my toddler's attitude.

Leaving the House

When I became a mother of two, leaving the house seemed scary again. I was scared to go to the grocery store, especially for the first time, because I had no idea what to expect. I wasn't even sure how I would manage to get the kids into the shopping cart, and back out to the car and into their car seats safely. I remember parking and thinking, *Okay now what do I do? Do I get the toddler or the baby first?* It seems simple, but it really stressed me out.

Two things were helpful. I found I could put the baby into my carrier or wrap, and then walk over and gently help my toddler out of the car seat and car. Another option was getting my toddler out first, and walking around to the baby's side with her. I would have her hold my leg while I got the baby out. Basically, the rule was I needed to feel her touch the entire time. This way, I knew she was right there because I could feel her holding onto me. It also gave her something to do so she didn't just run out into oncoming traffic.

I remember seeing an idea one day where you can put a bumper sticker or magnet of a hand print on the car next to the door. The rule is, the toddler must touch the handprint at all times when they are not holding your hand. So, as you load the baby in and out, the toddler is always right next to you with their hand on the sticker. I bet you could even create a magnet on one of those photo sites with a handprint if needed. If you don't have a sticker or magnet, the rule could be the toddler needs to touch the door handle at all times. Of course, if they challenge you and let go, they get a consequence, because as we all know "challenging" is a part of everyday life when you have a toddler around.

Then, once inside the store, things didn't get much easier. Even on a good day, I had constant anxiety just waiting for one of them to start screaming. Overtime, the anxiety decreased, and not to worry, one day you will have an anxiety free grocery trip.

Going outside used to be easy when I had just one child. We would simply head outside for as long or as little as we wanted. Now, with two, I had the challenge of making sure the baby was happy and the toddler was being safe all at the same time. Not only does the baby need to be happy and not screaming, but he also can't be too hot or cold and must be out of the sun to avoid sunburn. One idea I received is to set up the Pack 'n Play right outside when playing or even swimming. You can put a fitted crib sheet around the top of the Pack 'n Play so it completely covers the top. This will keep bugs and sun out and the baby in a comfortable and safe spot. Mommy win! I also used the stroller quite a bit, especially when we were taking walks. Both of my babies loved a walk in the stroller; the problem was always when the stroller stopped.

The Big Kid Bed Transition

If you have your second child pretty close to the first, like I did, the time will likely come when you will wonder whether you should use two cribs or switch your first child to the big kid bed. Guess what? I bet whichever option you chose will work out just fine. Everything typically does.

For us, our daughter had not even tried to climb out of the crib yet, so I hated to mix things up too much, but on the other hand, we hated the idea of purchasing another crib. We already had a double bed she could use in the house, so we decided to go ahead and transition our daughter to the big girl bed before the new baby came. I believe this was a great decision for us, but as I will say over and over, every child and family is different, so you do what is best for you. One advantage of using two cribs is while the baby is young, you will hopefully have both children safely in their cribs at night. It is one less thing to worry about.

For my daughter, we put railings on all sides of the double bed and we went with it. Luckily, we were able to move her into a totally new room, so we still had the crib just in case it failed. Either way, if you choose this option, you can get your child excited about picking out a new bed, new sheets, or even decorate a whole new room before the big move. We started the move at naptime, and it went perfectly. She just stayed put in the bed. I think because she never climbed out of the crib, or even tried, she just didn't notice any difference in the big bed. At first, she didn't even think about climbing out, even at night. This really helped with our transition. I guess this is one of the positives for making the move earlier rather than later.

Although thankfully it took some time, eventually, she did learn she could climb out of the bed. This presented us with the secondary problem of her not being able to climb back into the bed because it was too tall. At this point, we tried the "cry it out option" again. We had a gate at the door and the expectation was she needed to go to sleep. We checked on her in increasing increments like we had done when she was much younger. We also added a two-step stool to the side of the bed so she could climb back in. Even if they don't get back into the bed and fall asleep on the floor, this never hurt anyone. If they are uncomfortable, maybe it will even motivate them to get back into the bed the next time. For my son, before he started climbing out of the crib, we simply moved him to a big boy bed in his fun, newly decorated room. He loved it and transitioned very easily at almost two-and-a-half years old.

All in all, the moves worked out fine for us. Remember, whatever option you choose, everything will be okay. Of course, neither option is completely without challenges, but as with every challenge up to this date, it too shall pass and you will get through it.

If you choose to go with the big kid bed option, know there is no wrong way of doing it either. Some people move their child to a whole new room with a new bed and get their child really excited about the move. Some put a new toddler bed in the same room with the crib and allow the child to sleep there while lying next to them for a little while at first. From what I hear, some children may actually prefer the new bed to their crib and want to switch on their own. Some remove the crib entirely and replace it with a toddler bed with no looking back. I think the key is to go with your mommy intuition. You know your child. You know their sleep habits. You know their determination, and whether they may be likely to start climbing out of the crib as soon as baby two arrives. Again I will say, whenever I find myself worrying about something, it usually works out just fine in time. I don't think this situation is any different. Go with your gut.

A little disclaimer, if you choose to change to the big kid bed, and especially to a new room, I would recommend doing it at least a couple of months before the baby comes so the child does not feel like the baby arrived and took their room and crib away. There is already enough potential for jealousy, we sure don't need to add to it. Luckily, we were nicely transitioned by the time the new baby arrived.

Tips for Making Life Easier

When you have more than one child, anything you can do to make life easier, no matter how small, is awesome. Fortunately, there were some things which made my life easier when baby number two arrived. If you have two floors in your home, minimize the amount of times you need to take the stairs. Having a place to dispose of diapers both upstairs and downstairs is nice. You don't need a top-of-the-line disposal unit in both places. Any place where you can easily and un-stink-ally (I know, that is not a word, but trust me, it is important) dispose of diapers is great.

Also, have a place where you can comfortably change the baby upstairs and downstairs. We kept a portable crib downstairs with a changing area, diapers, wipes, and ointment. It was at a nice height, so I wouldn't need to bend so much with all my soreness. I put the things I used most downstairs along with plenty of activities for my oldest so I could stay in one place most of the day. I chose downstairs so I had access to food and drink, which we all know toddlers need multiple times a day. Know that avoiding the stairs may not simply be a preference either. You may be medically unable to go up and down the stairs much in the beginning, so take any help which is offered and this is a time you should not hesitate to ask for it.

Once I had two children, I don't think there was ever a time in my life when I craved a shower more and when having that said shower was more impossible. A life-saver for me was actually having a second portable crib (or enclosed space) in the bathroom. If it fits in the bathroom, this is a great place to put a baby or toddler safely along with some of their toys for entertainment while you take your likely put-off-for-too-long shower. Really, any safe place for a baby to sit while you shower works. You could use a bouncer, which allows you to strap them in; one with little toys hanging up top for your baby to view is nice. The key words are "strap in." You would be surprised how easily babies can jump or roll themselves out of things. Unfortunately, I speak from experience. You can also put a little swing in there with you. Anything that holds a baby safely will work. Just be sure your toddler is somehow separated from the baby at the time because, I don't know about you, but I definitely couldn't trust my toddler around the baby without my close proximity. For this reason, choosing my toddler's naptime as my shower time worked best.

Another tip, get your first child used to a smaller booster seat for the table before the new baby comes, so they won't think the new baby stole their high chair. You would be surprised how territorial toddlers can be even over their high chair if they feel it is theirs. My daughter wants to do everything her little brother does and wants the things he wants (even the baby toys), so any little bit helps.

As you can see, there are plenty of challenges when you go from one child to two, but I swear the great moments make up for it. I don't think much can compare to the feeling you get when you see your two children loving each other. Shared little hugs and kisses will melt your heart and the connection you witness between them can change your life.

POTTY TRAINING STINKS,
LITERALLY

As soon as your child is born, there is going to be someone telling you about their friend of a friend who had their child potty trained at "six months old" or "She has been fully potty trained since she turned one." I even got an, "It is true, it is on video." There is a major difference between being fully potty trained and using the bathroom on the potty. Once again, I will say that every child is different. Some children can become very excited about the potty and start wanting to potty on it right away. Other children don't even want to be near the potty. My daughter was interested in the potty right away and immediately started going to the bathroom when I put her on it. This lasted for a few weeks until the newness faded. Then, she was on to bigger and better things. If this happens to you, don't fear. Take it as a positive. Your child likes the potty and does not hate it. It might make potty training easier down the road. If your child hates the potty right away, don't worry, potty training stinks, figuratively and literally, for everyone. I am quite confident there has never been a single person who has used the phrase, "I love potty training."

"They" have a lot to say about potty training. There are plenty of methods I have heard about over the last couple of years. There are even videos out there which encourage you to watch them for ten minutes because "they are going to tell you how to potty train your child in three days without fail" only to end with, "all you need to do is purchase this guide." I will never forget even my dental hygienist at a cleaning brought up potty training when I told her my daughter was 18 months old. She told me she potty trained all of her grandkids. She took them outside during the summer months and put a potty out there. She let them run around naked and by the end of a few days, they were all fully potty trained. This was an interesting method, but I think there is value in it. I have heard of methods out there anywhere from the lackadaisical "just leave the potty out, let them use it when they are ready and when they choose to," to the more extreme methods which encourage children to clean up their own poop and pee when they have accidents. Well, I think one thing is for sure, as my pediatrician would tell me, there is no need to rush—most children go to kindergarten diaper-free. Don't worry, whatever method you choose, it will happen.

Our Potty Training Approach

I personally chose to use a little bit of all of the information I took in. We did a three-day approach in a more relaxed version and this worked really well for my daughter. We made a big deal of going to the store and picking out my daughter's favorite new underwear and made a big deal of when we were going to start potty training and wear no more diapers. My daughter was quite excited and especially loved picking out her new big girl underwear. You can find thicker training underwear too in some pretty cute patterns. We went ahead with the regular underwear, but if you want less of an accident to clean up, you might consider this option. "They say" you should throw out all diapers and use underwear from the time you start potty training on, even at night. I even heard someone say to throw them all out, or you might be tempted to give up and put the child back into diapers. I personally decided to keep the diapers in the house just in case.

I will say potty training was quite a difficult time. When you go to the store to pick up underwear, you may also want to pick up some wine to enjoy a nice glass at the end of your first potty training day.

We decided to start potty training shortly after my daughter turned two, which also happened to be shortly after I had a baby. I am sure having a potty-training toddler and a newborn did not help my cause. Potty training with a four-month-old present was extremely difficult, but at least it was short-lived. It was difficult to give my daughter and the baby the attention they needed and especially to nurse while watching my daughter like a hawk. There were quite a few times I had to unlatch my son while he was nursing and put him down only to hear him scream in order to put my daughter on the potty. Just remember that pretty soon, your child will be potty trained and although right now the process seems daunting and never-ending, when you look back, it will be only a tiny snippet of time.

Day one, my child woke up and I put her in her underwear. She was quite excited. We used only shirts and underwear. Pants would be too hard to pull off in time at the start. We stayed in the family room all day. She had a little toddler table and I pulled out tons of little activities we could play with right in that area. I put a towel under my daughter's chair or under her bottom if she was sitting in case of an accident for easier clean up, and the potty seat was always placed right next to us. I placed a couple of baby chairs and rockers near me, so I could entertain my newborn right there beside us. I told my daughter over and over, "Tell me if you need to go potty." The first time, she did not tell me and I noticed her start to have an accident. I immediately put her on the potty and she finished there. I reminded her gently she goes pee-pee in the potty and not in her underwear. I made sure to praise her with any success. Even if she only finished on the potty, she received praise and of course treats.

Someone had told me not to ask, "Do you need to go potty?" Not surprisingly, if you ask, many times a toddler will tell you no because they do not want to go, when in actuality, they need to go. So, I kept telling my daughter over and over (about every ten minutes) all day, until I lost my voice, "Tell me when you need to go potty." I did this for two days and really by the end of the first day, my daughter was somewhat potty trained. At some point during the second day, we put on pants. On the third day, we went out for a quick dinner. She did great. For quite a while, I told my daughter every so often, "Tell me when you need to go potty," as a reminder. Eventually, this piece was no longer needed. Another idea I heard was to give your child plenty of juice, popsicles, water, and fluids during potty training. The more they need to go potty, the more opportunities for practice.

There are other ideas out there, but this idea is what worked for us. This may work for you, or another idea may work better. It is all trial and error. I have seen little watches you can put on your child's wrist which vibrate at a set time to remind your child to go use the bathroom. There is also simply putting your child on the potty every 20 to 45 minutes even if they do not need to go, and eventually they get used to it. You can offer treats after every time they go on the potty, or you can even do a special song and dance around, whatever works for your child. I do find it is best to offer some kind of incentive.

We always talked about listening to our bodies. We talked about how our body will tell us when we need to go and it is very important to listen to it. I asked my daughter to let an adult know right away when her body told her she needed to go. Children's potty training books are also quite helpful. We started reading these even before potty training began, so my daughter could learn what potty training was all about. There are plenty of TV shows and movies out there which can also increase the potty training excitement.

You can make potty training a fast process or a slow one. I think it's all about preference. Before we started with the three-day potty training, I used a potty sticker chart for quite some time. The pediatrician told me if I wanted to start slowly, I could put a sticker chart up in the bathroom and give my daughter a sticker each time she went on the potty. She received two stickers if she told me she needed to go and went without being asked first. She really enjoyed it, but we kept her in diapers the entire time. She still peed in her diaper many times because she could. Once we switched to the faster approach, she became fully potty trained. Like there are many methods of transportation to get you from here to there, there are many ways to go about potty training a child. Fast or slow, they will all get you there eventually. Choose a plan which works for you. Even mixing multiple methods can be effective.

Naptime and Nighttime Potty Training

Naptime and nighttime training seemed like a whole new beast for us. I decided to go out and buy some disposable training pants which pull up and down for naptime and nighttime only. I remember spending way too much time searching the internet and worrying if maybe I should have stuck to all underwear even at night. I had the irrational worry that my child would get used to wearing disposable training pants at night, get used to having accidents and never be fully potty-trained. Lots of what "they say" told me this is just what would happen. Then, others told me their kids transitioned out of the disposable training pants fine when they were ready.

I was so worried about it, I brought it up during a girls' trip at a winery tour, of all times. The girls assured me that it is okay; their children were also in disposable training pants for some time. For some of them, the children had stopped needing them and others said their children were still in them, just in case and that it was okay with them. If it was one less thing they needed to worry about, then great.

Both responses were reassuring to me. Basically, whatever you decide, whatever works for you will be fine. In the end, they are all potty trained. Well, my daughter was fully potty trained, even at night not long after all of this worry, which basically meant all the time spent reading, worrying, and talking about it was wasted. Lesson learned. This was another reminder that I needed to stop worrying about every little thing and start enjoying life.

So what did we decide to do during naps and at night? At first, we put our daughter in disposable training pants. I did not call them diapers. I told her they were big girl underwear which were just a little thicker and okay to throw away. I acted like they were real underwear. After a few days, as she was doing well, I kept her in her underwear for naptime. I made sure to have her go potty right before she went down and I reminded her every day to call for Mommy or Daddy if she needed to go. I gave her a few extra treats if she woke up dry. She did pretty well. Over time she did have a few accidents which I think is to be expected. Accidents are bound to happen while they are getting used to it.

For night time, she stayed in disposable training pants for a while longer. When she woke up dry, she earned a few extra treats. I gave my daughter plenty of drinks all day long and then limited drinks after five. Don't worry, I would always give my daughter a drink with dinner, but I would not necessarily encourage her to drink it all gone either. We always tried our best to potty before bed. Even if she had gone potty soon before, we made potty time a normal part of our bedtime routine. My daughter actually challenged this for a while and would say she didn't need to go. We stuck with it, however. We read books on the potty and always tried.

When she started waking up dry more often than not, we tried the real underwear. It took an accident or two and her realizing she did not like waking up wet, but she got it for the most part. You may be thinking, *Changing sheets is such a pain.* My daughter is in a double bed with a regular mattress surrounded by railings, so it isn't exactly easy to change. I did what I could to make life easier. I already had a comfortable mattress pad over the entire mattress and purchased three very large, soft, waterproof, non-fitted mattress pads that covered over half of the bed. I put one on top and one on the bottom of the bed, slightly overlapping. Now, if an accident happened on the top half of the bed, I removed the top pad, and if on the bottom of the bed, I just needed to remove the bottom one. I always had an extra change of sheets and an extra clean mattress pad on hand for easier changes. I am glad I went ahead and put my daughter into the underwear at night, because it worked for her. If it hadn't worked, I would have put her back into the disposable training pants, and I don't think this is a decision we should ever feel bad about.

Venturing Out of the House

There were times throughout the potty-training process when I felt we would never comfortably leave the house again for more than 30 minutes. I remember for a few months, trips out were painful because I was so worried my daughter would have an accident. I packed a few paper towels and some antibacterial wipes, a change of clothes, new undies, and the foldable potty seat for every outing just in case. I was unreasonably scared I would be caught in the middle of a store with a mess on the floor and with nothing to clean it up. I also bought something called a piddle pad. It is a little waterproof pad which goes into the child's car seat to keep it dry in case of an accident. Genius, right? Less mess to clean up is always a win in my book. We learned the hard way to keep a portable potty in the car at all times. These ideas were helpful, but early trips out were still pretty anxiety inducing for me.

One day, I braved the grocery store alone with my newly potty trained toddler and new baby. It went fine; it was really quite funny actually. Well, at the time it wasn't, but looking back, it is pretty funny. We arrived at the grocery store. My son went into the baby carrier (it's a life saver) and I took my daughter out of the van. We walked in; I put my daughter into a cart and the diaper bag in the back.

"Lili, do you need to go potty?"

"Yes."

I left my cart outside of the restroom and we all went in. I struggled to get my daughter's pants down and get her onto the potty while my son was wrapped to my chest, but I somehow did it. *Great.* And I wait. *Great, she poops. Now we should be good to go.* I was so proud of her for telling me, so I promised her a treat. I began my shopping. All went well. My son fell asleep right away in the wrap. My daughter was being so good. We went through the entire grocery list. My son woke up as we were unloading the groceries onto the conveyor belt. With a crying baby and an antsy toddler, I paid and made it out to the car. I put the groceries into the back of the van, returned the cart, and strapped my daughter and then son into their car seats.

"Awesome. It's time to go. This wasn't so bad," I said. Famous last words.

"Mommy, I need to go potty." The dreaded words.

I thought, *Oh dear. What am I to do now? I have groceries which need to stay cold in a car on a hot day, but she is newly potty trained. I better listen or we will end up with an accident.* I put my son back into the carrier, ran around the car, grabbed my daughter, locked the car, and ran inside. Someone was in the family stall, so we ran over to the regular stalls. My daughter doesn't love the sound of multiple toilets flushing. It kind of scares her. If there are electric toilets, forget about it. I put her onto the potty anyway.

"Mama, I don't need to go."

I wait anyway. She won't go. Taking deep breaths to try to keep my sanity, we headed back to the van. I strapped my daughter in and noticed my son had a blowout poop. I laid him down on the van floor to change him. It was everywhere, up his entire back, all over his shirt and pants, even on his neck. I removed his clothes, took off his diaper, and dropped the diaper on my foot. *Great, poop is now all over my foot.* I cleaned it all up with the somehow very last wipe I had (I guess I forgot to restock before leaving the house) and put him in a new diaper. He rode home naked with only a diaper as I also happened to forget a change of clothes. Not the best trip, but at least we had groceries and no accidents, and at least I figured out the importance of the portable potty, because you never know when your child will have to go "right now!"

Believe it or not, eventually, we felt like we could leave the house again as we got more and more confident with my daughter's potty training. Now, I never have to worry about her. She always tells me when she needs to go.

Potty Training Setbacks

Keep in mind with potty training, as with all things in life, there will be setbacks. Some children have an easier time going pee-pee on the potty than they do poo-poo. For my daughter, it was the opposite. She hated pooping in her diaper, so she pooped on the potty 100 percent of the time right away. Our challenge when it came to accidents was more with pee-pee.

We potty trained my son at the same age and used the same methods as we did for our daughter. Our son's issue, on the other hand, was with pooping. By day five, he was pretty well pee-pee potty trained. We didn't even need the disposable training pants at night, because he somehow just always stayed dry. We learned later, however, he was holding his poop. The "holding" behavior became progressively worse and his gastroenterologist told us it was an extremely common behavior especially for boys. This seemed like a huge setback at the time, but we made it through. The doctor helped get us into a good place where our son was completely cleaned out. After that, we made sure to give him plenty of fiber and liquids, lots of fruits and vegetables, pear juice, and vitamins. We gave him lots of encouragement and had to up his reward for pooping to small toy surprises instead of candy. Yes, I definitely bribed my son to poop. I will admit that to get him to poop the first time after his clean out, I bribed him with a pretty huge toy, but hey, it worked so I am glad I did. Eventually, he got it and we were good to go.

Every child is different, but remember that no matter the child, eventually, it will happen. There will be accidents. I distinctly remember one time when my daughter had an accident at night. It was an accident which happened after I thought maybe we were out of the woods, because she hadn't had an accident in quite a while. By the way, that is something else I have learned as a parent: Never feel like you are truly out of the woods, because most likely you are not, then you won't feel so bad when something you don't expect happens. Back to the point—after the accident, I immediately asked my husband, "What did we do wrong? Is something wrong? Does she have a bladder infection? Is there something we should do differently? Did we train her too early?"

I remember my husband saying, "Why did it happen? Because she is a kid...that is all."

Hmm...amazing, I thought. Yes, it could be as simple as that. She is a kid. Things happen. Then, I realized I should try using this phrase way more often when answering all the other simple questions I had.

"Why did my daughter bite her brother?"

"Why did my son smack his sister?"

"Why did my daughter paint with her milk and spill it all over the floor?"

"Why did my son pee on the floor?"

"Why did my daughter use that bad word?"

Then, we can answer each question with "because they are kids." The answer is not that we did something wrong as parents. They are kids. I realized I could focus less on what I did wrong to cause the behavior (because we didn't cause it), and more on if there is any way we can help them learn from the behavior.

When the accident happened, I had worried we were back to square one again, that we would need to start over. It wasn't true. Accidents were always just little setbacks and they worked themselves out. So, I am telling you now, if your child has an accident, don't worry about it at all. Just move on. It will likely work itself out, and remember, it isn't something you did wrong either.

"They say" you should never yell at your child if they have an accident as it could cause problems with potty training. Well, I will admit, I remember yelling at my child at least once (there were probably plenty more) because I was so frustrated with the accident and having to clean it up. At this particular time, I remember within three hours, my child had four accidents. By the fourth time, I yelled. I felt horrible, like I ruined everything, like we would be back at square one. Once again, this wasn't the case. If you do happen to yell, don't fret; there is always the next time to try to remain calm. By the fourth accident, however, I thought, *What is going on? Does my daughter have a bladder infection?*

To the doctor we went. Turns out, there was no bladder infection. Constipation was the cause. I couldn't believe it. I never realized constipation could cause a child to have accidents. She was having pee-pee accidents, not poop. The doctor told us what to use to help with my daughter's constipation and by that evening, she was back to being potty trained.

The doctor told us when there is a blockage of stool and their systems are so tiny, it can put a lot of pressure on the bladder, which makes them feel like they need to go immediately, even if they just went. So, again, don't worry yourself over accidents. If you are concerned, ask your pediatrician. I did a little more research at the time and I remember reading something like if you potty train too early, children can be more likely to have issues with constipation and with potty training in general because they were too young to learn how to properly control their bowels. Again, this is what "they say" and I am not even sure if this is accurate information, but what it does tell me is there is no harm in waiting to potty train (maybe it is even beneficial), even if there are those kids out there who are "potty trained by the time they are one."

HOUSEWORK: ONE STEP FORWARD, THREE STEPS BACK

On TV, families have time in the morning to talk and cuddle in bed. The parents are in no rush to get their day started. The youngest children come in to join them in bed. They laugh for a while before heading downstairs to make a huge breakfast which usually includes juice, waffles, eggs, bacon, and lots of fresh fruit. They are never in a hurry. The oldest child comes down and grabs a piece of fruit. Then, the husband walks into the kitchen. He grabs some orange juice to go, not in a plastic cup, but in a real glass and says something like, "I've got to go." The mom is like, "Go ahead honey, have a great day, love you." What she doesn't say is, "Never mind the starving children all around the world, I will just throw all this food out." This scenario is so unrealistic. In real life, or at least in my life for sure, there is simply no time. I can hardly even find time to eat a package of mini muffins, much less make a breakfast like that.

A friend received a gift one year which said something like, "If you have a messy house, a dirty oven, and sticky floors, then you are the best kind of mom." Well, hallelujah, that would be me. Finally, I am doing something right. Sometimes, I feel my life is laundry, cleaning, cooking, and repeat. Keeping my house together is just exhausting and it feels like there is no end anywhere in sight. I mean, let's face it, there really is no end in sight. There will always be something to do, always. Not only that, but as a mom I find myself putting out fires left and right, and cleaning up mess after mess.

One day my son forcefully threw his entire bowl of rice across the room. While I was cleaning up this mess, I looked up and somehow my daughter had a newly empty salt shaker in her hand. Needless to say, this was not one of my best days.

Even if my house is somewhat clean, there is always going to be the "junk area." Don't all of us have them? You know, the area where you pile up the junk you have no idea where to put? For me, it is on the little desk area under my microwave and even in the drawer below that. If that wasn't enough, there is also one in the office. Then, there are the kids' toys which are consistently strewn around the house. They are everywhere! I cannot even finish cleaning them up before the kids have made another mess with them. Even worse is when you step on one of those tiny little toys lying around. Ouch! I have given up; I don't think my house will ever be completely clean—well at least not until my children grow up and move out one day.

I have just had to accept that it will never be finished, and the meals and the house will never be perfect. I will simply live my life, and do the best I can without killing myself over it. I found striving for perfection when it comes to meals and cleaning only makes me feel like a failure because it just isn't going to happen. I know there will come a day when I will miss all those toys which used to be everywhere…the constant reminder of those sweet little babies which will have grown up. So, I might as well try to enjoy them while I can.

I have so much mommy guilt when it comes to keeping the house straight. I feel guilt when I clean instead of playing with my children. I feel guilt when I play with the children when I really need to clean. Sometimes, it is a lose-lose situation.

The guilt feels never-ending. I have to try to remind myself to let some things go. "They say" it will be there tomorrow, and unfortunately, it will. I found myself feeling like all of the dishes needed to be clean or in the dishwasher by the end of each night, but do they really? They do not "need" to be there. I may "want" them there so the next day is easier. But, does it really hurt for them to sit in the sink for a day? Yes, they may be a bit more stinky when I go to clean them, but it isn't the end of the world, right? Sometimes, I have to remind myself of this, let some things go, and instead play a game with my daughter or read a book to my son. I have learned these moments will fill you up way more than a full dishwasher. The kids grow up so fast, in the blink of an eye. We don't want to miss it. I tell myself that there will be plenty more days for me to do dishes for the rest of my life, but I will not be able to get the sweet little moments back once my children are grown.

Tricks of the Trade: Housekeeping

I have learned many things when it comes to housekeeping. I learned a baby wipe can have multiple uses. When my newborns have leaked poop on their clothing and I was unable to apply spot remover right away, I found if I wipe it off as best as I can with a baby wipe, it comes off much easier later. Wipes have also been helpful when cleaning the carpet. My son may spill milk on the carpet. I think, *I should get the carpet cleaner, but is it okay for children to breathe this stuff?* I'll use a wipe to clean instead. Later, during naptime, I can go back and use carpet cleaner. Carpet cleaning is like a necessary evil for me. The smell is always horrible. Once, in my haste, I even went to spray it and accidentally had the nozzle turned to the right instead of down at the carpet. Imagine my surprise when I sprayed, and the cleaner shot four feet to the right, almost hitting my son in the face. Whew, it was close. Wipes are actually very handy little cleaners, and I always have them on hand or at least within close reach. Wipes also work on hardwood or tile. They can clean up juice and leave no sticky residue for ants to find. So, when you don't have time to grab the hard-surface cleaner or carpet cleaner (which is most likely locked up with an impossible lock in the cabinet), grab a wipe.

I have learned there are two indispensable mommy items. You will want to find a good laundry stain remover which actually removes stains (you would be surprised how many don't), and you will also need some good lotion. I wash my hands a million times a day. They become extremely dry without lotion. When it comes to stain removal, soaking seems to work well for us. I was recently introduced to the stain bar. It is like a bar of soap, but for stain removal. You should be able to find one in the aisle with the regular stain fighters. All you do is wet the fabric, rub the bar against the stain, wait one minute and throw it in to wash. It is amazing. It has even cleaned dryer-set stains left after multiple cleaning cycles. In conclusion, apply your stain remover, wash your hands, then lotion up.

Speaking of laundry, there was a day when I was doing the dreaded and never-ending laundry with the kids in the room with me. I turned around and saw my daughter in the laundry basket and my son playing with the vacuum, both looking up at me and smiling huge smiles. I thought to myself, *I officially love laundry…*Well, at least I did for that day, or maybe that minute. I guess this was one of those reminders to look for the joy in everything. In that moment, I found great joy.

I have learned to get creative when doing chores around the house. I try to involve my kids even when they are little. This is especially helpful if, like me, you are feeling guilty about doing chores instead of playing with the kids. I believe involving the kids in the cleaning process can teach our kids how important it is to help around the house and to all carry our share of the household chores. One day, I picked up my children from church childcare only to hear, "Your daughter told us she wouldn't help clean up because Mommy cleans up after her at home." Oops, pretty embarrassing. Well, there are worse things which could happen, but I realized it really is never too early to encourage our children to help clean up.

I try to make taking the clothes out of the washer and dryer fun for them. They can help hand me items to fold. I will give them a big, over the top "Thank you" when they hand me an item which makes them laugh. I act like they are handing me things too fast and I can't keep up. I drop clothes and act like I am so silly; I need their help again to pick them up. They like to try to help me fold the clothes. I always tell them good job even if it's hardly folded. You can put some toys in the laundry room while you fold laundry, so when they become tired of helping they have something else to do. The reverse is also true. They may become tired of the few toys and decide to help you with the laundry.

My kids also like to wipe down their areas after they eat. I try to make cleaning up their rooms and playrooms somewhat entertaining. We race to see who can clean up certain areas first, or to see who can find the most blocks. They can fill their laundry bins by playing "basketball." They love to help me load and unload the dishwasher (after I unload all the sharp items). Again, it is never too early to teach them how to clean up and involving them helps me get some things done around the house as well. Anytime I feel like I can overlap playing with the kids and cleaning, I feel like I am winning.

I have learned the hard way not to wear white while eating— this goes for me and for my children. As a matter of fact, don't even buy anything white, ever. If you are caught around meal time in white clothes, I would say just remove the clothing. Your children can always eat in the buff...maybe not you! I don't find much that is strange anymore, but that actually might be.

I have learned the hair dryer can be quite useful. One day, I actually found myself drying my son's onesie with my hair dryer while he was wearing it. Yes, I sound crazy, right? If your child is like mine, he hates to be changed, especially at naptime after lunch, and he is almost always wet or dirty after lunch. I would have to change his post-lunch clothes almost daily, which would cause him to cry and scream and get him all riled up right before he was supposed to settle down and sleep. Therefore, one day when he spilled some juice on his onesie, I grabbed my hair dryer, put it on low air and low heat (if you try this, be very careful not to use it on high heat, it could burn them), and just blew his onesie dry for a few minutes while he finished eating. I am sure I sound and looked insane, but then I could just take him upstairs calm and get him to sleep with much less of a fight. Even if this is too weird to try, just know there is a mom out there who is strange enough to blow dry her son's clothes while he eats. Maybe this will help you feel better on an especially crazy day.

I also used the hair dryer many times on my rocking chair. My kids would spit up and it would always seem to go right onto the rocking chair, no matter how many burp cloths I had surrounding us. My rocking chair pads did not have covers which could be removed, so I could only spot clean with laundry detergent. Drying them with the hairdryer worked like a charm and I didn't find myself stressing out and strategizing to find a good time to wash them so I had the longest possible amount of time until I would need the rocking chair again.

I learned never to underestimate the burp cloth. The best burp cloth is a cloth diaper. From what I have seen and experienced using, these are the thickest and largest burp cloths. At first, I thought these old cloth diapers should be extinct, especially with these new cloth diapers which have snaps and cute prints. Nevertheless, I have found many uses for those good old cloth diapers.

Of course, you can use them to burp the baby with good

coverage. You can put them on a changing table over the cute changing pad cover so you won't need to remove the entire cover for wash quite as often. I love to keep one handy at the changing station to dry my children's bottoms completely before applying diaper cream. Drying completely helps prevent diaper rash. You can take diaper cloths along with you for the unexpected spills or messes. With a baby and a toddler, there are days when my daughter, my son, and I go through three clothing changes each. This means a ton of laundry and I already don't have time for the regular amount. I like to put a diaper cloth over my son's lap in his high chair while he eats. The cloth catches most of the food rather than his pants. This means one less outfit added to the laundry queue.

Lastly, and yes this is the strangest, is to use it as an overnight or naptime tissue when you have a sick child. When my toddler is sick, her nose runs all night and I would hate to leave a box of tissues in her room. Who knows what she would do with them? Maybe eat them, but one thing is for sure, the tissues would no longer be in the box in the morning. If they don't have something to use to wipe their nose, snot gets everywhere. I give my daughter an old diaper cloth. She actually finds comfort in having it when she is sick, and uses it to wipe her nose should it start running. Anything I find which saves me time as a parent, I use, and the diaper cloth sure has saved me a lot of time.

I have learned there are many times when I really need something and it is wet. How is everything always wet or sticky when you have toddlers around? Maybe I need a blanket or clothing which has been sitting in the washing machine and I have forgotten about the laundry altogether. This happens more often than not. You would think throwing the single item in the dryer would dry it quickly, but I learned that is not the case. For me, a single item gets all stuck to the sides and never seems to dry. I found throwing the item in with one or two dry towels does the trick. Somehow, it dries much more quickly.

I learned that putting a towel under the high chair can be a huge timesaver. The amount of food which ends up on my floors and walls is outrageous. The towel is great because you can simply shake it out when plates or crumbs are dropped. Dropped plates, bowls, and cups are bound to happen when you have a toddler...daily.

I have learned—as a means of saving time when cleaning— you can use some chemical-free cleaners. I am not saying to go and throw out all of your cleaning supplies, but if the cleaning materials are safe for children, you have no worries in cleaning right next to them or even letting your children help you. I find using chemical-free mopping to be very helpful, as my son can run right behind me through the wet marks and I don't need to worry about any chemicals harming him.

Tricks of the Trade: Meal Planning and Cooking

I learned pretty quickly that it can be difficult and overwhelming trying to have dinner ready for the family each night. Whether you are a stay-at-home parent or a working parent, it can be impossible to find time to plan out meals and prepare them, and planning healthy meals each night...forget about it.

When my husband and I both worked, I remember one of us always rushing to pick up our children from school, and the other rushing home to make dinner. We kind of fell into the "fly by the seat of our pants" mindset when it came to dinner. We would often pick up last-minute items on the way home from work each night to quickly throw together a meal. Turns out, this ended up wasting a lot of our time, and it really is precious time which can be spent with family. By the time dinner was on the table and we ate, it was just about bath and bedtime. I remember feeling so sad and guilty because I hardly had any time at all with my children before they went to sleep. It was really tough.

As a stay-at-home mom, I sometimes felt like I was staying

home just to prepare meals, clean, and do dishes or laundry. When the children are home all day, they are constantly making messes throughout the house. Three meals a day need to be prepared. All of the dishes from each meal pile up in the sink. I still felt like I didn't have any quality time with my children even being with them every second.

Thus, it is always a good thing to do whatever we can to make our lives go a little more smoothly. I found a time once a week when I could plan out the weekly meals and write down all the ingredients I needed. Picking up the items on my list is even easier when I use the grocery store pick up and online ordering service. I have learned, as a mother of two young ones, that online shopping can be delightful. It's surprising how we can find so many things we want to buy online, but when we see that shipping fee of $5.99, we change our minds. Well, that $5.99 or even $10.99 can be worth it when you don't need to leave the house with two children under the age of three. When buying groceries online, the five-dollar convenience fee or any shipping fees can be worth not having to spend the five dollars on items I end up buying to avoid a tantrum.

I have learned that there are plenty of ways to minimize a difficult meal prep. Never underestimate the slow cooker. The slow cooker may literally be my new best friend. Cook the meal on low while you are at work, or cook the meal on high for a few hours as soon as you walk in the door. Experiment with slow cooker meals when you can. They make life easier and they are delicious. I recently learned you can stick chicken breasts right in the slow cooker with any seasoning or spices you choose, cook it for three hours on high or six hours on low, bring out a couple of easy sides and voilà, dinner is served. I always thought you needed to put some kind of liquid around the meat in the slow cooker, but it is not necessary. The chicken makes its own broth while it cooks. I have even cooked a whole three to four-pound chicken in the slow cooker on high for two and a half to three and a half hours.

Then, there are freezer meals. You can make a large meal one night and freeze half. Eat the second half another night. This works great for smaller families when you find yourself throwing out a large portion of casseroles or meals which go uneaten. You can even put together an entire meal—raw meat and all—in a freezer bag, freeze it, and cook it later in the oven or slow cooker. This eliminates all meal prep. I am all for the ideas which give me extra time to either get things done or to play with my kids. I will take any help I can get.

You can minimize meal prep by cutting your vegetables ahead of time. When dinner time comes around, all you need to do is throw it together. A little side tip: when cutting onions, bite on the end of a wooden spoon. I don't know how or why, but it stops me from having tears roll out of my eyes, unless you actually want an excuse to cry. In that case, omit the spoon and allow yourself a good cry. Sometimes, we need to simply blame it on the onion.

Letting Ourselves Off the Hook

I have learned, when all else fails and if feasible, hire a cleaning service. We did not want a monthly service, because we would be locked into a monthly payment for one more thing, but every so often, we hire a cleaning crew for a whole house clean. This is something which could even be a nice Christmas or birthday gift request. Really, what is better than a perfectly clean house? Best gift ever, right? After hiring a cleaning service for the first time, I remember thinking, *Now, our floors are so clean, we could literally eat off of them*...which believe it or not, happens quite frequently in our house with the baby, toddlers, and dog.

As a mom, I always feel like I am rushing around trying to get everything done. It's like I cannot wait to check every single item off my list. We all have a "to do" list, whether it is in our heads or on paper. I find myself believing once I check everything off my list, I will finally be able to relax. However, have you noticed the list is never finished? I mean, literally, even the very second you "finish" all of the laundry, there is one other item which ends up in the basket. Even the clothes you are wearing are dirty. We have to face it. There will never be a time when all of the chores are done. It is impossible. There will always be something to do. After straightening the entire house and having a cleaning service come through and do a full clean, I thought I would be done with cleaning for a while, but no—there was a new list the very next day.

Although I enjoy having a list to check off (it really makes you feel good to make that check), I realize my goal cannot be to finish the list. It is unachievable. My goal now is to do what I can while making sure to still enjoy moments with my kids. If it means the vacuuming or laundry waits another day, then so be it. If a friend or family member drops by, then so be it. If the house is a mess when they do, then it is just that—a mess. I usually feel if someone comes by, the house must be clean because if not, they may judge me. You know what, though? If they want to judge, let them judge. I would much prefer to have happy kids and a happy mindset than a spotless kitchen.

On the other hand, never feel guilty about taking time to clean, cook, or get things done. The house eventually does need to be cleaned. Meals do need to be prepared. We cannot put everything off, so never let that "mommy guilt" set in when you are getting things done. If it makes you feel better to clean the house while the children play independently, go for it. "They say" an unorganized home can negatively affect your mood. The bottom line is it always feels good to get something done. We feel that sense of accomplishment which everyone requires at least every once in a while. Don't feel like you cannot get anything done because your child must be entertained all waking hours of the day. In fact, I believe there are many benefits of independent play. I believe boredom leads to creativity. Do you ever just sit back and watch your kids play, without actually playing with them? They can be very creative when we sit back and give them the tools they need.

I do take time out of the day to straighten, clean, and cook and I think my children are better for it. They are able to play with toys independently. Through this independent play, they become more autonomous which is a great skill to develop. It will take them far.

As you can see, I have learned a lot. I have learned that the amount of paper towels, trash bags, and diapers I can go through in a day is shocking. It is never ending! I have learned to just expect the toilet paper roll to need a refill. I have learned it is impossible for laundry to be washed, dried, folded, and put away all in one day. I have learned never to underestimate the amount of mess two tiny children can make. They have already given me gray hair. But mess by mess—I have learned that the messes are not what are significant in life. It's all about the love.

TO WORK OR NOT TO WORK?
THAT IS THE QUESTION.

Staying home with kids is physically exhausting. On an average day, a short trip from the playroom to my daughter's room would probably involve bending down to pick up six stray toys, picking up a piece of clothing which somehow came out of the laundry basket, putting a hair tie back in its place so my son doesn't eat it, moving a toy car out of the way so someone doesn't wipe out, grabbing that last pile of clothes and taking it with me, and likely correcting at least one child for something they are doing wrong. It is seriously exhausting. I think the emotional exhaustion can come into play too when you are constantly putting out fires left and right, feeling mommy guilt over all of the tiny mistakes I feel I make each day, and dealing with tears as someone is bound to at least get a bump or a bruise. Being a stay-at-home mom isn't an easy job. You work long hours. In fact, the hours never end. You get no break, not to eat or even to pee. It is not an easy job.

Moms don't get sick days. The children still need to be fed. They need to be put to bed. They still require our undivided attention. Unless someone literally takes our children away from us for an entire day and night, our job is still there, sick or not.

Also, I am sure you have noticed that the "man cold" is right on. Even if my husband and I come down with the same illness, the "man cold" is somehow worse by a long shot. I will be taking care of myself and the kids and then I find myself having to fully take care of my husband, schedule him a doctor's appointment, and even tell him step by step instructions on how to navigate to and enter the doctor's office. I ask, "Can you not use your GPS and make a phone call? Do you hear what is going on over here?" All the while, the children are screaming and whining.

Being a stay-at-home mom is tough work. Sometimes I feel so alone, like no one understands how the day goes. I'm alone a lot with three kids, and seem to always have to make decisions, one after another. It can be mentally and physically taxing.

For working moms, life is just as exhausting. When I worked, I would say my job was more mentally or emotionally exhausting than my stay-at-home job is now, but then I had to come home after a long day, switch gears, and do all the mommy stuff before finally being able to settle down. I spent a lot of my days worrying about how my daughter was doing at daycare all the while trying to get all my work done. I remember feeling like I needed to give one hundred percent of myself at work and another one hundred percent of myself at home or else I would let everyone down. It all just felt unattainable.

In this situation, I found I needed to change my mindset. I had to stop telling myself I needed to complete the impossible task of giving two hundred percent, and focus instead on just being me. I needed to "be me" when I was at work and "be me" when I was at home. If I needed to get home a little earlier to take my child to the doctor, for example, I stopped "being me" at work a little early and started "being me" at home a little sooner, but I never gave less of who I was. Rather than focusing on giving one hundred percent, I simply focused on doing what I did at work. What does being me mean? I believe I am a hard worker.

I care enormously about people. I always want to do my best. I just needed to be myself and realize what I was giving should be just right. Of course, it is exhausting. No matter how you do it, whether you work or stay home, being a parent is tough work.

Let Go of the Guilt

I often felt guilty because, rather than always feeling fortunate to have the opportunity to stay home, there were plenty of times I took it for granted. I felt like I didn't always appreciate it as much as I should. As a stay-at-home mom, I feel like I am either disciplining the kids, yelling at them about something, or saying no all day long. I find myself thinking, *At least if I worked I would only be disciplining them for three hours a day, rather than 12.* Some days, by the time breakfast is over, I am thinking, *Is it time to go to sleep yet?* To be honest, sometimes the second I wake up I find myself wondering how I am going to get through the day. When we finally make it to the bedtime routine, I am not sure where kids get all that extra energy and screaming right before bed, but I can somehow make it through knowing that in a few short minutes, I will be on the couch with my husband watching one of our favorite shows. I am sure I either sound pathetic right now, or you are right there with me. There were even times when I felt I didn't even like staying home and I wanted to just go lock myself in a room for a few minutes to be alone. Sometimes I did just that.

One particular day, there was mess after mess which culminated in my daughter dumping half of a glue bottle on the kitchen table and then rubbing her fingers through it, smearing it across the table. When I noticed, I just lost it. I yelled more than I should. I later felt so guilty about yelling. I felt like I couldn't take another mess that day. I made sure my children were safe and then shut myself in the pantry for a few minutes and cried. When I say cry, I mean it was a you-could-see-drops-of-tears-all-over-the-pantry-floor kind of cry. I got it out, and realized sometimes you simply need a good cry.

The bottom line is that we have to stop allowing ourselves to feel guilty, and we have to understand that no matter which way we choose to do it, whether we work or whether we are staying home, we are doing the most important job in the world, raising our children. There is no "right way." It likely won't be an easy job either way, but if we just do the best we can, meet our children's basic needs, and love our children as much as possible, then we are doing it right. We are great moms and we need to stop thinking we are less than amazing for the job we choose for our family, whatever that job may be.

Value Yourself No Matter What

There were times when I found myself seeking the praise of others, like my husband or my family, for example. It was like I needed someone to tell me I'm a good mom or like I needed them to recognize how much I was doing, and to tell me I was doing a good job. I started to wonder why I felt I needed this validation so much. The more I thought about it I realized, as a stay-at-home mom at the time, deep down I wondered what I was really contributing to my children and family. My husband was contributing financially, but I was not. I think I somehow wanted to be sure I was contributing in a way which mattered to someone. It was like I needed to hear praise from others to feel like I was valued, so I could know that I was contributing in a meaningful way. It was either this, or I felt like I needed to defend myself by saying things like, "Do you know what I do all day? I work too. It is hard work too." I even felt this way as a working mom. I felt I hardly saw my child during the week, so I wondered if I was contributing enough to being a parent. I wondered if my paycheck was contributing enough to account for my time away and the costs we had as two working parents. Just think about how much undue pressure these types of thoughts cause.

Once I came to the realization that I was doing these things, I asked myself, *Why should my value be contingent upon the praise of others?* Whether we are a working parent, a stay-at-home parent, or anything in between, we are all parents. What we are doing, whether it be at home or at work is contributing, and being a parent is always meaningful. Sometimes, it may feel like we are accomplishing nothing as parents, but what we are doing is raising our children. We are guiding them, teaching them, loving them, caring for them. All these things together help shape them into the adults they will one day become, and that really is something. What I have to remind myself—and what I will remind you—is to not feel like you need praise from others to know you are valuable and don't feel like you have to be a superhero or a supermom to be a contributor. You are contributing with every word you speak and every action you complete and even those words and actions you don't complete, because let's be honest, in my home there is a lot less completing and a lot more starting an action and being interrupted.

Let's stop questioning ourselves and stop feeling like we need to do so much and be so perfect to be valuable, or to feel like a contributor. We contribute every time we tie a shoe, blow a nose, clip in a bow, when we pick up a dropped cup, wipe away a tear, when we remind our children to say thank you or sorry, when we make a meal, or even purchase a ready-made one, when we give a bath, a kiss, a hug, when we say goodnight, when we laugh with our children, read a book, play with them, and yes even when we put them in time out. The list goes on and on. We are parents, and you know what? That really is something! What could be more worthwhile or valuable, really? If we can feel good about what we are doing on our own without needing the help or input from others, it will only make us better, happier parents in the end. No matter which way we choose to do it, there is nothing more valuable than raising a child.

RELATIONSHIPS

"They say" marriage isn't easy. I would have to agree with this one. When you are taking care of children, it really can cause a strain on your marriage. I mean, children are great. They are amazing, even. They do, however, take up a lot of our energy, both emotionally and physically. No longer are we just worrying about ourselves and our significant other anymore. All of a sudden, you are putting the livelihood of another person (or people) ahead of your own. Of course this can cause a strain on your relationship with your loved one who had previously been put first. All of the attention gets put on keeping the children happy, comfortable, healthy, and safe, and the attention moves away from keeping your spouse happy, comfortable, healthy, and safe. Society even tells us that kids come first. If there is one last piece of candy and you really want it, but your child is begging for it, what are you supposed to do? Many of us feel like we need to give it to our child. Children first, right? Sometimes, I just really want that darn piece of candy!

Marriage is challenging. It is not a walk in the park as one might think. After all, you are two different people who come from two different backgrounds. When I give my children a sippy cup I always match the tops with the bottoms. It just makes sense to me. They go together, so I put them together. My husband, on the other hand, grabs the first top he sees and puts it with the first bottom he sees. No matter the color, no matter if it is even supposed to go together. As long as it fits together, in his book, it is fine. It used to irk my nerves when he did this. Now I am over it, because at least he is getting a sippy cup and it didn't have to be me.

This shows you though that we are different people. We have different ways of thinking, different upbringings, different experiences, and different parenting ideas and styles. It isn't always easy to mesh all of these differences, but just like the different cups and tops which fit together and work, so can we as a couple. My husband is the guy who when our daughter asks for milk, he brings it to her in a tall shot glass. Yes, it is the perfect size for her, but really? I guess whatever works, right? It actually did end up being easier for her to drink and she didn't spill it. See, we meshed. Meshing takes time and practice, and time is one thing you do not have a lot of when you have children. If married life is difficult right now, know you are not alone. Stay strong. You can mesh, and you will only become stronger because of it and you will only love each other more for it.

The Four Magic Words

I have learned a lot in the last few years of having children. Some things I have done have made our married life harder, but along the way I have learned some great ideas which have helped keep our marriage strong.

I believe, for the most part, that my husband and I have a great marriage, but it has taken practice and I will not lie to you, we have been through some tough times. I recall a recent argument I had with my husband. I'd had a tough week. I was staying home with my two children, who were both sick. There may be nothing worse than having two children who are very sick at the same time. It is so difficult to give each sick child all of the attention they need when they are feeling so yucky. It is also hard to deal with the almost constant crying and whining which comes from the child who isn't getting the attention or love at the time. It tugs at your heart and makes you physically and emotionally exhausted.

Slowly throughout the day, I felt like I was about to lose it. I told my husband when he got home and he was actually quite supportive. I had told him recently if he could use these four "magic words" more often, it would really help me: "How can I help?" I said it would help me feel less like I was constantly nagging him, if he was able to ask me how he could help instead of me always telling him what needed to be done. He actually asked me this a few times on this particular night and it really did help me keep it together.

"How can I help?"

"You can put the chicken on the grill."

"How can I help?"

"You can spend some time with CJ and straighten up the mess from dinner, while I spend some time with Lili."

I went to put my son to bed and he kept refusing his sippy cup of milk (because it was room temperature instead of warm). I continued trying to give it to him calmly and he kept hitting it away, kicking at me, arching his back, and the list goes on. Finally, I put him down and went to warm the milk up some more. He drank it until it was gone and then proceeded to cry because he wanted more. Finally, I got him to relax and fall asleep. I went downstairs and started to cry. I ended up yelling at my husband about how I feel so alone sometimes. As a stay-at-home mom, I find myself wondering how one can possibly feel so alone all the while getting no alone time at all? I told him I am home all day with no adult interaction. I told him by the time he gets home from work, dinner and cleaning are done and I am exhausted. To add to all of this, I feel like no one ever listens to me. I stay home all day and tell the children what they should be doing. No one listens. My husband comes home and I finally have some adult interaction, and he is so tired that he doesn't listen. It makes me go crazy sometimes. Then, we put the kids to sleep and just start all over again the next day. I yelled at him about trying to find a way to help out more. We argued and told each other how we felt. We came to a resolution, to both put ourselves in the other person's shoes and try to support one another more.

There may be times when you feel this way—when you feel all alone, when you feel you are holding the world up on your shoulders, when you feel like you need help. I cannot tell you the number of times in talking with friends when we find ourselves saying "men!" as the answer to some conversation about something silly or frustrating which our husbands have done. "Men, men, men." I read a quote in Deborah M. Coty's book, *Too Blessed to be Stressed,* that made me laugh. It was, "Men, so many stressful things start with that word—menstruation, menopause, mental anguish, ménage [the French word for housekeeping], even menace." I mean, men truly can be a pain in the butt, but on the other hand, I cannot imagine not having my other half there to help me out. Seriously, single mothers and fathers impress the hell out of me. They must be some of the strongest people on the entire planet. I simply do not know how they do it. I am not sure I could do all of this child-rearing alone.

Cool Down

Situations like this help me realize a few things. It is always better to try to "cool down" before arguing if at all possible. Don't walk into a conversation when something else has already made you hopping mad. Sometimes, at least for me, it is very difficult to be rational when I am extremely angry. I usually find I end up saying things I don't mean in these moments.

This brings me to my next point: Sometimes we say things we don't mean during an argument. If this happens, I try to apologize or accept my spouse's apology. After all, we have all said things before in anger which we honestly did not mean.

What is most important here, however, is that we did communicate what we felt. If you do wait to "cool down" before having a conversation with your significant other, make sure not to postpone the conversation forever. Even though you might feel calm later, it is important to share how you felt so you can work through it together and so a similar situation does not occur a few weeks, or even a few days, later.

Stay Positive

Lastly, take a moment when you are angry or frustrated and ask yourself, *What did my spouse do great today?* Had I asked myself this early on in our argument, I would have thought about how my husband worked so hard all day to provide for our family. I truly feel lucky to have my husband there to support me, and to allow me to be able to stay home with my children and see all of their accomplishments and catch all of the cute and funny little things they say and do. The days aren't perfect, but they are worthwhile nonetheless. I would have thought about how he took care of my son so both children could receive some one-on-one time from a parent that night. I would have thought about the fact that he used those four magic words when he noticed I was stressed like I had asked. He followed through. In the moment, I hadn't even thought about it. Well, after our argument, I did, and I felt horrible about yelling.

Especially when wound up in the day-to-day life with kids, I can become so frustrated with my husband, but there are so many things he does great as well. I have learned I need to try to focus more on these things. For example, my husband encourages me to get out of the house and spend time with friends. I remember one night in particular when he encouraged me to go to dinner with friends. When I got home, he gave me a play-by-play of everything that had occurred while I was gone. He literally showed me with body motions exactly how he put the baby to sleep. It was super cute. These are the moments we need to remember. I am sure they are there. It is just much easier for us to focus on the negatives, but all focusing on the negatives will do is make us more frustrated.

Here is a perfect example. We leave dance class and I always feed my son in the car before we head home, finishing up with his bottle. He has a very rigid feeding schedule due to his reflux. On this particular day, he screamed the entire way home. He was screaming so much, I pulled over at a school to check on him and maybe try to burp him. Of course, there happened to be a police officer sitting in the parking lot staring at me, probably wondering what on earth I was doing. Luckily, I didn't speed by him trying to rush home distracted by a crying baby. There is not much which can distract you or make your blood pressure rise more than a screaming baby, especially in the car.

I get home all flustered, just in time to make a quick and fresh meal, fettuccine alfredo. My daughter cried out, "Mama, CJ spilled my juice all over the couch. Can I have more?"

I pull out all of my ingredients and look into the fridge. *Where is my heavy cream? I know I put it on the shopping list for my husband to pick up.* I am so thankful my husband does most of the grocery shopping, but I swear, there is always one item missing! Shame on me for not being 100 percent thankful, right? Yes, my husband forgot the heavy cream. He was upstairs using the bathroom for the 20 minutes he could have used to work out, like he has been trying to start again, but instead wanted to "help with the kids." I didn't see how much "helping" he was doing by sitting on the toilet. I yelled, probably way too loud, and asked my husband to go back to the store and get the heavy cream while I shredded cheese.

I heard a "boom" and looked over to my right. My son was in the spice cabinet again. My daughter wanted to "help" get him out of the cabinet so she threw him back onto the floor on his head. I picked him up and ran him around to different lighting to check to see if his eyes were dilating. I am no doctor, however, "they say" if the child's eyes aren't dilating equally, it's a bad sign. He seemed to be okay, but I would still watch him very carefully all night; another night of worrying for the books.

My daughter called out, "Mama, I have a boogie in my nose. How can I get it?" and then "Mama, I got it!" All I could do at this point was laugh. At least that night my daughter told me her meal was delicious. I learned a couple of things from this situation. One, never have a spice rack in a lower cabinet. Why does the perfect space for spices always seem to be in a bottom cabinet? Just to make life harder for parents? Two, we ended up laughing over a "boogie" and everyone enjoyed the meal together as a family. I was reminded not to sweat the small stuff.

These moments also remind me that I need to stay calm. Even if I get frustrated by the many things going on at once, it typically all ends up okay in the end. Sometimes, I feel like all I am doing is yelling at my husband, when really he doesn't deserve it. He immediately offered to go to the store to purchase the missing ingredient when he could have simply told me to make something else. I realized I needed to stop looking at the bad and the negative and look for the positive. Rather than focusing my attention on the fact that my husband forgot an item at the grocery store, I should be focusing my attention on the fact that he goes to the grocery store so I don't have to with two kids in tow. That is a good man right there. At times, especially when you are having a tough day, or when you are in a bad mood, it is so easy to immediately look at the negative or to look at what isn't going right. I had to challenge myself when I start looking at the negative things, to stop and think about what could be positive in the situation.

Put Your Significant Other First

I remember reading something about "emotional abuse" towards your spouse once. "They" said we could actually be unknowingly emotionally abusing our spouses by constantly yelling at or putting them down. This article really made me think about how my yelling and demanding comments may have made my spouse feel. Anyone ever used any of these lines: "You have to use the bathroom again? How could you possibly need to use the bathroom so often and for so long? There is no way you go in there and actually use the bathroom for 30 to 45 minutes daily!" These are statements I find myself yelling at my husband probably way too often. At one point, he even shared he was scared to tell me when he needed to go. If you are one of those people who uses these lines as often as I do, don't feel bad. It is hard. At least in my situation, it seems like a vacation to be able to sit in the bathroom for even five minutes without any distractions. I saw a quote on social media one day which said, "I birthed an entire child in the time it takes my husband to use the bathroom." Both my husband and I laughed hard over this one.

I don't believe that it is "emotional abuse" when we raise our voices, however, it does pay off to practice empathy by putting ourselves in our spouse's shoes and thinking about how they may feel in certain situations. This can help put our behaviors into perspective and can help us change them if needed. I guess my husband deserves some alone time too. After all, he was at work all day with no opportunity to use the bathroom and comes home after a stressful day to usually at least one child, if not two, screaming or doing something crazy. That can't be easy either.

The "bathroom" dilemma wasn't the only problem. I realized over time, it got to the point where my husband would come home from work and I would be so wrapped up in my day-to-day challenges that I had stopped asking him about his day and it wasn't even just that. I had stopped even saying "hi" on most days. Instead I was usually greeting him with negativity. I would just jump right into asking him to help me with this or that, or I would immediately start complaining about how crazy the day was. Of course it happens—hanging out with multiple young children all day is difficult to say the least—but, as I started thinking more about it, I realized I may actually be hurting our relationship.

"They say" men are programmed to fix things while women are more likely to understand sometimes you just want to "get it out" and talk about it, no action required. When faced with a problem, I have learned men see a need to fix it. I realized the issues and complaints I was sharing with my husband were not something that needed fixing in my mind, it was just something I needed to vent. On the other hand, for him, it was likely overwhelming to be slammed with all of these complaints which he felt he should fix the second he returned home each day. I realized how tough it must be to be faced with so many issues which are not fixable. I realized it may even make him feel like he has failed.

Feeling like you failed is not a good feeling to have and constant negativity is never good for anyone. I wondered, *Why am I doing this?* I mentioned earlier in this chapter how putting our children first can cause a strain on a marriage. Well, I had definitely started putting my children in front of my husband and my marriage. It seems putting your children first is a reasonable thing to do, but it can definitely end up impacting your marriage at some point.

So, what did I do? I tried to focus more on building my husband up instead of inadvertently putting him down. I tried to minimize the negative comments and use more positive ones which I hoped would make him feel special and good about himself. After all, he is a wonderful husband and father. Most importantly, I started trying to put my husband and my marriage first at least sometimes.

Things soon started to change for the better. I started to become a happier person. As I gave love and support to my husband, I started to feel so much more love and support in return. This may sound silly, but our love started to grow. My children even started to notice. With a huge smile on her face, my daughter started saying things like, "Mommy, you really love Daddy," or when we went on a date, "Did you go see a movie about a Mommy and Daddy loving each other?" I found there were many benefits to putting my husband first. As we did this, our children witnessed a strong, loving marriage, which I believe can be a huge protective factor for children. It can help our children feel safe and secure. I think a strong and loving marriage or a strong and loving family equals strong and loving kids. For us, I even saw it increase our family happiness as a whole. Although it seems like once we have children we need to put them first at all times, I found this may not always be the best practice.

Try Not to Keep Track

Sometimes I found myself almost "keeping track" of who did what around the house. Has anyone else ever had a conversation like, "I am doing everything around here! When is the last time you have taken out the trash, or loaded the dishwasher, or done the laundry?" Usually these conversations would occur when one or both of us were in a bad mood. When in a good mood, I found it easier to see all of the things my husband was doing to help me out and to make my life easier.

I have to be careful about "keeping track" of every little thing each of us does. All it does is make me on-edge and frustrated with my spouse. I have learned I should try to focus on what my spouse is doing, rather than what he is not doing. After all, it is not about the number of things you do for the family. It is about how you can together provide for your family as a team. You can both bring different things to the table and these things are not all of equal weight. Rather than watching for things your spouse does and "keep track," watch for the helpful things they do and acknowledge it.

These small changes have helped build up my marriage, and in turn, they've made life a lot easier. Honestly, if I call my husband out less, he seems to appreciate what I am doing more, and then he in turn starts doing more. It's quite an interesting dynamic. Now, don't get me wrong, true teamwork is important. It takes a village to raise a child, right? I just find it best to focus on what we are both doing to contribute, rather than to focus on each little item each person does and how often it is done. This "keeping track" does nothing but build frustration and it never makes anything better. It only makes both of us feel bad.

Communication is Key

There are times when you have an issue which needs resolving on your hands. How do you know? I am not a marriage expert here, but I feel an issue needs resolving if:

1. You frequently feel there is a problem.
2. It is something which truly bothers you more often than not.
3. It does not only come up the moment you are in a "bad mood."

If this is the case, communicate, communicate, communicate. My husband and I have always practiced "get it out," and I think this has been invaluable in our marriage. When in doubt, communicate. I don't think good communication can ever make a situation worse. We tell each other when something is bothering us, in a calm way and away from the children when we have some alone time. Once, I found myself raising my voice at my husband, and my daughter said, "Mommy, God says not to yell or whine. He says to be good." That made me quiet down pretty quickly. Not only this, but it is hard to have a meaningful conversation with little minds around listening in. With some privacy, we get it off of our chests and talk it through. We try to come up with a compromise or a solution. "Getting it out" only seems to make our marriage stronger.

Always remember to be real. If you feel hurt, put it out there. Tell your partner how you feel. It is never good to hold it in. I believe the more we hold in, the further we grow away from our spouse or partner. Think about it: you have this whole side of you which you are keeping to yourself and not sharing. Marriage is about two becoming one, which I believe even means to share the tough things. If you are holding it all in, one of two things could happen (maybe not, but I think it is possible): you could either drive yourselves apart or you could just explode once it is too much to hold in. Neither option seems very healthy in a relationship.

Once you talk about it, let it go. Try not to hold grudges. Try not to bring it up again at a later date. If you can erase it from your mind somehow, that's even better. There is no need to continue bringing things up which have been resolved. After all, don't we all deserve a clean slate every once in a while?

Find Time to Enjoy Each Other

It is so important to save some time for yourselves as a couple. I think it's the single strongest factor which keeps love alive. My husband and I had not been away for more than one night on a single occasion until our oldest was almost three. Three years was a long time to not have any true time alone as a couple. We didn't even realize how much we needed this time until we actually went away. We stretched a friend's wedding weekend out and ended up driving up the California coast for a week together. The trip was amazing and we had plenty of time to spend talking and enjoying each other's company without distraction. We even learned a few new things about each other. Who knew there was more to learn after years of marriage and life with kids?

I encourage everyone to take time away together if you have the opportunity. If you have the opportunity to travel the coast of California, even better. What a relaxing and rejuvenating trip it was. No matter how you do it, whether it is short trips or a long one every so often, or even frequent day trips out, taking this time will help keep your marriage and your bond strong. If you don't have the ability to do this, merely finding time alone (even after the children go to sleep) to do things together is beneficial. You could sit down and play board games, watch a movie, cook, talk—anything you can do together. Whatever you do, don't allow yourselves to feel guilty being away from your children. I assure you, allowing time to recharge your relationship will do nothing but benefit you and your children in the end. What do "they say?" Absence makes the heart grow fonder? Well, I would agree that a little time to recharge never hurt anyone.

Don't Push Away Those You Love

When you face difficult situations, don't push people away. I went through some tough times where there seemed to be no end in sight, and it was easy to yell at those around me, especially my husband and my family. I found myself so frustrated, and at my wit's end. I felt like I had no energy and strength left. I thought it was easier to be alone, but it wasn't. And if you have done some yelling, that is okay too. Don't be hard on yourself. I believe the open and honest relationship I have with my husband, where we don't hold back and put everything out on the table can be positive, even if there are times it comes out in yelling form. Even though some yelling took place during these tough times, I also leaned on my husband. Lean on your husband or partner, your friends, your family. Difficult times can bring you closer together or tear you apart. I found in the end, when we made it through tough situations, our marriage only became stronger. When you have someone, or multiple people who stick by you and help you navigate the tough times, you know you have found the right people to have by your side.

I don't think parenting is necessarily supposed to be easy or all fun and joy. I think the hard times which come hand in hand with parenting define your relationship as a couple and can bring you closer. When you look back, you will remember the tough times, but you will more likely remember the amazing ones. You will remember how you stuck by each other. This only makes your love grow. It made me feel better just taking the pressure off and realizing life isn't easy. Marriage is not easy and that is normal. Relationships are not easy. Raising babies, toddlers, children, and teenagers is not easy. It isn't supposed to be easy. When things get tough, you are not alone. These are the things which shape your life and your relationship. These are the things which make you stronger as a person and as a couple. It is okay if you have some turbulence in between. It will only make you stronger in the end.

There may be times you find yourself wondering, *Is it worth it to keep trying?* There is a line in the Hallmark movie, Karen Kingsbury's *A Time to Dance*, which I believe answers this question nicely. It is, "A marriage is a house. You invest in it, you make the repairs, and you love it because inside is everything that ever meant something to you." So, keep on trying.

Let It Go

It wasn't just the relationship with my husband which was strained. There was a time after having my first child when I started feeling like I was struggling with all of my close relationships. It progressively became worse especially after my second child was born. I am not sure if it was the hormonal changes of having a baby and being pregnant, but the actions of others I was close to started frustrating me. I think when I became a mom myself, the way I saw my relationship with my own parents changed. It was like I had a new lens on the relationship. I found a new appreciation for my parents and for what they went through raising me and my sisters. On the other hand, I started comparing the relationship I had with my own child to my parents' relationship with me. Even though I had always valued my relationship with my parents and know they are wonderful parents, when I did this, I found myself becoming frustrated with their actions.

The bottom line is that you cannot change others; you can only change yourself. As a school counselor, I told my students this time and time again, but I wasn't taking my own advice. The more I thought about this, the more I realized I was actually playing a huge part in my frustration.

There were five valuable questions I started to ask myself when I was experiencing frustration in a relationship:

1. What can I personally change to make this better?
2. What am I doing which may be making this situation worse?
3. What am I really mad at here?
4. Does it really matter in the scheme of life?
5. Will this matter ten years from now?

The truth is, if it won't matter ten years from now, it probably isn't worth our time today.

I started letting things go and this really helped me. I learned never to underestimate the power of forgiveness. I found holding onto frustrations only strained my relationships more. It is hard to imagine just how much weight can be taken from one's heart until you forgive. Finding it in your heart to let it go can lead to so many wonderful experiences. Always remember that no relationship is perfect and no person is perfect. People will make mistakes. When they do, finding it in your heart to forgive can make a huge difference.

The best part is, as I changed my mindset, my relationships truly started to improve. I mean, there were still arguments from time to time, but without all that built-up anger I would carry around, things went much more smoothly.

Don't forget to take care of your relationship with yourself too. It is important to take care of ourselves. We cannot beat ourselves up over our mistakes and we cannot continue putting ourselves down. How are we supposed to have strong relationships with others when we don't first have a strong relationship with ourselves?

RECHARGE YOUR HEART

I think it is important to eat the center cinnamon roll…at least sometimes. This probably makes me sound even crazier than I actually am, but I am serious. Many want that center cinnamon roll when you make them in the round pan. It is so soft and squishy and there are no burnt edges. I usually feel like I should save it for my husband or give it to my child, but sometimes you need to just eat it. As moms, or parents, we give and give and put everyone else first. But, sometimes you need to take care of yourself first. Sometimes you need to do something for yourself so you can stay strong. So, do it and don't allow yourself to feel guilty. You may think it is wishful thinking to suggest we all require some "me time," and I get that. I barely have time to shave my legs, or much less to even shower, but that is what makes finding this time even more important.

One morning, I went to my biannual dentist appointment. As the dental hygienist cleaned my teeth, she asked the dreaded question, "Have you been flossing?" Hey, I was quite proud of myself that I even made it to the appointment at all. Flossing daily? Now that was just too much to ask of a mom with two kids.

I replied, "Well, not as much as I would have liked to floss. I have done my best with my newborn and my toddler around. I am often too exhausted at night to even think about flossing." Wrong answer. I think I must have given too much information again, because the dental hygienist seemed determined to help me figure out how to floss.

She said, "Most people don't realize you can actually floss anytime. It doesn't have to be at night. It can be during the day when you are watching TV. You can just grab a piece of floss and floss as you watch."

I responded, "Great idea," so as not to take away from her excitement, but I was thinking, *Yeah right! In our household, we are lucky if I brush my own teeth and both of my kids' teeth at all. Much less watch TV.* Is this why "they say" women lose an average of one tooth per child? No time for brushing, or especially flossing?

Moral of the story, however, is it is important to find time for yourself, somehow. It may not be easy, but if you want to be able to take good care of your children, you must first take good care of yourself. This goes for both your physical and emotional health. It is like on the airplane when they say to put the oxygen mask on yourself first and then put it on your child. You can't protect your child if you are incapacitated.

Being a "super mom" doesn't mean you are so strong you don't experience or feel emotion or that you can keep going and going even in the face of adversity. I believe being a "super mom" is actually realizing when you have hit your limit and knowing you need to ask for help or support. As a stay-at-home mom, there were many times where I found myself struggling with exhaustion, frustration, and many other emotions. The truth is I never truly got a break. I felt a little selfish thinking this way at first, because I thought, *What am I talking about? I am staying home all day, every day. Shouldn't this qualify as a break?*

It took me a few trips out alone when I finally realized that I wasn't really being selfish. I would leave the house alone, drive to the store, listen to music, yes, even bad music with plenty of cuss words if I wanted, and I would listen to it as loud as I liked. I would jam and smile and relax. I would browse the store calmly without an antsy or yelling toddler. When I came home, I found myself feeling like a new woman. I thought, *Is it really possible a simple trip to the store alone makes me feel like a new woman?* It sure did. I hear people say they need a manicure or a massage. That would be lovely, but I am thinking, *Heck, I would be okay with just ten minutes in the car, just me and the radio.* This sounds a bit pathetic, but it illustrates just how little time we as parents have to ourselves.

When I worked, I didn't get a lot of breaks either, but I at least had time alone to drive to and from work. I had a few minutes here and there to talk with other adults and actually enjoy those conversations. I wasn't getting these moments at home. If I went somewhere, I had two children tagging along, one of whom was likely whining, crying, or screaming at some point—or let's be real, multiple points—throughout the trip. I was hardly even getting a second of alone time throughout the day. I mean, I didn't even get alone time to use the bathroom. Have any of you out there been in the middle of using the toilet yourself (without privacy of course) and your toddler says, "I have to go potty?" It has definitely happened to me, multiple times. It would be so invigorating to have ten or fifteen minutes of peace to use the bathroom. Wow, my definition of invigorating sure has changed. I used to think *spa*. Now, I think *toilet*!

The lack of privacy you have as a mom is real. I remember shortly after having my son, I had to wear those bulky post-delivery pads. I had to take my daughter with me to use the bathroom and she asked me, "Mommy, are you wearing a diaper?" I mean, what do you even say to a potty-training two-year-old when asked that question? Yes, Mommy is wearing a diaper, but you can't? I ended up telling her no, it was just a big Band-Aid Mommy needs since her brother came out of my tummy. Even that sounds horrible, but what else do you say? I know a better alternative would be to put her somewhere safe when I am in the bathroom, but sometimes it's hard to even do that. If I left her in front of the TV, who knew where she would end up when I came out. If I put her in an enclosed space, she would probably scream or cry and wake up the likely sleeping newborn. So, there you have it. Many times she ended up in the bathroom with me.

Then, there are the tampons. There is bound to come a time when your child spots the tampons. They are brightly colored and wrapped like a gift of sorts. Maybe my children are just strange, but it's like they are drawn to the things. There have been many occasions when I find them playing with one, or the whole box, and many more occasions when my daughter has asked me, "What are these Mommy?" Again, how do you answer this question? I just told my daughter every time, "They are Mommy's toiletries." So, far she has accepted that. If she asks what toiletries are, I just respond with "toiletries." Eventually, she lets it go. If it's that time of the month, how do you find the privacy for that? The last thing I want to do is scar my children for life. So, it's true, there really are no breaks. If you thought you would at least be able to pee in peace throughout your life, I hate to say it, but you are wrong.

Even after the kids went to sleep it didn't seem like a true break because I was still on duty with the monitors in my ear to ensure everything was okay. Once, my husband told me to just turn them down, but I couldn't even do that because then I would worry about the kids. You would think I would get a break when my husband came home from work, but no, still no break. First, he needed—and also deserved—a break too after working all day; and also, I would say I am the key person on duty most of the time when home. For example, one day my husband came home from work and he took my son upstairs with him to put him in the portable crib while he changed so that I could have a second to eat my dinner. How sweet that he offered to take him off my hands so I can have some form of peace (well, as much peace as I can get with a three-year-old still present).

Not one minute later, I heard him yelling something from upstairs. "Oh no...Lauren!!!!" He ran down the stairs, his arms stretched straight out from his body like a mummy, barely holding the baby under his armpits saying, "He has a huge poop. I think it's on me. It's all over my arms. It stinks. I need to take a shower now, right away!" I am like, "Seriously? It's just your child's poop. Get over it." Man, the amount of poop I can deal with on a daily basis is insane. Even when I am slightly "off duty," I would say I am still "on duty." No wonder we all feel crazy at times, or maybe even all the time.

How Can I Find "Me Time?"

If you are finding it difficult to find enough "me time" I challenge you to keep trying, because it is definitely important. Try to get creative. I think it is possible to have some "me time" with your child. Think of the things you enjoy doing or things which have relaxed you in the past and try to do them with your children. If you like to bake, bake with your child. If you like to garden, garden with your child. If you like to scrapbook, scrapbook with your child. The list can go on and on with exercise, yoga, art, photography, and so on.

I loved to take pictures of my children, so one day, I made a little play camera for my daughter. We used a soap box and a toilet paper roll. I just cut a hole in the box in the center to fit the toilet paper roll. I let her decorate the camera with stickers. She loved taking pictures with her camera when I took pictures with mine. There are lots of ways to be creative and do some of the things you enjoy. This is not exactly "me time" because you still have the kids with you, but it can be "good for the heart" time. A happy heart is always a good thing.

Another way to find that true "me time" includes hiring a babysitter, even for just an hour or two so that you have some time to yourself. It is good for you and for your relationship. I feel like my husband's and my relationship definitely gets put on the back burner, but it is really important to find time for that relationship as well. It is easy to feel like we shouldn't use a babysitter unless we have somewhere we need to go, but the truth is having a couple of hours to simply relax can be even more rejuvenating than having a night out. Other ideas include letting your partner or a family member watch the kids, or even simply take the monitors away from you after the kids are asleep so you can take a bubble bath or even just a shower in complete peace, without worrying that the kids are going to wake up. There is nothing worse than just starting your shower during naptime and your child wakes up screaming. If you have neighbors with children, you could make a plan to watch each other's kids every so often, so you can squeeze in a quick trip to the store or a quick break.

Another time I may get some "me time" in is during naptime. It was amazing when I finally had my two children on the same nap schedule. This was short lived, however, because my daughter chose not to nap most days pretty early, soon after age two. Even though she tried not to nap, I found she still benefited from quiet time. On the days she had no time to herself, she was a mess by dinner. So, mid-day, I had my son nap, and my daughter spent time in her room. She could choose to nap, read quietly, or play with her animals and dolls, but the quiet time was non-negotiable. There were days I felt bad about it, but remember, it is good for them to get some time to let their brain recharge, and it is good for you to let your patience recharge. This still allowed me the "quiet time" I needed.

I remember asking my pediatrician at our two-year appointment if it was important for my daughter to take a nap every day. His response was, "Yes, it is absolutely essential." He paused, then added, "For your sanity, Mom." I laughed, but it is so true. He encouraged me to ensure my daughter had some quiet time even if she didn't find herself napping every single day; that it would be good for the both of us. You do what you feel is best for your situation and your child. If quiet time in the room is best for you, great, give it a try. If skipping the nap all together, or if playing a movie for your child to help them settle down works for you, then go with that.

Another way to get creative is to use your time wisely. For example, while your child is eating lunch or playing happily, you can get something done. I like to pull my child's high chair around to face me in the kitchen and do the dishes while he eats or has a snack. Sometimes, I schedule in a little TV time so I can get one thing done. "They say" never let your child watch too much television. Who knew two letters, TV, could cause so much trouble? You better not watch too much TV, or else, right?

Once again, don't let what "they say" get to you. You decide what is best for your family. Of course, I am sure it is never a good idea to use the TV all day, every day. Nothing is ever good in excess, but if an hour or two of TV time a day is what works for you, then I say go for it. My husband always says, "Nothing is a problem until it becomes a problem." If you start to notice TV is becoming a problem, you go back to the drawing board for a new TV plan. So far, my kids make no trouble when we say, "It is time to turn off the TV," even if it is mid-show. If we start experiencing trouble with this, I will come up with a new plan, and maybe a break from television.

Time with other parents can also be beneficial. Finding opportunities to get together with other adults with the kids present may not exactly be true "me time," but it can provide you with much-needed adult interaction. There are groups out there which you can participate in stroller walks together or exercise groups where you can actually exercise with your baby, even using your baby as a weight or the stroller as a bar. Even finding parents in your area to go to the playground with, walk around the mall, or have play dates with can be very helpful. Looking for a MOPS (Mothers of Preschoolers) group in your area is another great idea.

Moms, do try to get creative with your schedule. Find ways to have some time for yourself, because it can immensely impact your level of happiness...and even your sanity.

"MOMMY FAIL"

For me, parenting is like cutting wrapping paper. The scissors start to glide, then they catch and you are like, "Oh poo... Somehow I messed it up again."

I put my daughter in ballet at two and a half years old. She should be able to listen at age two and half, right? Well, that is questionable and it depends on the day. It seems listening actually varies moment to moment for a two-and-a-half-year-old. The other kids in her class were anywhere from age two-and-a-half to five. One day, the teacher asked them to take off their ballet shoes to do some stretching. Then, she asked them to put them back on. All of the other children, even the two-year-olds, put their shoes back on. Lili just sat there waiting patiently. I was thinking on the other side of the glass, *Oops, guess I should have taught her how to put her shoes on.* Mommy fail. Oh well, don't sweat the small stuff. It could have been worse, right?

As I have mentioned, even at three, I have my daughter spend some quiet time in her room while her brother naps. One day, my daughter screamed out for me. I worried she would wake her brother who wasn't feeling well and needed the rest, so I literally ran up there and told her to stay in her room because naptime wasn't over. She said, "But Mama—"

I cut her off and said, "Go back into your room. Naptime is not over yet. Mommy decides when naptime is over."

She went back into her room without a fuss. Later that night when my husband was putting her to bed, he called for me and said I had to see something. I thought, *Oh dear, what now?* I went in and my daughter had somehow pulled her wooden monogram over her bed down. It was double reinforced too. I said, "Lili, how did you do that?"

She responded, "I wanted to do something cool, like the Croods do." (She had recently watched the movie, *The Croods.*)

She literally had tried to climb up her headboard and up her monogram. Thank God she didn't get hurt. I don't know how I didn't hear it, especially with her video monitor on. Maybe I shouldn't have let her watch that movie so much without explaining we don't climb things like the characters do. I could not stop myself from laughing and had to leave the room to pull myself back together again. I am thankful for my husband who was able to keep a straight face while he handled that one. Mommy fail.

I will never forget the first time I clipped my daughter's nails. It was such a scary experience for me. I always made sure to take my time and I clipped them while I was nursing. While feeding on each side, I would pick up the hand on top and clip away. This was the only way I could keep my children still. I will never forget one time when I accidentally clipped one nail too short. I clipped a tiny bit of the skin which separated her nail from her finger. She didn't seem like she was in pain, but I was so worried about it. I remember telling myself I was the worst mother ever. I felt like it was the lowest of all lows to clip my daughter's skin, the thought that I could have hurt her. Mommy fail. I spent several days feeling bad and worrying, but it never seemed to bother my daughter once.

I am here to tell you that you will make mistakes and it is

okay. Your child will get hurt and will fall and there will be times when you cannot get to them quick enough or prevent it from happening. We are all human. I think almost every mom has had a clipping accident, and plenty of other accidents along the way. When it happens, it is best to block that negative, or what I call "stinking thinking," and instead of telling yourself "I am the worst parent ever," tell yourself, "Here is one of those accidents/mistakes which are bound to happen" and move right on. Do not question yourself as a parent because the fact you are concerned means you are a great parent. I found when I was sitting around questioning myself and feeling bad, it took my focus away from my children. Not only that, but it would put me into a bad mood which affected me, and in turn, affected my kids. Trust me, your children will love it way more if you continue playing with them rather than stew over what you did, right or wrong. There will be things you might feel you did wrong, but I promise you are going to do a billion more things right.

One day, I ventured out with my two children to get some last-minute clothes, bathing suits, and supplies for the beach. I was looking at shirts for my daughter. As I looked over at her, I saw she was bent over grabbing one of the shelves and shaking her butt super fast. She seemed to be twerking. I thought, *Where on earth did she learn this?* Mommy fail for sure. However, the next thing I knew my son was laughing the loudest, most adorable baby laugh I had heard to date. It was well past his naptime and his irritation had disappeared. I had started to tell my daughter, "Stop that right now, young lady," but stopped in my tracks and said, "Never mind, go ahead and dance."

When these moments happen, it is all in how you look at it. You live and you learn. You learn from your mistakes. Mistakes make you a better mom because you grow. Don't let fretting over mistakes make you miss the good moments, because they are what life is all about.

It was another one of those days when I was quite flustered. It had been one bad thing after the other. I yelled at my dog—I mean really yelled at her. I cannot even remember what she did wrong, but what I do remember is when I yelled at the dog, my daughter looked terrified and literally ran away. I felt horrible. I felt like I scared my daughter. Mommy fail. In the end, I had to stop beating myself up over it. It was just one of those "I'll do better tomorrow, it will be a new day" kind of things. We all make mistakes.

My very young toddler was trying to blow those fluffy dandelion flowers like his sister was doing. It was so cute, so I told my daughter to hold one up for my son to blow, solely for the purpose of taking a cute photo. As I snapped the photo, he took a big bite out of it. I ran over and started scooping the seeds out of his mouth. This is one of those times when I should probably have been paying closer attention to my children instead of taking a photograph. Mommy fail. I will admit, the photo is priceless.

My baby sings rap songs, not "Old MacDonald" or "Twinkle, Twinkle Little Star" like other children do. My children also enjoy singing the "Happy Birthday" song, specifically, "Happy birthday kaka [meaning poop]." Double mommy fail.

Then there is poison control. There was the time when my son ate fish food. My daughter went to feed the fish. Before I could get to her, she grabbed a fist full of fish food from the container and completely missed the bowl. It somehow fell right down into my son's mouth. I seriously couldn't even make this stuff up. I called poison control. Let's see, my daughter also took a big bite out of a lip balm. I called poison control. As I told you, my son took a bite out of a dandelion. I called poison control. On separate occasions, both of my children ate chalk. I called poison control. My son ate some of his diaper ointment. I called poison control. My son ate a small tube of his baby toothpaste. I called poison control. Mommy failures. Thank goodness for poison control, but I am waiting for them to show up at my door for all my calls. My husband always jokes with me about this, but I always tell him I will continue calling. I doubt they are going to take my kids away for calling and making sure they are safe. They may take them, however, if I don't call.

Then, there was that day when I missed my son applying this same thick, pink diaper cream as a facial mask. When I turned around it was all over his face, and all in his hair. What I did learn that day was diaper ointment is great in lieu of hair gel; hair gel which lasts for five days and many, many washes even after trying four different shampoos. My son had a super fancy mohawk for a week. Mommy fail.

One day I was at the doctor's office with my first baby who had been feeling so ill that she eventually needed a blood test. As I was talking with the doctor, I had my daughter sitting in my lap. She told me to watch out for the bandage on her finger as a lot of children end up putting them in their mouth and swallowing them. After speaking with the doctor, I stood up to leave. When we approached the waiting room, I went to check for my daughter's bandage and it was gone. Sure enough, it was in her mouth. Thank goodness she hadn't swallowed it. I remember feeling so stupid because the doctor had just warned me and I still somehow missed it. Mommy fail.

Then, there was the time at the doctor's office when my daughter had a rash. As the doctor was talking with me, my daughter started saying "boobie, boobie." At first, we were like, "What is she saying?" Then she continued to say "boobie" over and over and continued to point at my boobs. This was way after I had stopped nursing, so I have no clue where this came from. I know my face was as red as a beet. Again, where does she learn this stuff? Mommy fail.

When something is falling, like a sippy cup or spoon, has anyone ever swung their arm quickly to get it and accidentally bonked their child in the head? Maybe it is just me who has done that. There was also the time while I was opening a honey packet so carefully across the table for my daughter, and my son pushed my entire cheeseburger onto the floor. Mommy fail.

One of my strangest "mommy fail" moments came when my husband and I took our children to a major theme park during the Halloween season. My husband had free tickets from work to go to the local theme park, but we had yet to go. It was the end of September and we decided we were going to head up there one day after work. We arrived around 4:30 and thought we would have at least until 8:00 to walk around. We figured on a week night, this should be plenty of time for the children to enjoy the kids' rides. Well, it turns out, although it was not even October yet, it happened to be the first night of the Halloween scary stuff.

As we entered the theme park, we were met with bloody, dismembered hands and feet hanging all above us. As much as I tried to avert my daughter's gaze, she definitely saw them. Thank goodness she didn't realize they were bloody, as she pointed, laughed, and said, "That is so funny, Mommy! Look at those feet!"

First mistake: We were already there, so we decided to try to enjoy ourselves and figured we would leave before dark. There was a sign which read that children should be accompanied by an adult after six, which was when the festivities would begin. Second mistake: The children's area was just next to the front gate area, so I figured if we stayed there, even if we left a little after six, it would not be too much of an issue to leave the area and head directly to the front gate.

As 6:00 approached, the kids had had enough fun, so we started preparing to leave. Of course, my daughter needed to use the potty, which took some time and we ended up walking out of the park about five minutes past six. I had been there a few years prior and it wasn't very scary at all when walking around the park, so I figured we would be just fine. Third mistake: I should have paid more attention to the clearly seasoned park goers who had draped sheets over their children's strollers, and many even had heavy-duty headphones over their children's ears—and this was in the children's area. After taking note of what other parents were doing around us, we put the hoods up on both of the kids' sweatshirts. My husband ended up holding my daughter against his chest and told her to keep her head down and her eyes closed, just in case. I put my son into the mommy-facing carrier, hooked the covering over his head so he wouldn't be able to see much, and we started to head out.

It was not even a second after we left the children's area when scary people started coming at us from everywhere. I am not even kidding when I say everywhere. Up ahead, I saw a lady in a black dress holding an umbrella, only there was no head. It was just the body. I yelled out to my daughter to close her eyes. Of course, she didn't. I squeezed my son to my chest so tight that he was crying. I did not want him to see any of this. I looked behind me to see what was in my daughter's line of sight and there was a man walking right behind me with a huge butcher knife in his hand, wearing a white apron covered in blood. Even his face was painted, making him look terrifying.

My heart was beating a mile a minute and I screamed to my husband, "Cover her face! Cover her face!" Of course, he didn't. He had no idea what was behind him. I started running to catch up and a ghost lady came out of nowhere and snapped her fan in my face, right next to my son's head. I jumped at least two feet in the air. Finally, my husband made sure my daughter's eyes were closed and we literally ran out of there. I was shocked how scary it was even right at the front gate. I was shocked these scary people would come towards young children. As we walked out of the entrance, my daughter started to cry. Here is the conversation that ensued:

I said, "What is wrong honey?"

My daughter responded, "I want to go home."

"Why sweetie? Did something scare you?"

My husband says to me, "Shh. Stop. Don't bring it up."

"Of course I need to bring it up. I am not going to hide it. Did you see what she saw?"

My daughter interrupted, "Yes, something scared me."

I held my breath. "What did you see that scared you?"

"I saw a dress."

"Oh, that is not scary, just a dress?"

My daughter disagreed. "Yes, it was really scary."

After thinking back to what I saw, I said, "Did the dress have a head on it?"

"No."

Trying to think quickly, I said, "Oh, I am so sorry sweetie. Mommy and Daddy forgot to tell you there were going to be people dressed up for Halloween today. Unfortunately, some people dress up scary for Halloween. I prefer to dress up as something pretty like a princess. She must have dressed up as a dress. Her head was just under the dress. There were holes so she could see. That is so silly. I cannot believe someone wanted to dress up like a dress."

My daughter laughed out loud and said, "Oh, that is so silly. I would have liked it much better if the dress was not black. It should have been pink and purple."

"I agree. Did you see anything else that was scary?"

My daughter said, "No," then paused. "Mommy?"

"Yes, honey?"

"I am going to be sunglasses next year for Halloween."

Thank goodness, she did not realize the man with the knife covered in blood was scary. I guess she just assumed it was a regular person who spilled his smoothie or something. I cannot describe how happy I was that she only saw the dress. Even that took some explaining. Afterwards, my husband said, "I felt like we were in the movie *Escape* trying to get out of that theme park." Mommy fail. Lesson learned. I will never enter a theme park even close to October with the children again.

There was still one particular "mommy fail" moment which tops all the rest for me. Yes, it even tops the theme park. It was a moment which scared me more than anything else thus far. I was still trying to get used to life with two children. I will be honest, it is not all roses and butterflies as it may seem—it is rough getting used to caring for two children at once. It does become smoother, but on this day, it clearly hadn't gotten too smooth for us yet.

My two-year-old was playing quietly and I had my four-and-a-half-month-old in his high chair, trying to feed him some baby food. I noticed it had gotten too quiet. It couldn't have been more than 30 seconds of quiet since I last heard my daughter, but I went to check on her anyway. I noticed the front door was wide open. I was immediately shocked and scared. I had no idea she even knew how to open the heavy front door. She never had before, but when it comes to toddlers, I have learned that there is a first time for everything. I looked outside, and she was across the street playing with rocks. Thank goodness we live on a small, quiet street with hardly any traffic. I yelled out for her and ran across my front lawn and across the street screaming. She saw me and immediately started to cry. She was crying like she was so scared and was asking me to help her. It was like the second she saw me, she realized she was wrong and became scared. I would have much preferred her to realize she would be scared before she actually ran out the door, but we live and we learn. Mommy fail.

I will admit, this was a time when I literally yelled at my child and she was sent to her room for way longer than the "two minutes for a two-year-old" rule. This was followed by a serious discussion about what happened. Hopefully, my daughter learned not to run out the door alone anymore and I asked my husband to put a latch lock on the top of our front door so she wouldn't even be able to do it again. I felt absolutely horrible. I beat myself up over it of course. I was lucky. Something horrible could have happened. The thoughts which crossed my mind were, *She could have been hit by a car or someone could have taken her. If I hadn't noticed so quickly, she could have run away and I may not have been able to find her.*

The thing is, however, I did notice right away and I did go out there to get her immediately. That should count for something, right? In the end, everyone was okay and I learned a really important thing about toddler-proofing: don't forget the doors. Once again, I will say, we are not perfect; we are going to make mistakes. Beating ourselves up over the mistakes we are bound to make at one point or another does nothing to help the situation. If anything, it will only make things worse. I have learned, even if we make a mistake, we have to try to focus on what we did right in the situation, rather than what we did wrong. There is typically something we do right, even if it is making a change to make it less likely to occur in the future.

I bought my daughter a tablet after our second child was born. It was one way to keep her calm, quiet, occupied, and next to me while I nursed. One day as she played a letter game, I asked her, "Did you learn any new letters on your tablet?"

She replied like a little teenager. "*Honestly*...not really."

I had never heard that statement out of her before, so I asked, "Where did you learn those words from?"

"Benjamin, from *Peter Rabbit*," she said.

Oh yes, of course, from a television show. I know. These may not really be mom-of-the-year moments, but let's take the good with the bad here. She used the word "honestly" correctly in a sentence. That is great work for a newly three-year-old, right? At least she knows what "honestly" means. I can't be too bad of a parent after all, if she understands that word.

If we let ourselves believe we are a failure, there can be some really great things we skip over and miss. In fact, when I was a school counselor, I always used to tell my students that we all make mistakes. It is what we do with the mistakes and how we learn from them that matters. We cannot let "mommy fail" situations like these get to us and make us feel any less than what we really are—extraordinary parents!

It really is all in the way we look at things. My dad was watching my daughter one day and he came downstairs with his forehead bleeding. He was completely calm but from the shocked look on my face, he said, "It's okay, she didn't mean to." I braced myself as he told me how she accidentally dropped a drum with metal edges on his head. I am not sure how "accidental" this was when it comes to a toddler, but he sure believed that it was. Really, when it comes to Papa, every negative thing my daughter does is an accident. I felt pretty bad about it but moved on hoping it was—as he said—an accident.

A few days later, my dad came back to visit. As soon as he walked in, my daughter ran over to him and said, "Papa, how is your head?" We can look at this situation as, my child is a bully. Maybe this is a bit of an extreme, but you get the idea. Or we can look at it as, my child cared enough to remember what happened a few days earlier and checked on my dad immediately after he walked in.

We were in the car one day and I was letting my children eat while I drove, and they were eating fast food. Some would say this is two mommy fails already, but some days, I just go with what is easiest. I had given my daughter a container of fries and she spilled them all over the car. I kept it together even though I was so frustrated at the thought that I would soon be cleaning up all of those fries with two screaming children who were ready to get out of the car. I handed her some more when we came to a stop, and then she dropped those too. Already in a bad mood from the hectic morning, I yelled. I felt so guilty for yelling at her. She listened and when I stopped yelling she said, "I still love you when you're mad, Mommy." It was so sweet and I felt a little stab in my heart because I had just yelled at this sweet little person. Yet again, I felt like I failed, but on the other hand, the fact that she was able to say such a sweet comment in that moment is reassuring. I grab ahold of the little bit of optimism and think to myself, *Just maybe I am doing something right?*

Maybe I Am Doing Something Right

I question myself all the time as a parent. I feel guilty and I wonder if there is anything I am actually doing right. I feel like as parents we don't truly know how our children are doing until they grow up. It is the test of time, right? Maybe we can actually tell if we look close enough.

There are times I find myself thinking, *Wow, I must be doing something right.* I compare having one of these moments after a long and crazy day to when you are extremely hot and thirsty: you take that first sip of ice-cold water and you feel its cool sensation going all the way down your throat. Just like that feeling, these moments are refreshing—revitalizing even. These moments show us we are doing a good job after all. I am not going to share some of these times with you to brag or boast. I am going to share them because there are honestly many, many days when I feel like a complete failure as a parent, when I feel I have done yet one more thing wrong which will ruin my kids. Let's face it, it is way more likely for a toddler to do something wrong or test you than to do something right. It is the stage, it is not you. Even so, I have great moments, and I know you do too. Unfortunately, sometimes it is just so easy to skip over our great moments or forget about them, only to remember those which are less than great.

As parents, we have to take the bad with the good. There are going to be times when we feel we failed, but we cannot let these times define us. Let those moments when you feel you must have done something right define you. Let it define you when you hear sweet words come from your child's mouth, or when you see your child is kind to her dolls, her siblings, or to others. We all have these moments. Value these moments rather than the negative ones. You have to know in these moments you are doing something right. Keep them in your mind for the ten minutes later when you are feeling less than great. It really does only take ten minutes. That is life with a toddler.

One day, I was waiting on hearing from the doctor regarding my son's sleep study, so I was already on edge, and my son decided to stand up on one of the toddler chairs in the playroom. As I went to get him down, the chair fell. Of course I saved him, but not myself, as somehow the chair landed really hard against both of my feet. I started crying because of the pain, along with all of the other built up emotion I was feeling.

My little baby boy came over and started patting my face and rubbing it and saying "Mama, Mama." It was the sweetest thing. Then, my daughter came over with her fairy wand and said, "I have magic, Mommy. I can make it all better." Then they both hugged me. It was just the sweetest thing. In this moment, I thought, *Man, I make plenty of mistakes, but thank God somehow my children learned how to show care and love.* Mommy win.

Another day, I started pulling the door to my daughter's room closed, and accidentally pinched her hand. She cried out. I said, "I'm so sorry sweetie. I didn't see your hand there."

She replied, "It's okay Mommy. When we fall down, we just get back up."

I said, "Aww, where did you hear that?"

"You told me at soccer, Mommy," she exclaimed excitedly.

I thought back and remembered telling her this at soccer about six months prior after she fell down and hurt her knee. That is a pretty long time ago for a three-year-old. Mommy win. I realized in this moment that there are great things we do and say which rub off on our children without us even realizing it. This one she vocalized, but imagine how many more great things are in those little heads which we don't even hear.

One night, as I was putting my daughter to sleep, she was talking so quietly I could not understand her. I asked her what she was saying. She responded, "I was saying my prayers. Dear God, thank you for helping my brother feel better and keeping him safe. Thank you for letting us stay in this house. Thank you for making me and putting me in my mommy's tummy. Amen." The prayer stole my heart. Mommy win.

There are plenty other examples of "mommy wins:"

When my son is crying and my daughter says, "It's okay CJ, I am right here. It will be okay."

When we were at ballet, a little girl gave my one-year-old son two crayons and he said "thank you" clear as day and completely on his own.

When I called my son "booboo" and my daughter said, "He is not a booboo, he is one of my people and he is my friend."

When my baby boy walked over to my toddler, who was lying on the floor, and gave her a big kiss on the face, and then, she responded, "I love you too, CJ."

When my baby is screaming in the car and will not stop, and my daughter says in her sweet voice, "Calm down CJ. There is no need to be upset. It is okay."

When I put my screaming son in the portable crib because I had to use the bathroom and my daughter went over to him, rubbed his head with one hand, rubbed his belly with her other hand through the crib mesh and said, "It's okay CJ, it's okay," over and over again.

When my daughter said, "When I get older, I'm going to draw a heart and write 'I love Mommy and Daddy and CJ and Jesus.'"

When family was leaving, and my daughter said, "Thank you for the cake and my toy, and thank you for CJ's toy too," because she knew he couldn't say it yet.

When my daughter told me (even when I had never said it to her before), "I love you more than all the birds and owls, to the moon and all the way back to me."

All are mommy wins.

One morning when my daughter woke early, we were lying in my bed watching a show. She reached over, rubbed my arm softly and said, "Mommy, I'll take care of you." Then, she gave me a gentle kiss on the cheek. Mommy win.

One day, after my daughter dropped a storage container, my 18-month-old son walked over, picked it up, and put it in the cabinet where it was supposed to go. He is forever taking out all of the storage containers from the cabinet, but this time he put it in its correct place. Yes, it was a dirty container, but it was so sweet of him to help clean up. Mommy win.

These moments are certainly there, we just need to grab ahold of them and preserve them in our memory. I think it is a great idea to write these things down. They are very easy to forget, but it is so powerful when you are feeling down and you read over all of the amazingly sweet things your children have said and done...and don't forget, you are the reason they do them.

Then there are those times when you find your child has

learned something important. These moments can be just as meaningful. I went to get my daughter after her nap and found saline spray in her hands. Mommy fail here; I guess I should have been more careful about leaving it in her room. I said, "What are you doing with that spray?"

My daughter responded, "I planned to give it to you once you came to get me, so I had it in my hands." She actually used the word planned.

I said, "But, did you spray it?"

She said, "No, because I didn't know how to spray it, but that's okay because you know everything."

See, what did I tell you? Mommy knows everything. This is something super important and valuable, right?

Okay, in all seriousness, let's all just lose the term "mommy fail" and replace it with "I must be doing something right." We aren't really failing after all. We are simply learning. I think those moments when we feel we must be doing something right must be the universe's way of telling us we are doing a good job, mistakes and all. So, don't allow yourself to feel like you have ruined your kids forever based on one thing you may have done wrong.

There have been times when I have gotten so frustrated at my children and I have yelled. I worry my children will turn out just like me in this moment, but we cannot be so hard on ourselves. The truth is, that moment is not who we are. Think of all of the amazing things our children see in us. If you still don't believe me, there are some amazing people out there who have come from pretty difficult upbringings. There are also people out there who have really struggled who have come from fantastic upbringings.

I am not saying we should be as horrible as we can and not to worry about it. I am simply saying that we cannot assume every small issue, mistake, or mishap that occurs will ruin our children forever. I believe it is a mix of genetics, environment, temperament, and upbringing that shapes us into who we are. Think of the number of siblings who could not be any more different from each other, even being raised in the same home by the same people. We just have to do our best to model what is right, provide discipline, and encourage our kids to be the best that they can be. Never allow yourself to forget this: For all the fails, there are wins. I believe, in the scheme of life, the wins are what make the difference.

DISCIPLINE: FACING THE CONSEQUENCES

These days, how could we not feel like bad parents based on the things we see and hear? We are receiving all kinds of information from friends, our parents, the news, the internet, articles, and most of this information is conflicting. A big one when it comes to discipline is "they say" you should never yell at your kids. I know you have seen or heard this one. I have seen article after article with titles like, "How to Get Your Kids to Listen without Yelling." When the day is done, I think we all feel like we failed in some way with our parenting based on something someone has said or we have read. It is so confusing. I even saw somewhere that we should be careful how often we tell our children good job or remind them to say they are sorry. I thought I could count on encouraging my children to say they are sorry when they make a mistake as a good parenting practice, but if I always listened to what I read, I could not even count on that. And I mean, how could saying those words possibly be a bad thing? How can we feel good about ourselves as parents when everywhere we look someone is telling us we are doing it wrong? Well, the truth is, we are not failures, we are great parents.

One day, my daughter said, "Yesternight, I saw the moon

too, Mom." Yes, she used a completely made up word, but it made perfect sense. Some toddler advice we can all take: when in doubt, make it up. Do what you think makes perfect sense. When in doubt...to be honest as parents that is pretty much always. I never know exactly what the right thing is to do. I especially doubt myself when it comes to discipline. When disciplining my children, I always wonder, *Did I say or do too much or not enough?*

I was telling my husband about the horrible mother I thought I was yet again after a day of what felt like constant discipline and he told me, "You are not a bad mom, you are parenting. If someone says parenting is easy, it means they are not parenting." He went on to say, "Parents who don't feel like parenting is difficult are probably the ones who end up with the most issues down the road." Okay, I guess this is a little extreme, but I bet some truth is there. It is not easy to discipline our children, but in the end, they need to be disciplined to learn right from wrong. If you feel like you are crazy, do not fear, you are probably the best kind of mom. Even when you feel you are doing everything wrong, you may be doing everything right. Disciplining makes us feel pretty crappy. I mean really, no one enjoys disciplining their children. It usually leads to them being upset or lots of tears. No one wants to see their child cry. Of course, it is going to make us feel like horrible parents, but the fact is, discipline is essential if we want to raise well-rounded, respectful children.

I will never forget the time my father-in-law told me, "It is easy to bring a baby into this world, but it takes a lot of effort to raise the child properly and effectively." This is so true. Bringing the baby into the world, literally delivering the baby, is not a walk in the park, but it is nothing in comparison to raising a child properly. Parenting isn't easy. It is very challenging. So, when you feel that challenge, don't allow yourself to believe it means you are a bad parent. It likely means you are a good parent and you are doing it right.

Again, there is no way to really measure how we are doing either. I guess we won't know for sure how we did with parenting until our children are much, much older. It is a scary thought. Still, sometimes we simply have to go with it and do what we think is best for our children, even when we don't know exactly what the best thing is. We have to try not to take things too seriously and if we make a mistake, try, try again. We need to use that mommy intuition and do what we feel works for our kids. You are the parent. You know best. Through trial and error, we've found some things that work when it comes to discipline which I will share. Try any ideas you like, but remember, you know what is best for your children.

Everyone has a day here or there when the "terrible twos" or "trying threes" have peaked. Maybe your "three-nager" has really come out. At these times, you might feel you are about to go off the deep end, or lose your mind. One such day happened for my husband and I at the post office when we were trying to obtain a passport for my one-year-old son. We arrived before they opened, thinking we would be first. Apparently other people had the same idea because about 15 others had already arrived. We waited for two hours and when they were finally ready to take our son's picture, he started crying, arching, and refusing to stay still. I am not sure why my son does this arching behavior (maybe it is from his reflux), but he arches his back so quickly he would probably fall out of our arms if we weren't used to it. We put him down for one second and he arched his back while standing, fell down, and landed on the back of his head first on the concrete floor. Of course, I was now worried that he could have major head trauma. The lady who was helping us literally shrieked at the top of her lungs when this happened.

Next, my three-year-old daughter, who had done pretty well for a three-year-old up until this point, just lost it and started trying to roll around on the dirty floor while we tried to pay. I tried to pull her up and threatened time-out, but nothing worked. I felt like every eye in there was judging me. Finally, I took the kids outside to wait for my husband. Change of scenery worked. In this moment, I felt like I couldn't take it anymore. I felt like every person in there saw it and thought I was an unfit mother.

The truth is, we all have moments like this, where we feel like we are at the end of our rope. My best advice when these moments hit is to first, realize you are not alone. I can assure you, all parents feel like this from time to time. Second, choose your battles, and third, realize that this too shall pass. Soon, the situation will end, we will all move on to a happier moment eventually, and we just need to try and keep it together in the meantime.

Preventative Measures

I will begin with preventative measures because I always feel we win when we can prevent the negative behaviors from occurring in the first place.

The Yes/No Balance

Sometimes, with three children, I feel like a broken record that says, "Stop, no, don't touch that, put that down, leave your brother/sister alone, do not hurt your brother/sister, hot, that is dangerous, you are going to hurt yourself, freeze, don't even think about it, one-two-three..." on repeat all day long. On a side note, yes, I am that mom who is yelling "one...two...three" as loudly as possible in public to get my daughter to do as she is told while praying she actually makes a change by the number three, because if she doesn't, what on earth am I going to do next? At least it works for now. I cannot even imagine the day when "one...two...three" stops working. Anyways, there are definitely going to be many, many times when you need to tell your toddler no and, no matter what "they say," I believe it is okay to do just that.

I believe it is actually good to tell your child no. It is an important word for them to learn and clearly understand. "No" can help teach our children right from wrong, which is one of the biggest jobs we have as parents. "No" also helps teach self-control and respect for authority which are of huge importance when you think of the future of our children. Someone is going to tell our children no, even if it doesn't end up being us. It may be a teacher or a boss, even a friend, or all of the above. They will need to know how to respect the no when they receive it.

I remember reading something once which talked about how we should not tell our children no. It suggested that rather than telling our kids what not to do, we should tell them what to do. It actually gave the example of, if your child is drawing on the wall, then rather than telling them no, we should tell them something like, "Draw on this paper instead." I remember thinking, *Are you kidding me?* When my daughter colored on the wall, the very first thing I said was "no" and that was not the end of it. We definitely even had a time-out afterwards, and I am sure yelling was involved.

Although I clearly do not agree with this extreme, I do agree it is helpful to find a balance between yes and no and find opportunities for saying yes when appropriate. I will give "them" that at least, because I do find the more my kids hear "no, no, no," the more they start to push back or rebel. I try to find times when rather than saying no, I can teach instead. My daughter loves to learn, so this works well for her. For example, rather than telling her no, you cannot jump on your bed, I tell her beds are made for resting and I explain what could happen if she jumps on the bed.

Offering Choices

I have found providing my kids with choices is another way to find a good yes and no balance and it also helps decrease some of the opposition. I try to let my children pick simple things, like which socks they would like to wear, or even which outfit (when I am feeling brave). Other ideas include:

Which fruit would you like with your lunch, apples or bananas?

What would you like to play with, puzzles or blocks?

What would you like to use: markers or paints?

Which plate would you like to use for dinner?

Would you like to take a bath before or after dinner?

Would you like to read one or two books before bed tonight?

Here are two outfits. You choose which one you like best.

The key is to offer options which are feasible for you. Also, it usually helps to provide only a couple of options. Otherwise, you could sit there for days waiting for them to sort through every possibility. Choices help my daughter feel empowered, which helps her be a little less oppositional later. For us, more choices equals fewer tantrums, which is always a good thing when you have a two or three-year-old.

I believe choices can help our children learn limits, if used correctly. If we allow our children to choose between two reasonable options, they can learn a bit of independence, while also learning independence is not limitless. For example, you might say, "Would you like cereal or pancakes for breakfast?" They get to choose between two reasonable options, but they do not get to ask for filet mignon with eggs. There is a big difference between "cereal or pancakes, your choice" and "choose what you would like for breakfast." These types of choices allow our children to feel they have a say, but also teach them they cannot always have whatever they want whenever it is wanted. There are limits. In the real world, you have the opportunity to make choices for yourself, however, we do have to work within the limits of the situation. We cannot simply go around doing whatever we want at all times. We have independence to do as we please, but we also must follow the laws and the rules. Hence, it is quite important for our children to learn about limits.

I love one example of choices my father-in-law shared with me. He told me when he took my husband and his sister to the grocery store when they were young children, one or both of them would always ask for something. I am pretty sure this is a common occurrence in all of our lives. When we are at the store, there is going to be something our children see and they want it. The stores do a really great job of putting these "child-friendly" items in just the right place, at just the right level where my kids will see them. Then, if you get through the entire store, you have to face the candy and toys situated just opposite the register. Whew! Sometimes, this issue leads to lots of whining, and maybe even a tantrum if they are told no.

When my husband would ask my father-in-law for something, if it was reasonable he would say yes, but he would tell him "you can only choose one thing." My husband would agree. Then, later in the store, my husband would see something else he wanted and ask for it. My father-in-law would respond with, "Remember, you can only choose one thing. You pick which item you would like to keep." My husband would choose and they would keep moving. So, on most days, his kids would end up with only one item, and they wouldn't be crying. I thought this was a pretty neat way of using choices. I thought, well, if I am willing to purchase the kids one item at the store, it might be worth a try. You could of course put limits on price, or only use this in certain stores if needed.

So, finding ways to say yes from time to time can be

advantageous. Remember, I don't think saying no is a bad thing. Most of life is about finding a good balance, so in my mind, finding a nice balance of yes and no could never be a bad thing. On the other hand, there will definitely be those days when you find yourself saying no 90 percent of the time, and this is okay too. On these days, I find myself becoming frustrated beyond belief. It helps when I remind myself there will be better days ahead and I try to keep moving forward, all the while looking for that yes/no balance.

Teaching Patience

Another preventative measure in our tool kit to increase good behavior is teaching patience. I believe more patience can lead to less negative behavior. I tried to practice patience with my children starting at a very young age. I did this by allowing them to wait for something, while slowly increasing the wait time. For example, when my children were hungry and in the high chair, I would first rush to get their food. Slowly, over time, I would increase the wait time for the food. At first, I had them wait for as little as five seconds. While they waited, I repeated something like, "Wait, food is coming," or even just, "Wait." If they waited even a few seconds, I congratulated them big time. I made a big deal by clapping or telling them how great they did. Soon, I increased the wait time to ten seconds, then 15, and so on. If we can teach our children to delay gratification a little, it can make a big difference later on when they really want something they are not going to get. I don't know for sure, but it may even help prevent some supermarket or restaurant tantrums, and that would be pretty remarkable.

How to Stop or Change a Behavior

In addition to the "no, no, no" days, there may also be days when you find yourself yelling. Earlier, I said "they say" you should never yell at your kids. Once again, I say, we can't always believe what "they say." Maybe you feel in that moment, when something horrible happens, you should yell at your child. Maybe you do yell at your child. Does this mean your child is ruined forever? I say, absolutely not. I have thought about this topic a lot. Why? Because it has brought me a lot of mom guilt. "Mom guilt," it is a very real term and we really do feel it quite often.

My child might do something I feel is unacceptable, like maybe they hit their sibling for example, or maybe they do something I feel is unsafe, like jump into the pool without swim-wings before they can actually swim. In these moments, and plenty of others, I know I am guilty of yelling at my children. I mean, really yelling. Then, I feel guilty. I will admit, it is not just yelling about the dangerous things. There are days I find myself feeling horrible about yelling at my children over something completely silly. There are times I even find myself struggling with a temper which comes out of nowhere. Who knew such little people, my children, could require so much self-control.

Later, I find myself having the repeated conversation with my husband. I will say, today this happened and I yelled, I mean, really yelled, loud. I will go on to say how horrible I feel, that I am the worst mom and that maybe I should not be yelling at our children. My husband always responds with, "Stop it, you are parenting. Sometimes, you need to yell." Bottom line is, we cannot beat ourselves up and feel guilty or question every little thing we do as parents. These questions and this guilt is only going to wear on us, and when we are worn down, I bet we will yell more and maybe even parent less in general.

One argument I have heard "them say" is if we always yell at our children, we will model this behavior and teach them it is okay to yell at people. I have also heard that yelling will squelch our children's individuality, or leadership qualities, or "spark" and that these qualities are necessary for their success in the future. On the other hand, I have heard "them say" our children actually should be exposed to yelling. One day, they are going to get "yelled at" by a teacher or a boss, and they won't be able to handle it. I have found myself wondering, *Would it really be the worst thing if a little bit of that individuality or spark they are talking about was squashed? Could there be a fine line between some of that spark and a little too much entitlement? Could that entitlement even lead to a bit of disrespect?*

One day, a friend shared a quote on social media by Peggy O'Mara: "The way we talk to our children becomes their inner voice." I am not sure if this is true or not, but it sure is an interesting quote. At first, it made the "mommy guilt" come on strong. I thought, *If I yell at my children, their inner voice may suffer.* The more I thought it over, I realized what this quote really tells us is we need to teach our children right from wrong. Their inner voice must know right from wrong, believe it, and live it. There are many ways to teach right from wrong and I believe yelling may be included in that lesson at times.

I am not saying I identify exclusively with either side here. I see where both sides are coming from and I think we can learn from each. I am not saying we should all go around screaming at our children day in and day out, but on the other hand, I don't think it is the end of the world if yelling takes place. I think it is all about a balance of discipline and love. We need to stop feeling guilty about the way we choose to parent our children and feel good that we are parenting. And, once again, I don't think it really matters what "they say." I think it is the parents who know what is best for their child.

Providing Consequences

Providing a consequence can go a very long way when you are trying to stop a behavior. It is important, however, to make sure the consequence is appropriate. As I studied in graduate school,

I learned about providing natural and logical consequences. Basically, this means the consequence should fit the crime. So, a natural consequence for not wearing a coat, for example, is your child will be cold. Next time, they may want to wear a coat so they will avoid being cold.

My daughter loves to draw and color. She uses markers almost every day. It becomes so frustrating, however, because she never puts the tops on the markers and when she is done the markers and crayons are literally everywhere. When, she refuses to clean up, I might say, "If you do not clean up your mess, I will take the markers and you will not use them at all tomorrow." This is a logical consequence; if you do not clean up the markers, I will take the markers away. Always make sure to follow through.

Time-out can be a very effective consequence for children. I find time-out can be quite beneficial when trying to stop a toddler behavior. I specifically recall the stage when my daughter learned to bite and hit. Unfortunately, she usually bit me. What worked was trying to limit my scream (seriously, it is painful), and immediately placing her into time-out. After a few times, she got the idea.

Time-out can start at a pretty young age. At about 16-months-old, my son was pulling a cord out of the wall. I said, "Stop, do you want time-out?" He stopped and walked into the other room. I went to look for him and found him on the stairs where his big sister has time-out. So, even at 16 months, he understood. Up to this point, my son had time-out in the portable crib. We always do a minute per year of age, so we put him in there for one minute. During time-out, I believe removing yourself from the room is key. What really makes this time-out—and not just sitting in the crib—is removing any interaction for the entire minute.

For my three-year-old, we do time-out on the stairs. I have seen people use an actual "time-out chair," but we chose to simply use the stairs because most places you go, you will find stairs. You can usually even find stairs outside, like the front steps for example. Consistency is key, and let's be honest, there will be a time, or many of them, when you will need to use time-out while you are not at your own home. If only they would always be perfect little angles when we leave the house; I will keep wishing.

I have talked about providing choices to prevent negative behavior. Choices can also stop a behavior. When your child is doing something you don't like, you can provide two choices, one of which would be to stop the behavior and the other choice would be a consequence. So for example, "You can either stop whining or I will put the game away. You choose." Another example would be, "You can either give the toy back to your brother, or you can go to time-out. You choose." The key here is either option works for you. If they choose to give the toy back, great, the problem is solved. If they choose to go to time-out, they will receive a consequence for their behavior.

Once they are older, you can use more advanced choices. For example, "You can either clean up your room, or you will lose TV time later. You choose." Sometimes, simply saying no can lead to tantrums and whines. I like this approach, because the toddler feels they are making the choice, but in the end either choice stops the behavior.

Tantrums and Whining

When it comes to toddlers, tantrums and whining are like breathing. It is just going to happen. I once saw an interesting quote about whining. "Fun parent drinking game: Take a shot every time your child whines. LOL, don't do this, you will die." I laughed so hard when I read this because it couldn't be more true at my house. My daughter was quite the whiner. If I gave her something, it was, "*No, I don't want that!*" If I asked her to do something, it was, "*No, I don't want to!*" I could go on and on. They wouldn't truly be toddlers without the tantrums and the whining, but there are things we can do to try to minimize it. First, accept that it is okay when your child has a tantrum or whines. You are not alone. I used to always feel embarrassed, but then I realized, it is just a part of life. I felt much better when I changed my thought process.

What ended up working really well for my daughter was reminding her to use her words. I would say matter of factly, "Liliana, I do not understand whining and crying. Use your words so I can understand." Of course, I could actually understand what she was saying, but I did not respond or acknowledge the words until she was able to calm down and use her words correctly. She caught on pretty quickly that if she wanted help with something, she would need to voice it in words rather than whine. Of course, she still whined from time to time, especially when she didn't get what she wanted, but over time, things went much more smoothly. I am not a behavioral expert by any means, but this is something which worked for us.

You can use this technique for tantrums as well by stating you do not understand screaming or crying, and asking them to please find their words. I also remind my children to "use their words" when they are fighting over something. They may be pulling an item back and forth and don't want to share. They may end up pushing or shoving one another out of the way. The first thing I remind them is to use their words. I explain they can use their words to ask for help. They can also use their words to tell each other what they need or want before pulling, pushing, or shoving.

There were a couple of stretches when my daughter's whining was out of control. It felt like most of the words which came from her mouth were whines. I was getting super tired of the behavior, so I decided to give her time-out every single time she whined. My husband and I stuck to it. I told her the plan ahead of time and each time she whined, I put her right into time-out. Each time, I reminded her to use her words. It didn't take long for her to figure out she should stop. Now, I am not saying she never uttered a whine again, but the whining decreased substantially.

When I was in graduate school for counseling education, it was impossible not to learn about the importance of empathizing. As a counselor, empathizing or reflecting is essential when working with a student. It is important for the student to feel heard. We want to use active listening (which basically means really focus on and listen to what the person is saying), and then we want to reflect back what they are saying (or empathize). Basically, you try to put into your own words what they have told you. This helps the student feel like you understand them. Out of habit, I started using this technique in my daily life when talking with family, friends, and even with my children. I found empathizing is quite effective in minimizing tantrums (and even whining too).

So, how do you do it? First, make sure you are at eye level. Then, empathize by putting into words what your child is trying to tell you. Once they calm down, you can explain your position. You can explain why they cannot do or have something and then you can even try to redirect with something else. Remember, for younger children, the fewer words you use, the better.

Reflecting back what the child is saying (or trying to say) even works with my newly one-year-old. For example, when my son is crying and I can tell he is reaching for his milk, I might say, "You want milk." Usually, once I put into words what he wants, he calms down quite a bit. In the car, when he is literally screaming, I will reflect his feelings by repeating, "You are so mad, you do not want to be in your car seat." He literally stops crying every time and looks at me as if to say, "You get it." This doesn't mean he doesn't ever start crying again, but it at least it gets him to calm down initially so I can either distract him or sing to him, or do something to help keep him calm.

This even works if my child loses it in a store. If they are screaming, I try to voice what they are screaming about. For example, "You really want the toy." I repeat it until they calm down and stop their tantrum. Then, once they are calm, I will use other techniques. Techniques can depend on age. I might try distraction, by giving them one of their own toys to play with. I might try explaining, "I know you want this toy, but we cannot buy a toy right now. When we get home we can [insert activity here, for example: play with any toy you chose, color, go outside, anything my child enjoys]." Many times tantrums occur because our children cannot communicate what they want, or when they really want us to understand how much they want something. Putting their thoughts into words makes sense. They will feel understood.

Never underestimate getting on eye level with your child. It may seem silly, but this makes a huge difference. One day my daughter was literally freaking out because she wanted different juice. I think you can imagine what a toddler freaking out looks like. I got down right at her eye level and empathized. "You want a different kind of juice." She nodded. I said, "Mommy already has this kind of juice opened. We cannot open another one until this one is finished. Once you drink all of this juice, I will let you choose the next bottle to open." Then, she hugged me really tight and said, "Okay, Mommy." Getting down to eye level makes a huge difference. I bet if I wasn't on eye level, I would not have gotten that hug, and in fact, I bet she would have kept screaming.

When it comes to tantrums, there is always the option to ignore. Sometimes, if you simply ignore the tantrum, it stops. If the child is having a tantrum in order to receive something like an object or your attention, once they find the tantrum is ineffective, it may stop. This technique can be difficult, especially if you are in the middle of a store and everyone is staring at you.

In the end, do what you feel is right. Don't be ashamed of a behavior which is completely normal. I will say it again: different techniques work at different times and for different children.

There was a period when every time I entered my daughter's room after her nap, her room was destroyed. All of her clothes were out of her drawers each day without fail. I felt like I tried everything to stop the behavior. I remember I tried sternly asking her to stop taking the clothes out of her drawers. I tried time-out while I cleaned up the mess. I tried having her help me clean it up and match every single pair of socks again, however this seemed like a game to her. It backfired because she loved it. Finally, I simply moved the plastic drawers which held the socks and other items into the closet and she lost interest. Sometimes it simply takes avoiding or changing the situation. I also learned a very important lesson here. When it comes to discipline, never forget the phrase, "If at first you don't succeed, try, try again." When a behavior is tough to change, it doesn't mean you are failing. Sometimes, it takes some time to change toddler behavior. Try not to become discouraged if you are stuck in a tough spot. Hang in there. The best part is, sometimes it is simply a stage which passes on its own.

How to Get Our Children To Do Something

So we talked about some ways to get our children to *stop* doing something. Now, how do we get them *to* do something? This can be just as challenging.

Focus on Wording

Something I have learned as a parent, probably the hard way, is to be careful not to ask a question when you need your child to do something. In other words, do not offer a choice when there is no choice in the matter. If it is bedtime, do not ask your child, "Are you ready to go to bed now?" or "After I finish this story, will you go to sleep?" I found if I ask my daughter these questions, she is likely to respond with "No." Then, you have to start the negotiations and it can become quite a battle. If you need your child to do something, I found it is best to tell them directly what they need to do.

If it is time for bed, I try to say, "Okay, it is time for bed now. Head upstairs and get your pajamas." There are still bedtime battles here and there, but I found if I say it like this, my daughter is more likely to head on upstairs.

Another example I find helpful is to steer clear of "Do you want to [insert activity here]?" So, "Do you want to brush your teeth?" or "Do you want some green beans?" The answer is going to be no more often than not, then I typically end up trying to convince her why she needs to do whatever was asked. At dinner, you might not ask, but simply put the green beans on her plate if it is part of the meal. When it is time to brush teeth, you might say, "I'll race you to the bathroom. It's time to brush your teeth." If you want your child to help you by giving their sibling a cup, you might say, "Give your brother his cup," rather than saying, "Will you give your brother his cup?" Again, the latter will likely lead to a no.

Of course, if I say, "Give your brother his cup," she still may not do it. If that is the case, I may ask again and add the word "now" to the end, or I may even utilize time-out. If I ask, "Will you give your brother his cup?" and her answer is "No," then I find myself in a long discussion about why she should do something when an adult asks and while this conversation continues, I end up giving the cup to my son myself. Without realizing it, I have reinforced the behavior. She said no and she didn't end up having to give the cup to her brother anyway. I am not saying this idea is fool-proof, but I do find statements rather than questions to be much more effective overall.

Along these same lines, I have and will continue to use the

phrase "because I said so" with my children and I try not to allow myself to feel bad about it. "They" might say that you should never use these words, because you should always provide an explanation to your child. You might hear the latter will empower children to question things and explain why they don't like something and that if we encourage this, it will lead to strong, influential minds. I believe that "because I said so" could actually be an important phrase for our children to hear. Why? Well, there are times when a child needs to do something just because the responsible adult told them to do so.

In school, children need to do things just because their teacher says so. As adults, when our boss tells us to do something, we typically do it. We typically do not ask why. Yes, I am sure there are situations when you feel the request from your boss doesn't make the most sense. Maybe there is a better option, but typically, we do not go around asking our boss, "Why should I do that?" each time we are given a directive. So, yes, I do believe the old "because I said so" phrase can be beneficial for our children. Bottom line, I believe it can help teach them respect for authority, which is what I would call vital. Again, do what you feel is right for your parenting style, use the phrase, or don't, but don't let yourself feel bad should you chose to use it.

Another challenge I think we all face as parents of toddlers is transitions, especially getting our toddler to move on when they are doing something fun. Maybe it is time for lunch, for example, but your child is swinging on their swing set; or, maybe one child is swinging on the swing set, and it is another child's turn. I have found using a timer works wonders in these situations. I will say, "Okay, we have three minutes left," and I will show my daughter I am setting the timer. You can use an egg timer, the timer on your stove, or even the timer right on your cell phone. I could always simply tell my daughter, "You have one more minute," but nothing works as well as hearing that ring when time is up.

I remember learning at one time or another that toddlers do best with short, quick sentences. The fewer words you use when speaking to a young child, the easier it is for them to understand and follow through. I find if I go on and on about something, they will always lose me. Hence, I started to try to use one word when I want my children to do something. For example, if I want them to put on their pants, I may say "pants" pretty loudly and I hold out the pants. It works much better and faster than if I say, "Okay honey, now it is time to put on your pants. Come put your pants on now. Did you hear me? Come over here and put on your pants." If you want them to put the fruit snack wrapper they just threw onto the floor into the trash can, you can simply say "trash." It sounds strange, but I found if I say the word loud and clear, it usually works pretty well.

The Importance of Modeling

We may not realize it, but modeling can be huge for getting a child to do something. When children are young, they may not say much, but then you find out little by little they know much more than we think. I remember asking both of my kids when they were very little to do something, and they surprised me by doing exactly what I asked. I had no idea that they could understand the words I was saying. At first, I remembered feeling so proud and excited and I remember thinking, *Wow, my child is so smart.* Then, as I thought about it more, I remember thinking, *Oh dear, this means they probably understand way more than I thought. Yikes, how many things have I said in front of them that I probably shouldn't have, just thinking they didn't understand it? Oops, too late now.*

We have these children who still seem like babies, but who understand what we are saying, and almost as soon as they can crawl or walk they are imitating us. My daughter used to wipe and clean all of the cabinets. My son used to pretend he was vacuuming everywhere. We see them cooking in a play kitchen. I mean, it's crazy just how much they pick up on from what we do and say.

This is where modeling comes in. Many times, we can influence our children just by what we are saying and doing, and by how we react to things. This does not mean we should never cry, yell, or show emotion. We are all human. We all experience feelings of anger, sadness, fear, and so on. Our children can learn a lot by how we deal with these feelings. Crying can teach our children that it is okay to cry, and we don't need to hold everything in. It can even teach empathy. When someone is crying, they are sad. I never bought into the idea that we shouldn't cry in front of our children. I don't make a habit of it, but I do believe crying can be a therapeutic way of handling our feelings and I don't think we need to be ashamed when it happens. If we make a mistake, or do something which later we feel we shouldn't have, we can apologize and show them how we learn a lesson and make a change for the better. I put this out there, not to make us feel like we must be perfect human beings, but just as a reminder that none of us are perfect and even in our mistakes, we can teach our children very valuable lessons.

I feel lucky to say that my children typically say please and thank you, even though I never really taught it. What I did do was model the behavior. My personal experiences have led me to believe children can understand language way before they begin to speak. Since my kids were tiny babies, I always made an effort to say please when I asked them for something. So for example, "Give Mommy the cup, please." When they gave me the cup, I would say, "Thank you." If we model something, our kids will pick up on it, both the good and bad. My children picked up on please and thank you and started using these words on their own. Of course, there were times I would remind them to say thank you, but for the most part, they got it. My son began saying thank you at age 20 months, which makes me very proud.

I am sure they have picked up on plenty of other things I would prefer they hadn't. If we accidentally say something we probably shouldn't have, we cannot allow ourselves to feel like the worst parent ever. My daughter repeated "shut up" at age three. The worst part was she told me to shut up and it came out like a teenage girl, real smart-alecky with a dramatic pause in the middle. We must have said it to the dog, or maybe she even overheard me saying it to my husband long before…yikes. I know, that sounds horrible, right? If we slip up, use it as a teachable moment, with "Don't say that word. It is a bad word." This is where we can teach them that we learn from our mistakes. We can teach them that no one is perfect. Everyone makes mistakes. What is important is that we learn from the mistakes we make and don't keep making the same ones.

Unfortunately, even if we can control ourselves, we are not the only people from whom they may hear a bad word. I am sure we have all heard teenagers cussing loudly at the next table over, but the reality is, it is important for our children to learn just because someone says a bad word or does something wrong, does not mean they should. You know the saying, "Two wrongs don't make a right." It is important for us to teach our children this concept and we can start early. It can be invaluable when they enter school and they begin to see others make mistakes and for when they are introduced to peer pressure.

I will never forget the day when I was holding my almost two-year-old son while waiting for our ice cream at the ice cream parlor. I noticed the teenage girl next to us dropped her wallet. A minute or two later, she turned to me and said, "I just said a bad word and I am so sorry." I had not even heard the word, but how big of her to recognize she said a bad word in front of my son and to apologize. I would be very proud of my son if one day he did just that, made a mistake and apologized for it, even when he wasn't required to apologize, even if it was awkward. What a great lesson in the end. Everyone makes mistakes, even moms and dads. What is important is how we handle the mistakes we make.

Encourage Good Behavior

Another way to encourage our children to do something is to catch them being good. This was a line I heard a lot in a favorite graduate school professor's parenting class. I love the line even more because it actually works. The idea behind this is to catch our children doing something good and comment on how it makes us feel. For example, one day I caught my son cleaning up his blocks. I said very enthusiastically, "Wow CJ, it makes Mommy so happy when you clean up those blocks." Not only did my son continue cleaning, but my daughter literally ran over and started helping. Soon, the room was pretty clean. I think catching my children being good makes them continue to want to do good; it encourages them. The best part is, it is pretty easy to do.

Pick Your Battles

Never forget the art of picking your battles, especially when it comes to toddlers. I recall a blazing hot day in the summer. It was probably 100 degrees outside—at least it felt that way. I ran into an old friend at the shoe store. She apologized because her young toddler was wearing no shoes, running through the store. I responded, "It's okay with me. My daughter had to wear boots today in this hot weather." Never underestimate the value of simply letting things go from time to time.

Another one of those times which comes to mind is baking Christmas cookies with a toddler. I'll tell you, it is not an easy task. I remember telling my husband, "Oh honey, this will be great. We will make Christmas cookies, start a tradition. It will be so special." I clearly glamorized this experience. Have you tried making Christmas cookies with a toddler? Those speed fingers. They grab the dough faster than the eye can even catch and it's in their mouth. I wish my children were that quick when I say, "Time to clean up." I am thinking as the dough enters their mouth, *Ahh, salmonella!*

I don't even have any ideas to help you through this one. My recommendation is simply to be ready for a bit of a rough experience and have fun. Change your thinking. I don't know about you, but my siblings and I used to always lick the batter. My mom would say, "Only a little or you could get very sick." I don't really see how eating "only a little" would prevent salmonella poisoning if it was in there. The egg is probably fully mixed in, so "eating just a little" probably wouldn't keep us healthy, maybe just a little less sick, but we were always okay. Don't expect the experience to be perfect or you will only end up frustrated and disappointed.

This piece of advice goes for crafting and activities too. Your child might make a big mess or make something less than perfect, but to them there is nothing better than a blank canvas and new art supplies they can explore and enjoy. I always recommend picking your battles. Here, they can "win." Later, when your toddler starts throwing food across the kitchen or trying to paint with their ketchup, you can "win." Finally, when all else fails, go outside and play. It is unbelievable how far getting a little extra energy out can go with a toddler.

Remember, respect and discipline don't stop in the household. I was talking with my father-in-law about education and parenting one day and he said parents aren't the only people who raise our children. He said it is probably more like 40 percent parents (family), 40 percent teachers, and 20 percent friends. I thought this was such an interesting notion.

We take care of our children and teach them from home, but once they enter grade school, maybe even preschool, they are likely spending the majority of their time with teachers and peers. So, yes, teachers and peers can have a huge impact on our children. It is so important we teach our children to respect adults and teachers from a young age. It is never too early to start to teach our children the importance of listening to their teachers, even in nursery school. If we don't teach our children respect for their teachers, we may have a scenario more like 40 percent parents, ten percent teachers, and 50 percent peers. Let's face it, this could be bad news, depending on who the friends are. Peer pressure is real. It is important for us as parents to realize teachers are not just teaching academics. They are a big part of shaping our kids into who they are not only academically, but also emotionally and morally.

Teaching our children respect doesn't just start in school. It starts with teaching them how to respect us as parents and subsequently, all adults. Thus, we cannot underestimate the importance of discipline.

Let's say you are disciplining your child, maybe you even try all of these things—we still cannot expect our children to be perfect little angels. Sometimes, I feel what "they say" can impact the way we view our own child's behavior. It is really easy to see what "they" are saying on social media. We see so many perfect posts of all the sweet and perfect things toddlers are doing, and I believe it can make us question the behavior of our own children, even if the behavior is developmentally normal. Let's face it, they are two, three, or four-year-old toddlers. Expecting them to be perfect is simply irrational. It will only end with us parents questioning ourselves. It makes us question whether it is something we did or didn't do. We put so much pressure on ourselves...and for what? So we can raise the perfect children? It just isn't going to happen. No one is perfect. Everyone makes mistakes. Our children will make mistakes. Mistakes are a part of life and it is okay. So what do we do? We just keep loving them and do our best to guide and discipline them. We help them learn and grow from the inevitable mistakes they (and we) make along the way.

TODDLER TIPS

Toddlers can make life very challenging at times, but there are so many great things to love. I love the little dimples my three-year-old still has on her hands. I love the comments which come out of her mouth—sometimes so sweet, or sometimes just plain hilarious. Where do they get this stuff? My daughter was singing to her brother one day while I changed his diaper. She sang the line, "Boys are so sweet" over and over again. I thought, *Girl, I pray you will always believe that throughout your entire life.* Oh, the innocence. I love how their legs start to grow long, but they are still squishy and they may even still have knee rolls. I love how good it still feels when they wrap those sweet arms around your neck tight. I love how toddlers do crazy things, like run around and bite bubbles instead of catch them, or howl like a wolf when they wake up from their nap. I even love the little tiny fingerprints I find everywhere—on the windows, the drawers, or the doors just high enough where they can reach. I think those fingerprints are the true sign of a happy home. I love how they are so accepting of differences and how they love so easily. There is just so much to love.

On the other hand, my toddler throws full, blown out tantrums over butter. "I want a bite of butter." "Spray the butter in my mouth." "I can't see the butter." What's astonishing is the amount of times I have needed to explain that butter is, in fact, there. "Of course you can't see the butter, because butter melts." What can I say? She is truly my daughter. Or there was the tantrum because there is no such thing as a purple M&M. I mean, how dare you, M&M company, not make purple M&Ms? Let's also not forget a toddler's passion for dressing himself/herself. It typically includes wearing the same tutu, super hero, or princess outfit every single day. It is to the point where I dread the day I need to throw the particular outfit in the wash because it will be a rough day for me. "They say" a difficult or spirited child can one day become a strong leader. There are days—like when I have given her the wrong fork, the wrong spoon, or when she absolutely must have three things on the plate instead of two—when I wonder, *Can this behavior really make them a strong leader or does it just make Mommy weak?* Who knows, but I will hope for the best.

I found myself texting my husband one day, "What are we going to do with our daughter? She is so darn stubborn and she makes me want to throw things." This was when we were in the throes of the trying threes when she wouldn't eat and she wouldn't drink. She was getting ulcers in her mouth likely from too much "red juice," but red juice was all she would drink. When we stopped giving her the "red juice" she stopped using the bathroom. Even getting her to pee was a fight. I felt like I wanted to throw in the towel. As parents, no matter how much we want to, we have to hold on to the towel tightly. Toddlers need us. They need us to guide them and teach them right from wrong, even if it almost kills us in the process. So, hang in there, moms and dads. This too shall pass. Push through the bad and try not to miss all those great moments as these days will be gone before we know it.

Managing Medications

During the toddler stage a lot of things make life difficult, so I found some things which made my life easier. Life with a toddler is so frenzied that I found myself easily forgetting things, even important things like required medications. There was a time I was managing eight different medicines between two kids all at the same time, which can be enough to drive a person insane. Between my son's reflux, vitamins, and regular illnesses, medication could really add up, and things were unintentionally skipped.

Labeling my children's medications worked like a charm. I started writing the correct dosages directly on the medicine bottles with a permanent marker. I even wrote the correct use for the medication. Believe me, the prescriptions and creams will add up and you don't want to mix up the medications and cause a problem. This trick can also help if you have a babysitter or if you need to go out of town. All of the medications can be clearly labeled in case they are needed. You can be sure the babysitter will use them correctly.

It is definitely not outside of the realm of possibility to give the wrong medication by accident. There was one interesting night when we learned it is okay to put eye drops in the ear, but putting ear drops in the eye is dangerous. Luckily we made the first mistake, rather than the latter. My son had just gotten tubes and we had a bottle of ear drops we needed to use each day. I asked my husband to please go grab the ear drops for me as I held my sleepy son on the couch. He brought me the bottle and I put them right in without thinking, as if I was on autopilot. Autopilot happens a lot around here when the exhaustion hits after a long day. After I put the first drop in, I looked at the bottle and yelled out, "These are not the ear drops! These are eye drops." My husband and I both freaked out, and the next thing I knew, my husband is literally trying to suck the eye drops out of my son's ear with his mouth. Yes, it is hard to admit, but this is a true story. Now, this is the definition of unconditional love.

I called the ENT emergency line and told them what happened. They said "What? You tried to suck the drops out of his ear?"

"Well, yes," I said.

"Okay...well, it is fine. It is completely safe for eye drops to go in the ear. It is not, however, safe for ear drops to go in the eyes."

The next day, I took my son into the doctor's office just to make sure he was okay. I know, I may be a bit crazy. The doctor said the same thing, that everything looked good. She suggested I label the bottles with "eyes only" and "ears only." I did this immediately. This is always a good plan if you find yourself with both eye drops and ear drops in your home, and more likely than not, you will.

Another helpful idea is to put a chart on your child's medications which are given daily. I cannot tell you the number of times I couldn't remember whether or not I gave the medication to my child. The days start to blur together and I remember giving it, but I cannot remember to save my life if it was that day or the day before. Now, I use a permanent marker and draw a little chart on the side of the medicine bottle itself. For a ten-day antibiotic, I put M, Tu, W, Th, F, Sa, Su (for example) in one column and leave the other column blank. I leave the permanent marker right there next to the bottle, so I can simply check it off after I give it. This also tells you when to throw out the remainder. Usually, you don't use those toddler medications until they are completely gone. Who knew how frustrating "discard the remainder" could be to a parent who can't keep their days straight. You can use this for longer term medications as well (like a vitamin).

Toddlers and Tiny Objects

Another important tip we all learn pretty quickly is to keep your eye on your toddler if they are around tiny objects. Once something gets past that seal of a young toddler's mouth, it is not an easy task to remove it. I mean, it is almost impossible to get your finger in there. I wish they had sippy cups with a seal so strong. Maybe they actually wouldn't spill as promised. Once you squeeze your fingers in there to retrieve the item, it is very likely you will be bit...hard. Their teeth must be sharper than a shark's, I swear. Toddlers may also try to put things up their nose or even succeed at swallowing things which can be very dangerous. Usually, children who do this are repeat offenders. I learned this the hard way. You know the story when my daughter put a seed up her nose around 18 months old. Well, when she was about to turn three, she swallowed her earring.

After I went to retrieve my daughter from her nap upstairs, she said, "Mommy, my earring is gone."

"Where is your earring?" I replied.

"It's in my tummy. I swallowed it."

I actually let out a quick laugh. "You are joking right?"

"Yes."

"Okay, so where is your earring?"

"It's in my tummy."

"Lili, did you really eat your earring? Why did you do that?"

"Because it tasted good."

I would have liked to laugh in this moment, but realizing the earring was almost certainly in her stomach at this point, I rushed upstairs with her to search her bed and room as best as I could. I could not find the earring anywhere, so I assumed she was telling the truth. Not only was this an earring, which probably wasn't a great thing to eat, but it was a piercing earring which had an extremely sharp back which hurt my finger just touching it with slight pressure. Freaking out, I immediately called the pediatrician. She told me in most cases, earrings pass through the intestinal tract fine, but it was best to take my daughter over to a medical office with the ability to X-ray to ensure the earring wasn't trapped in her esophagus.

We headed over to our neighborhood urgent care center for children. Of course, my daughter got to put on a really cute gown covered with clowns while she had a picture taken of her tummy. Afterwards, she could pick any sticker she wanted and could look at the picture of her tummy on the inside. Apparently X-rays encourage children to swallow small things because they are so much fun.

Thankfully, it turned out the earring had already passed into the intestinal tract which meant she was likely in the clear, however...the doctor said, "You will need to search through her poop until it comes out, but that shouldn't be too bad since she is just recently out of diapers, right?" I was thinking, *Umm, I am not sure if I would choose the words "not so bad."* Then, the nurse brought me quite a few pairs of gloves and some potty inserts and she was my new best friend! I'll tell you what, those gloves were the best gift I had ever received. She told me if I did not see the earring come out within ten days, I should bring my daughter back for another X-ray. I thought, *Oh no, does this mean I could be searching through poop for ten days?* She instructed me to watch for any warning signs, like bloody stool, increased stomach pain, vomiting, and so on.

I spent the next few days searching through my daughter's poop. Of course, she found this so entertaining to watch. "Mommy," she would tell me, "you have to search through my poop now."

"Thank you for the reminder, sweetie, but how could I forget?"

While we waited, I tried not to take my daughter out, unless it was a very short trip, because the only bathroom option would be to rush back to the little potty in case she pooped. I definitely didn't want to miss the earring and be searching poop for ten days. Finally, on day three, I found the earring. It was a low of all lows sorting through poop. However, others found it quite entertaining when my daughter literally told everyone she swallowed her earring, but they should not worry because she would poop it out. My daughter really owes me one day for this one!

I mean, don't most of the toys out there say, "For ages 3+, small parts included?" Doesn't that mean a three-year-old should know better than to eat their own earring, or to eat anything small and inedible for that matter? Well, apparently not. I learned those words do not apply to my child and that I should always keep an eye on her when she is playing with small things. I also learned not to leave piercing earrings in your child's ear any longer than necessary. I recommend a twist back which you check every couple of days to ensure they are still tight.

This was a really tough day, but the day became even better when somehow a diaper made its way into the washing machine, which was a nightmare indeed. Luckily, the day came to a close with me watching my little girl talking to my little boy and he was just laughing and laughing. A baby's laugh is, hands down, the best sound ever. All the negatives and frustrations of the day were forgotten.

Baby-proofing/ Toddler-proofing

Speaking of toddlers being sneaky, one of my son's favorite things to do was run into the bathroom and stick his hands in the toilet (luckily this has since lost its appeal). He also loves trying to climb into the bathtub to turn on the water. One time, within the matter of a few seconds as I washed my hands, my son managed to fall headfirst into our bathtub trying to get in there to turn on the water. It was impossible for me to get him in time once I saw him start to teeter over. It was pretty scary as he landed on his neck, but he was fine. Of course, there are the dangers of them falling, but we also have the added danger of them turning on the water. If you can put something on your bathroom doorknobs to keep them from getting in, I would say do it.

This leads me to toddler-proofing. What is the deal with electrical cords? What is the appeal? Do all boys throw everything in the toilet and stick their hands in there? My daughter was never into the cabinets, toilets, or cords, but these are all my young son wanted to play with. Maybe it's a boy thing; maybe it's a personality thing. I am not sure. What I do know is toddlers are drawn to things they are not supposed to play with. This makes toddler-proofing quite important.

Most of the tables in our home are square. With toddler wobbles and climbing, it is very easy for them to bump or fall into the sharp corners. We used pipe insulation on the sides of our fireplace hearth and around our rectangular coffee table. Pipe insulation is usually grey and can be found at your local hardware store. Basically, it looks like a pool noodle, but it has a cut on one side where you can slip it around a pipe. Instead, we slipped it onto our fireplace edge. We used a size similar to a regular pool noodle on our fire place and simply cut the ends at an angle so you could meet two pieces together and make it square. For our coffee table, we used a smaller diameter which also had sticky parts along the edge. This worked great because at the opening, the sticky part adhered nicely to our table. You can find plenty of items out there for covering corners, but this worked really well and was not very expensive.

A big baby-proofing item is the cabinet lock. As we just built a brand new house, we didn't want the ones we had to screw into our new cabinets. Of course, I would use them if necessary to protect my children, but we tried other options first. I am glad we did, because I found a great product. We tried the drawstring type of cabinet closures and they worked wonders. Even my child who wants to get into everything wasn't very interested in breaking into the cabinets with those on them. He doesn't even mess with them. They are so quick and easy to open and close. You basically slide the drawstring closure down when you open the cabinet, and then slide it right back up tight around the knobs to close.

Before, when I had the plastic locks, I dreaded going in there to get the cleaner out so much that I wouldn't even use it. It took that long and it was frustrating because I didn't have time to open and close those locks every time we had a spill, which is pretty much all the time with toddlers. Then, there are the doors. It was a bad day for me when my son learned how to open a doorknob. Luckily, there are plenty of products out there to add to door knobs to help keep them closed if needed.

I believe there is a downfall of baby gates—well maybe I am actually the one with the downfall, but I will blame it on the gates for now. Baby gates are a must to keep children safe. Toddlers can be out of your sight in a second, and they are exceptionally fast. It only takes a few seconds for them to walk out of a room and make it to the stairs. We try to have a gate at both the top and bottom of the stairs because they can fall down from the top, but they can also start climbing up the stairs pretty quickly, only to fall back down.

The downfall with gates for me, however, is when you think they are closed. There are times when we parents may accidentally forget to close them. If we assume or expect our baby gates are closed and we let our young ones explore, it is kind of like a false sense of security. We think they are closed, so we let our kids go a little further into the hall then we normally do, and they fall. I will admit this happened to us.

We were moving some decorations back upstairs after Christmas. I brought the kids upstairs and locked the gate. My husband brought something up and went to make another trip. I was in the playroom with my daughter. Our attic pulls down into the room and I didn't want her trying to climb those stairs. My one-year-old son snuck out of the playroom and all my husband and I heard was *boom, boom, boom*, and then my son was wailing. I think my heart stopped. We both ran, me from upstairs and my husband from downstairs, and my husband just saw him roll down the last two steps and hit the side of his face on the hardwood floor at the bottom.

Parents of the year, right? We felt horrible. Our child actually fell down the stairs. I couldn't even stop crying because I thought I was the worst mother in the world. I had assumed the gate was closed and should have had a closer eye on my son. My husband went to get one more thing and assumed I would be watching the kids; hence, the "downfall" of gates.

To make matters worse, even when our baby gate was secure, my son figured out how to slide right under. One day, I looked over at the stairs. The baby gate was closed and my son was on the other side heading down the stairs alone. Then, let us not forget the issue of the gate actually falling down. After my son fell down the stairs, I called my mom because I felt like such a failure. She helped me feel a little better by telling me the story about how my sister pushed the gate over and fell down the stairs with it when she was little. Things like this happen to all of us and when these things happen, we cannot feel bad about them. It doesn't make us bad parents. It makes us human. In fact, my three-year-old daughter fell down the stairs the very next week. She had been walking down the stairs by herself for a while and did a great job, and I was quite confident she could do it…that is until she took a horrible tumble as well.

Remember, baby-proofing can help avoid disasters, but as you can see by the many little disasters we experience as parents, it cannot possibly protect our toddlers from everything. Things are going to happen; I promise you. It cannot be prevented. So, we cannot beat ourselves up over it when they do. We need to remember to cut ourselves some slack. We learn a lot when accidents happen, as do our children. Believe it or not, this is part of what shapes them into the adults they will one day become.

Removing the Pacifier

I have been told removing the pacifier can be another anxiety-inducing task for parents. Sometimes, the transition away from the pacifier can be pretty seamless, but I bet more often than not, it is a pretty challenging task. For some reason, my first two children never liked a pacifier. Some would say I am lucky, but my mom would always say things would be easier if they took a pacifier. She would tell me pacifiers helped calm all of her children especially when they were teething. I guess as with most things, whichever side you are on has its own set of positives and negatives.

I would say as with any major change, I would make sure to try this transition at a time when no other major changes are taking place. It may not be the best plan to try to take the pacifier away as soon as a new baby comes home or when you have just moved into a new house, for example. When you feel you and your child are ready, there are some great ideas I have heard about which may be helpful for you.

One idea is to let your toddler "sell" you their pacifiers; then, they can use their "earnings" to buy a new toy at the store. You could even make a little coupon to give them when they sell you their pacifiers, which allows them to purchase a new toy of their choosing. A similar idea is using the "pacifier fairy." They could leave their pacifiers in a special place for the fairy to come pick up in the night. In the morning, the pacifiers will be gone and the fairy will have left a gift (or maybe even a gift for each pacifier if you wanted) in their place.

As we know, pacifiers can be lost or torn. Once you and your toddler are ready, you could explain you will not be able to buy them any more pacifiers. When the ones he/she has go missing or break, there will be no more pacifiers. You may need to help a couple of them go missing, but sometimes—by the time you get down to the last one and it is gone—the toddler understands. This may or may not be your child. All these ideas depend on the child. If your child is struggling with letting go of the last one, I have heard people send the last pacifier up into the air on a balloon. You could tell them you are sending it to the pacifier fairy if you wanted. Maybe they could find a toy just for them the next day from the fairy. You could even say you are sending the last one away to a new baby or a little boy or girl who really needs a pacifier. The balloon will take it to the right place.

I have even seen a five-step system out there to help eliminate the pacifier. It looks pretty strange, but seems promising. There are five pacifiers in the set. The first pacifier looks pretty normal. The second has only the tip missing. The third has a little more missing off of the top. The fourth is about half gone and the last one is just a little area sticking up from the holder. Basically, you move from pacifier to pacifier every few days until there is practically no pacifier there. I bet this one depends on the age you are trying it as well. An older child may not even go for the first one with the missing top. It all depends on the child, but maybe one of these ideas will help make the pacifier wean a little less stressful.

Toddler Attire

Another helpful hint when it comes to toddlers: purchase some inexpensive "play clothes" to use for home and school which you don't mind getting dirty. You may even be able to find some inexpensive ones for resale. I cannot tell you the amount of time I spend using spot cleaner and soaking clothes trying to remove stains. This is a daily occurrence. I have found some pretty good stain fighters out there, but it is nice to have a set of outfits which you can just put in the wash without scrubbing every single stain first. It is a nice time saver.

Diaper changes aren't easy, especially when it comes to toddlers. You would think they would let you change their diaper which probably feels yucky on them, but that definitely doesn't seem to be the case. My children may or may not let me get the diaper off first, but then without a doubt, the second I undo those diaper tabs, they are on the move. I mean, there are kicks and twists and rolls. Some crazy acrobatics go on during diaper changes in our house.

As if wiggling toddlers weren't hard enough, sometimes toddlers don't want to keep their diaper on at all. They are pretty smart; they can figure out how to take that diaper off. My pediatrician shared a helpful hint for this one. Put the diaper on backwards so the tabs are in the back. This way, it is harder for them to find the tabs to pull off the diaper. You may not need to do this forever, but maybe just until your toddler gives up and stops trying to pull off the diaper. Perhaps this tip will come in handy for you one day, although, I hope you don't need it.

Bumps and Bruises

If there are toddlers, there will be many bumps and bruises. This goes for them, and for you, as a mom, as well. Is it just me, or does being a mom make us more of a klutz? One day, I actually went to the doctor because I had so many bruises on me I thought I had a health issue. My doctor ran blood work and everything was normal. Well, maybe that's just me, but it proves days with a toddler can seem like a war zone.

On one hand, I feel like I am a complete klutz, but on the other, I think motherhood has given me Spiderman-like reflexes. I could be having an in-depth conversation with a friend, and my child will drop the sippy cup. I can reach over, catch the cup before it hits the ground, and set it on the table without hardly breaking eye contact. It is not just sippy cups I can grab. I found I can reflexively grab a toddler just before they smack their head on the ground or just before they fall off a chair. I have seen people out there who are following toddlers around with both arms outstretched just waiting for them to take a spill. They likely will take a spill, so this is not a bad thing, but for me, I have gotten so used to it that when my toddler starts to wobble, I reflexively reach my hand out and catch them, no outstretched arms needed. Being a parent can do some strange things to us. If it gives us super powers, I'll take it. I need all the powers I can get for this job.

If your toddlers are like mine, they will always want a bandage or an ice pack. Sometimes, offering a wet cloth instead will do the trick if you want to save some bandages. Speaking of ice packs, it is always good to have some ready in the freezer because you never know when you will need one. Things certainly happen in an instant with toddlers. I tried putting ice in a bag and it always moved around and my kids had a hard time holding it. They always complained it was too cold, even with a napkin around it. The gel ice packs with fun designs usually work nice, but that requires going out and buying them. This sounds strange, but what always works for us is putting some ice in a children's sock (I put it in a plastic bag before putting it into the sock if I was worried about it melting everywhere), and then simply tie a knot in the sock. I would wet the sock a little so it was cold enough to work. My daughter thought it was cool and it fit into her hand nicely to hold herself. Let's face it, toddlers are quite independent. I know mine wouldn't let me sit there and hold it—it had to be her.

If you don't have an ice pack, do not fear. Put some bread and butter on it. Did you go back and reread that statement wondering if you read it correctly the first time? One day when we were in Europe visiting family, my son fell and hit his head on the concrete sidewalk. I grabbed him and everyone came running toward us wondering if he was okay. Before I could even speak, one of the grandmothers came running out with bread and butter in her hand. In a very concerned voice, she told me to put it on his head right away and squished it all up. I mean, he hit his head, so I was thinking someone would offer me ice. They were thinking bread and butter. Well, no ice came, only the bread and butter, so I went with it. Sure enough, he never got a single bump or bruise on his forehead. "They say" the bread and butter keeps the swelling down. I guess they were right.

Here is another interesting remedy. My husband fell off his bike as a child and bruised his knee pretty badly. It was very swollen. His grandmother put some raw onion on his knee and wrapped it up in a bandage. She said the onion would heal it, and my husband said when she took it off just hours later, it was almost completely healed. I find this interesting because "they say" an onion can cure you if you are ill. Have you heard people talking about how if you cut a raw onion in two and put it in the room with a person who is sick, it will soak up the illness, turn black, and the person will feel better? Well, if this is true, maybe the onion on the scrape actually works too?

There are plenty of ways to deal with the bumps and bruises, but most importantly, don't let them get to you. I cannot tell you the amount of times I felt like the worst mom ever because I looked away for a second and my child fell or even when they tripped and I told myself, "If only I was holding their hand, it would have been avoided." This is life. Kids play. Kids run. Kids fall. They get bumps and bruises. It would be nice to keep them in a safe, protective bubble, but we just can't. Remember, they learn and grow from these "ouchy" experiences as well.

Brushing and Flossing

Another toughie when it comes to toddlers is caring for their teeth. Brushing and flossing can be difficult. I find it hard to get the toothbrush in there and reach all of their teeth. I learned you can hold your toddler's head in your lap while they look at the ceiling to brush their teeth. It is easier to get to all the teeth this way and you can even hold their arms by their sides with one of your arms in this position if needed.

I always wondered if I should floss my toddler's teeth. We decided to give it a try. We used the little individual children's flossers. They can be found at many convenience stores and they worked nicely. I think the flossing even helped prepare my daughter for the dentist. We started flossing a little before my daughter's first dentist visit at age three.

Toddler Feeding Troubles

Unfortunately, toddlers can take the term "picky eater" to the extreme. Feeding a toddler can be challenging to say the least. If you want your toddler to eat, you may or may not want to roll up their mashed potatoes into little balls. My husband decided this was a great idea when my son wouldn't eat his mashed potatoes. Guess what? It worked. My son ate every single mashed potato ball he rolled. You know what else worked? My older daughter started rolling her mashed potatoes into balls too. She ate them all, which at the time was unusual during her picky eating phase, but she also continued to try rolling her food into balls for quite some time.

You never know what will work for your child. Some people might look at this as a win because both of my children ate that night. Some may look at it as a loss as my husband ended up encouraging my daughter to play with her food. In the end, however, who cares what "they say?" What matters is what you say. Don't be surprised if as a parent you find yourself doing all sorts of crazy things in order to get your children to do something. In the end, a little rolled up food never hurt anyone, so do what works for you.

My daughter went through stages where she hardly ate anything. She went through stages where she hardly ate any vegetables or fruits. She still hates chicken and beef, and won't eat much meat in general, unless it is sliced thin. I have talked to many parents whose toddlers are literally surviving on chips, chicken nuggets, yogurt, and macaroni and cheese and they still seem to be happy, healthy toddlers. As a mom, I found myself literally freaking out during these stages wondering if my children were getting all of the vitamins and nutrients their bodies needed. It started with worrying that my newborns weren't getting enough milk and I still worry today about their eating habits. I am no dietician, but there are recommendations for how many servings of each food group we all need per day. I will tell you, however, getting a toddler to eat the appropriate number of servings of fruits and vegetables a day can be a pretty impossible undertaking. When my toddlers were not getting those fruits and vegetables we are told they need, it was hard not to worry. It was hard to simply sit back and let it go, but strangely enough, this seemed to work.

The more I fussed over my daughter's eating, the worse it became. From all the worries, I got to the point where I was begging my child to eat. I might say, "Three more bites and then you can get down." Sometimes this worked, and I still do use it from time to time. It got to the point however, this was said at each meal by someone, in addition to "Yum, it is so good," and "Look at Mommy eating this. She loves it," and so on. When we had larger family dinners, it was coming from everyone at the table. Eating started to become a battle, so I decided to sit back a bit. I put the food on her plate and let her go. I stopped telling her she had to eat all of her vegetables, or meat, or how many more bites she had to take, and I just let her eat.

I found that teaching my children healthy eating habits worked much better than pressuring them to eat. I taught my daughter why it was important to eat a variety of foods. I told her about the nutrients we get from fruits and vegetables and how they help us grow. I continued to put all of the healthy foods on the plate, whether it was eaten or not, but rather than tell her to eat another bite of her broccoli, I would remind her of our conversations about the importance of eating a variety of foods. It was working. Somehow, she started loving broccoli again and she started eating her fruits and vegetables at most meals. Surprisingly, with less pressure, things improved. Now, she won't always clean her plate, but she does a great job eating at least for most meals. My son, on the other hand, cleans his plate each time. I think he might eat all day and night if I let him.

I will never forget a story my father-in-law shared with me. He remembers a night when my husband as a child refused to eat the dinner which was prepared for him. He said he wanted pizza and he wasn't going to eat anything else but that. My father-in-law told him, "No, we are not having pizza tonight, your mother made dinner for us." When my husband kept pushing for pizza and refused to eat, my father-in-law stood firm and said, "We are not having pizza for dinner. You can either eat what your mother has made, or eat nothing at all." A little while later, he said my husband became hungry and went ahead and ate the regular dinner. Once my husband finished his dinner, my father-in-law handed him $10. He said, "Thank you for eating the dinner which was prepared for you tonight. Now, with this $10, you can order pizza for dinner tomorrow night." I loved this story. My father-in-law never forced him to eat, and my husband received a great, logical reward after he chose to eat on his own. I've found that no force, but some positive reinforcement, can go a long way with young children.

People, even my own family members, believe a child should clean their plate each time. I will say it again: people will always have advice for you, but don't always go with what "they say." Choose the strategies which work for you and your family. Personally, I choose not to ask my children to clean their entire plate. If wasting is a concern for you, one idea to avoid that is to offer smaller portions so that it is easier for the child to finish and ask for more.

Giving small portions has not only made us less wasteful, but it has been quite instrumental in getting my toddlers to eat. I offer my daughter very small portions to start. I find if I load up her plate, it almost seems overwhelming to her and she won't eat much. If I give her smaller portions, she seems to ask for more. This also allows me from time to time to say, "No problem honey, I will give you more, but eat a little bit of the other things on your plate first," if needed. Also, while she is waiting for the next helping, she is more likely to eat some of the other food on her plate which may not be her first choice.

I have also heard the idea of putting all the options on the table and allowing toddlers to serve themselves, family-style. This could become messy, but giving your toddlers the opportunity to choose how much they eat of each item could prove helpful. You might be thinking, *My child would end up with a big plate full of only macaroni and cheese.* If this is the case, you could always introduce the rule where the child can choose how much of each food they want on their plate, but they must take at least some of each item on the table.

A fun food appearance is another idea we have tried. Arranging food in fun shapes (making sandwiches into butterflies), or fun plates and utensils can go a long way. I have even seen a plate with a bulldozer on it and you can scoop the food items around and then eat them.

I find it helpful to vary the foods I offer. I am not above using canned fruits and vegetables if needed to ensure my kids are getting their fruits and veggies. I will heat up a can of whole potatoes in the microwave and then cut them into strips so they look like French fries. My kids will dip them in ketchup even without any additional salt; sounds like a win to me.

I talk a lot about snacks in this book, because they have really helped me through tough situations such as waiting at a doctor's office or grocery shopping. I will say though, for the most part I limit snack foods for my children. My pediatrician once suggested this to me, and I went with it. It turned out the more snacks I offered, the less hungry my children would be at breakfast, lunch, or dinner, and therefore, the less likely they were to eat the healthy foods I provided them at these times. The more I gave them yummy snacks, the more they craved them and refused healthier options. If this doesn't work for you, an alternative to consider may be offering only healthy foods as snacks.

One more factor to consider is timing. My pediatrician has told me ever since my children were very small that young children do best on the 8:00, 12:00, 4:00 schedule. Have you ever noticed your toddler wakes up from their nap "starving" and they must have a snack? I definitely have. The idea from my pediatrician is to feed them breakfast at 8:00, lunch at 12:00, and dinner at 4:00. You can give them a dinner at 4:00 before they have had a chance to snack and then offer a snack at 6:00 or while you eat dinner. Maybe it's worth a try.

All in all, less pressure, small portions, and varied food options and appearance are all things to consider with a young eater. The only other thing I can leave you with is an "I feel your pain," and a big good luck.

Head-Banging

Then, if our toddlers didn't already give us enough to stress over, there is head banging (and just to be clear, I don't mean us as parents doing it, I mean them). Is it a boy thing? My daughter didn't do it, but there was a period of time when my son did. He would hit his head against things—the floor, the crib, the wall. He would even hit himself with his own toys. He would literally throw a fit when he wanted something and crumble down and start banging his head on the floor over and over.

I remember going to the internet for this one. "They say" it can be a sign of intelligence. I will choose to believe that piece of "they say" knowledge. Some of what "they say" will scare us, but I remember reading things which told me head banging was typically normal at his age. I remember my pediatrician didn't think twice about it and told me it was just fine and not to worry. Of course, I still worried about it, but it did not last long. My son outgrew it. So, we are living proof that sometimes things just need to run their course.

There were a few different strategies I tried to stop the head banging. I tried yelling no or stop pretty loudly so that he understood it was not okay. This made him laugh more than anything and kind of encouraged the behavior. I also tried ignoring the behavior at times. This was really difficult, because it is hard to ignore your baby when they keep hitting their head on the ground. My pediatrician actually suggested this. He said they would not allow themselves to hit their head enough to cause any damage, but if they hit it pretty hard just once, they may learn not to do it again.

There was one issue with the ignoring thing for me, which was when he tried to do it outside on the pavement. Sometimes, he would start having a fit and I would have to grab him quickly because he would throw himself backwards, head to the ground first. When he started doing this, I couldn't just ignore it, because I was scared he would get hurt. So, I simply grabbed him gently enough to keep his head from hitting, sat him back up without saying anything, and tried to move on to another activity. I felt this was kind of ignoring it, but also making sure he was safe. Sure enough, he stopped the behavior eventually and never banged his head on purpose since. Maybe it was a compilation of all of the strategies, so if you are having this issue, one or more of these ideas may help.

Our children are definitely going to go through different stages. Some of these stages can be quite difficult, like this one was for me. The truth is, they are usually just stages and they will grow out of them as quickly as they come. We will face plenty of stages and challenges as parents of toddlers. We just have to do our best in the mean-time to get through it and to keep moving forward.

Expect the Mess

Speaking of challenges, I can almost promise you there will come a day when your child poops in the bathtub. It is never pretty. I actually thought we had almost made it through without my son doing it, until it happened and I can see why someone didn't want to put me through it before that point.

After a tiring day of gymnastics class with both of my children, I was exhausted, probably more so than them. I put my son into the bathtub first and was about to get my daughter undressed when I saw it, right there in the bathtub...poop. It was just a little bit, so I thought, *I can handle this.* Imagining myself as super mom, I grabbed my non-potty-trained son quickly to put him on the toilet. I was so proud until he started screaming and I realized somehow on the way to the potty, more ended up all over his leg. When I put him down, it squished into the potty seat and all over the potty itself. He started to scream. I guess he didn't want to be dirty. Then, my daughter started to scream. I guess she didn't like the sight of poop. He was squirming and trying to jump off of the toilet, but by this time it had spread. It was everywhere. It was up both of his legs now, top to bottom. He tried to jump off and I grabbed him, getting poo all over my hands and even on my wedding and engagement rings. Yuck. He kept squirming, but I didn't know how to get him down because everything—including my hands—was covered. I touched the toilet paper to try to wipe it off my hands and then there was poo on the toilet paper roll. I just paused and thought, *I need to give up now because I have no idea how to clean up this mess.* By this point, I wanted to scream too.

As my son was trying to get off the toilet, he started to fall; his head was heading toward the bathtub. I grabbed him just in time. Whew, but now he had poop all under his arms. I put him down on the bathmat and, somehow, now there was poop on his feet, and therefore on the bathmat too. I noticed there was now poop on my sleeve. I grabbed the wipe container and got poo on those too. I started wiping poop left and right and finally cleaned it all up. What a disaster. I hope this was just the grand finale with no more tub poops to come. Unfortunately, I have learned as a mom, we can dare to dream, but be sure to prepare for the worst. Sure enough, that very night, my daughter threw up all over the kitchen. It was my second huge mess of the day and this one included the hardwood floor, counter, and cabinets. Thank goodness I bought that new container of disinfectant wipes. There is my next suggestion: when you have a toddler, always have disinfectant wipes on hand.

My last tip is to anticipate that when you have a toddler in the house, things are going to get ruined. We have learned the hard way that a baby becoming a toddler can be exciting and fun, but it is definitely not the time to purchase anything nice for your home. My husband and I were talking one day about changes we wanted to make in our house and furnishings we wanted to purchase. The kids were running around and playing as we talked. My husband brought me into the living room and told me we should keep this one chair because he thought it was so nice. I agreed we would absolutely need to find a spot for it. We walked back into the kitchen.

The next thing we knew, my daughter was yelling, "Mommy, Daddy, CJ is spilling his milk." We looked over and he had dumped almost his entire cup of milk across his lap. As we ran in, we noticed there was a milk trail across the entire floor, a huge puddle on the floor under him, his clothes were soaked and so was the chair we were just talking about. My husband ran over and started spraying the chair with cloth cleaner. Then I heard him yelling. Turns out, as he sprayed the cleaner on the chair it splashed up all over the wall. That was his favorite paint color and he couldn't even remember the color to fix it. Well, so much for the nice chair and the paint on the wall.

It is so easy to get wrapped up in moments like these and feel frustrated and down. After all, as parents we have plenty of them. In the end, we have to remember, it is just a chair. It is just our house. These are material things. What matters most in life are not things at all. It is those toddlers which matter most. Even with toddlers, we will all have moments when we feel our heart will simply explode with joy and pride. These are the moments we need to hold onto in our minds. I have learned that these are the moments which make all the difference when it comes to happiness.

DEVELOPMENT

"Mama, one day I am going to be a super model and fight all
the boys away." —My daughter, Lili

Development—it is intangible. It is something we can't easily
measure as parents, but it is always on our minds. Are we
doing enough? Is my child growing and changing as they should
be? What can I do to help them grow? I will touch on some of
my experiences here, but remember, there are no requirements.
There is no rule book. Any activity or experience you offer for
your child provides opportunities for learning, so even when we
aren't even trying, our children are learning every second of every
day. Never feel like you aren't doing enough.

My daughter was singing songs in my husband's language
before she was three. She was learning the language, slowly, but
surely. It makes me wonder, *How do children catch on to things so
quickly?* It seems their minds truly are like sponges at this age. I am
glad my kids are learning the language. I want them to interact
with their cousins and family and we will visit Europe frequently,
but a snapshot of the future pops into my mind: My children as
teenagers, speaking in another language right next to me, and I
have no idea what they are saying. Why can't I learn it as easily

as them? I think, *God, can you make my mind like a sponge like my two-and-a-half year old? Please? That would make things so much easier!* Well, I have accepted the fact that easy is not a term I will often use when it comes to raising children. Hopefully, I will be able to learn the language too, but if not, I will let you know how it goes in the teenage years. By the way, am I the only parent out there who is terrified of the teenage years? Based on how the three-nage year is going, I am terrified. As parents, we will face one challenging time after the other. It can be so tough, but we hang in there and we make it through. So, don't let development be another stressor for you. Remember, a child's mind is like a sponge, so you can't really mess up development too bad. Whatever experiences you share with them, they will soak right up.

My son would kick a soccer ball and shoot baskets at 11 months old. Why? Because we provided him with the opportunity to do it. Provide activities for your child even if they seem too young. Don't push, but provide. They can hold a ball in their hands and practice rolling it. They may not be able to do these things yet, but it gives them the opportunity to learn. On the other hand, if you don't provide every activity in the book, don't worry. Your baby will gravitate towards things as they begin to show interest. As always, I will say, do what works for you.

As a stay at home mom, I began to worry...I began to worry about whether my children would be behind educationally when they started school. I had thought about having my children do half-day preschool a few days a week for a year or so before they enter kindergarten, but for the most part, they would be home with me. It is great having them home, but I couldn't ignore my fear that I was doing them a disservice because they were not getting the educational activities other children were receiving in preschool. I shared my feelings with a great friend who gave me the idea of doing letter of the week. If you are feeling like me and are looking for something fun and educational, this is a nice option. I have found you can do as much or as little with it as you like.

We started letter of the week and my daughter loved it. We chose a letter and focused on it by doing activities which started with that letter. I will admit, sometimes it lasted longer than a week because I could not find the time to do activities as often as I would have liked. Sometimes it would become the letter of the month, but it seemed to work. For a nice art activity, we would design the letter on a piece of construction paper. We might do arts and crafts which started with the letter. Some weeks, we did math activities or even ate or made foods which started with the letter. It ended up being a great way to plan activities for the kids each week. For example, for the letter T, we made a big T out of brown construction paper to make it look like train tracks and added train stickers. We painted a ceramic tea cup, made tacos for dinner, and practiced telling time for math.

Some other examples of favorite activities included going on a treasure hunt for the letter X. I drew a map of our upstairs and my daughter had to find the X. At the X, I had left some supplies for a fun activity and taped a big X over them with painter's tape. I left Ziploc bags and paint. Once she found them, we put the paint into the bags. We taped them on the window with the painter's tape and she was able to use her finger to draw in the paint without making a mess. She practiced drawing her letters.

For the letter S, we played with sand. We also finger painted in shaving cream. It was quite therapeutic, even for mom. For the letter P, we played with a new Play-Doh set. For the letter L, we played with Legos. For the letter B, we baked something special. For the letter J, we made jewelry with thin Twizzler twists and "fruity loops" as my daughter calls them. The options are endless.

We had fun with it and my daughter even started to tell me or ask me what objects around her started with. I really owe my friend, because this was fun and it helped me feel better about providing my daughter some educational activities even while staying home. The best part is, they didn't cost an arm and a leg.

Even though the letter of the week is fun, it is definitely not essential. I still believe the very best ways for our children to learn are simply through play, exploring, and—our personal favorite— reading books. Children can learn so much through basic play and imagination. In fact, "they say" children learn best through play. You can make play even more educational by asking them questions or to count and name colors as you go. There are so many games out there which allow toddlers to count and sort by color or size. You can even make these games yourself. Your children can go on a scavenger hunt for anything which is the color red, for example. As children explore outside, or even when you visit different places in your community, they can learn a great deal. Just think about how much children can learn from a quick trip to the zoo or even on a simple nature walk.

Last but not least, there are books. I love the quote from one of my daughter's favorite Dr. Seuss books, "The more that you read, the more things you will know. The more that you learn, the more places you'll go" (*I Can Read with My Eyes Shut,* by Dr. Seuss*)*. I love books and so do my children. I say provide them, read them, let your children play with them. Touchy-feely books are great for younger children to play with. I don't think it is ever too early to start reading to your child, even when they are newborns. I believe it can spark a love of reading. As you read, ask your child questions about the story or about the pictures on the page. You can ask them to guess what comes next or ask them to summarize what just happened. Children can learn so much from simply reading books.

If you find development is stressing you out like it did me, try not to worry. By just being a parent and engaging your children in conversation and play, you are teaching them more than you even realize already.

Get Social

Of course, not only do we think about educational preparedness, but social preparedness as well. I believe this is a common worry of stay-at-home moms especially. I worry, will my children be socialized enough when they go to kindergarten? Will they be able to fit in? Will they be able to work well with other children? This may be one of the biggest pieces of mommy guilt I experience from staying at home. I wonder, *Am I doing my children a disservice?* The truth is, no we are not doing them a disservice. We are doing what is best for our family and for our situation.

So, what did I do to help with the guilt? I tried to give my children opportunities for social interaction. I allowed my children to participate in sports, where they had the opportunity to listen to a teacher while in a group. We also made an effort to schedule play dates with friends to allow for socialization. Don't be shy; reach out to parents of children around your child's age. You can make a new friend and your children can too. It is a win–win situation. We went to Sunday school, which I felt was a lovely learning environment for my children. There are "Mommy's Day Out" programs or mommy groups in general. I joined a wonderful mommy group in our area so I could connect with other moms while my children received childcare. You can sign up for mommy newsletters or social media pages to learn about things going on in your area. There are even partial day programs for preschool. You can find programs where your child can participate for just a few hours a couple of days a week. The more I kind of get out and get involved, the more I appreciate the days we are able to simply stay home and relax together. The appreciation is good because those drawn out days which never seem to end can become pretty lonely and monotonous.

What is really important here, however, is whatever decisions you make for your family, do not allow yourself to feel guilty about them. There will be plenty of opportunities for socialization.

There are even plenty of opportunities which are either free or inexpensive. The bottom line is, try to venture out if you can, no matter how intimidating it can be with children. When I first had my son, I was literally scared to go out with both kids. I had no idea how I would be able to handle them both alone. As time went on, things became much easier, but it is still intimidating as you never know what to expect.

I had just taken my children to gymnastics and somehow kept up with the two of them while they each tried to participate, or maybe my son actually tried not to participate. Either way, it wasn't easy for me, and I was more out of breath than my children by the time class was finished. We decided to run an errand. Bad idea—we made it out of the store by the skin of our teeth. A couple weeks before, we had tried to go get some food after practice, just the kids and me. There was a really nice older man who worked there who came over to check on us. He asked, "Who is your helper today?"

I was kind of confused and said, "I guess she is," smiled, and pointed to my daughter.

He replied, "I see. You are brave."

So, even other people know how hard it is to venture out with children. It's not only me. That day, the lunch had gone as well as it could have. Thus, I did not heed his warning and on this day, we decided to give it another try.

I took the children to lunch and met my husband. Things went great, until he had to rush to eat and leave to get back to work. Lunch went pretty well, with the exception of some honey which spilled on my daughter's clothes and my son finishing super early and becoming very antsy while we waited on my daughter; you know, the usual stuff. Then, the kids wanted to play in the play area. They were doing great together, so I sat down and watched. I thought, *Wow, this is so nice. I get a little break. I can sit here, watch them, and relax.* No! Not one second after the thought crossed my mind, I smelled something horrible. My son had pooped. I forgot his changing pad as it was laying out to dry after I spilled my entire coffee in the diaper bag a couple of days before, so I laid my thrashing son on his jacket and changed him. I didn't think it would go well to pull them both out of the play area so soon to find the bathroom. Well, as soon as I let him go, I heard my daughter say, "Mommy, I need to go potty." I guess we were making the trip to the bathroom after all. I corralled the children and took my screaming son, who didn't want to leave the play area, and my daughter to the bathroom.

There were only two stalls. As my daughter went poo-poo and took longer than she had ever taken before, I was trying to entertain my son so he wouldn't touch anything in the stall. I could tell by the things I was hearing there was a line a mile long waiting for the two stalls. I was holding up the line, and they were all listening to my craziness. I even told a made-up story to keep my son entertained. As we left the stall, there was a wet floor sign because on our way in someone dropped their milkshake. I guess they managed to clean it up while we spent an eternity in there. The sign was not lying. The floor was sopping wet. I slid the stool out hoping my daughter could reach to wash her own hands as I was already holding my son, and she couldn't quite reach. She literally almost fell off the stool as she tried to reach the sink as it slid out from under her on the wet floor. So, I put my son down to help her. Of course, he immediately started rubbing his hands across the wet bathroom floor to play in the water. My audience, the entire line, went, "Ohhhhh." I think they felt my pain. I picked him up and tried to wash both my daughter's and son's hands in the sink at the same time. Then, thank goodness, we headed for home.

It truly is intimidating to go out when things like this happen, but don't worry, you are not alone. All the parents out there are right there with you. Just do the best you can, and try not to feel bad or defeated. For every horrible experience, you are bound to have at least one great one.

Another place I enjoy visiting with the kids is the local library. Many times they have story times for children. Some even have activities or a craft to go along with the story. On one library trip, my son wasn't being himself. I don't know what hit him. Or, there was my other fear, which was, *Is this him actually being his new self?* If it was, I was not sure what I would do. He was screaming for juice or a snack, even though I didn't have one. He was taking all of the other children's toys and had no desire to share. I went to help my daughter find a book for a second, and he literally almost ran out the door into the street. I hesitated to take him back the next week, but we went for it.

Our next library visit started with my daughter picking out her big sister shirt to wear. She said, "I want to wear this because I care so much about my brother. I want to wear this to the library because I care about all kids." Right before we left, she put her hands on my cheeks and said, "I care about you." At the library, my son listened pretty well to the story and participated. When we went to play with toys after, as other children came to play with the toy he was playing with, he literally gave it to them and said, "Share." This happened more than once. The trip could not have been more different from the last. When we returned home, my daughter hugged her brother and said, "I will always be here for you," then looked at me and said, "I love him and he loves me too." When it comes to the development of toddlers, there is such a large range of normal. One day, you may have a perfect angel for a child and the next, don't be surprised if they turn into a wild animal. This also illustrates for every bad experience, there will likely be a great one. Don't feel like you failed if your child has a wild animal day, don't feel defeated from a failed outing, and don't give up.

I will never forget when my daughter was in daycare and I came to pick her up one day. I asked the teacher about her day.

She replied, "Well, she didn't do a very good job of listening today."

I replied, "Oh, I am so sorry. What did she do?"

She said, "Just things like, when we asked the children to come to clean up before lunch, she would not do it, and when we asked her to come to the table for lunch, she did not come. We had to go get her."

Even though she wasn't even 18 months old at the time, I felt horrible. I wondered why my child wasn't listening. Was it something I had done wrong? But, you know what? The more I thought about it, it was one bad report. It was the first bad report I had received, and the fact is she was not even 18 months old. Is it really developmentally appropriate to expect them to listen perfectly at that age? I think not. At age four, my daughter still has a hard time cleaning up after herself, but she is a good kid. I would go as far as to say, if you ever find yourself feeling like a failure when you have a toddler, don't. Whatever is happening, it is likely developmentally normal. If you have true concerns, talk with your child's pediatrician and I am sure they will help you feel better and I'm sure they will have advice as I promise you are not the only parent asking.

Remember, there is no rule book. If we do all or none of these things, our children will still develop at their own pace and it will be okay. It is so easy to compare our children with how other children are developing. After all, social media is right in our faces each day if we choose to use it. We have all the cute and exciting stories of our friends' great moments right at our fingertips. All the good things are posted and not a lot of the bad. We see the wonderful things our hundreds of friends' children are doing and wonder why our child isn't doing the same. Even without social media, it is easy to compare yourself to other parents and friends.

No matter what "they say," we must remember, everyone is

different and our kids are growing and developing in so many different ways all at once. It is impossible for two children to develop in exactly the same way, so just because your child may develop differently than another child doesn't mean they are behind. Just because another child is doing something doesn't mean your child should be doing the same. Every person in this world has strengths and weaknesses, and our children will too. And in the end, the weaknesses aren't all bad. After all, they are what allow us to grow.

VOYAGING THE UNKNOWN: LEAVING THE HOUSE WITH CHILDREN

With kids, I can never make it anywhere on time. Even if I plan ahead, something always happens right as I am about to leave and I am late. Here is a prime example: We were about to meet Daddy to do a little shopping. It is so nice to have two adults when you have two kids to handle. We were just about ready when my daughter had to go potty. Recently, she enjoyed doing it herself; I will rephrase, she must do it herself. I could not help her if I wanted to. She had to use her stool to climb up and down and wipe herself. She tried to climb up and right as I was approaching the potty to help, she slipped and her whole arm went into the toilet...time to grab a new dress. When I saw my husband, he said, "White pants, white dress, and a white jacket."

I replied, "Don't ask."

Then there are the days when you don't set the alarm clock. The children are typically our alarm clock, but you can bet your bottom when you are counting on your children to wake you, they will sleep in. My children wake up at the same time every morning. I find myself lying in bed praying they will go back to sleep so I can have just 15 more minutes, but no, they are up. If there is a time when I need to be up for something, and decide not to set an alarm because the children will wake me, sure enough, they will sleep in. I have learned, when in doubt, set the alarm.

Another day, I called my friend as I was leaving for her house to explain that I would be late yet again. I found myself saying, "I am so sorry I am late. I had to give my son an entire pharmacy this morning." Without fail, there is always something which makes me late. Then, I get into the car and stress the entire drive. By the time I arrive, my blood pressure is through the roof, and for what? The stress does nothing but ruin my day, and is it really the end of the world if we are a few minutes late? Nope, definitely not. If this is not enough to deal with, once you make it to your destination, you will likely have more issues to face. Getting out of the house with children can be quite stressful, but don't give up. The more you do it, the easier it will become.

The Grocery Store

Grocery shopping is one of those stressful outings for me. It can be a scary excursion with a baby, a toddler, or multiple children. I think all parents have some moments they would prefer to forget at the grocery store. I have many of these, but this particular one takes the cake. We left my daughter's dance practice and headed over to the store. We only needed a few items, not a full grocery shopping endeavor, so I was thinking it would be pretty quick and easy. Well, both children started crying and whining immediately, so I ended up giving them both lollipops right away. Probably not the best idea to reward the whining, but oh well, sometimes I do what it takes. All the while, my son continued to stick his lollipop all over the cart seat. I am sure it was covered in germs. Then, he decided to put the entire grocery cart belt clip into his mouth to suck on as I looked for an item. He then continued to try to stand up in the cart. The buckles don't even hold him down. Not ten minutes after I gave him the lollipop, he threw it on the ground where it smashed into a million pieces. I bent down to try to pick it all up, hoping he wouldn't jump out of the cart in the meantime. He was sticky. I was sticky. It was not a great situation.

Finally, I pretended the cart was a car and said "Vroom, vroom," as we maneuvered around the store. This was the only thing which kept him sitting. I think on a crazy scale, we went from one—when a nice lady stopped us and told me how cute my daughter looked in her dance outfit—to 100 when shoppers watched me zoom around the grocery store saying, "Vroom, vroom, vroom" and telling my daughter over and over, "Please walk a little further away from the cart or you will get bumped or run over." We made it to the checkout line and checked out. I paid and we headed out the door. Thank goodness...or maybe not. You know it's been a tough day when you actually leave the grocery store without your groceries. Yes, that is right; I literally forgot to take my groceries with me out of the store. I had to turn around and go back into the store to get my bags, all the while saying, "Yes children, I did actually forget the groceries." People saw me and giggled. I don't think they were rude giggles, maybe they were relating to my experience because they had been through a similar experience. I am sure this will be a funny story to me one day.

From these crazy grocery store experiences, I have found a few things which have helped. First, any kind of program where you can order your groceries online and pick them up outside of the store without having to leave the car is nothing short of amazing. No shopping, no issues.

If you have to actually enter the store, I have found that the more organized my list is, the better. Now, I hate to rewrite a grocery list, so I like to separate my list into sections based on where the items are located in the store. So, I will put a dairy section on the list, a frozen section, a meat section, a canned goods section, a baby section, and so on. You can do it however your grocery store is organized. Throughout the week, I add items to the appropriate columns. This way, I don't need to rewrite the list when I already have a million things to do before heading out the door; and the list is in a nice order to move smoothly through the grocery store, thus saving time. I know you know saved time is gold at the grocery store.

Packing the diaper bag is key when heading to the grocery store, I pack snacks, maybe even lollipops. I don't think lollipops are something awful. They have saved me time and time again. I pack a drink in case they become thirsty. I pack the things they usually whine for.

I also think of different ways the children can travel at the store. I bring my cart cover for my toddler to sit in, but I also bring my baby-wearing carrier (even when my baby got older). I like to have multiple places to secure my children in case they start to get antsy. I may start my son in the cart and later move him into the baby-wearing carrier as my daughter takes a turn in the cart seat. I find sometimes just doing a little swap-a-roo can make a big difference when toddlers become bored. Recently I saw a little baby hammock product which you can attach right to the cart. This would be a great place to put a younger baby while at the grocery store. It simply unrolls and attaches directly across the top of the cart. Never underestimate baby wearing when you are at the store. As a baby, my son always fell right asleep as I wore him through the store. Then, I would only have one child to worry about.

The Doctor's Office

Another stressful outing is a trip to the doctor's office. There will be plenty of times you will find yourself waiting in a doctor's office for an appointment. For me, even a short wait can seem like an eternity. You usually have to wait in the waiting room and then wait in the room for the doctor. At least there is a scenery change in the middle. I always bring easy activities or books along with me to help entertain my kids, for two reasons. First, it helps the wait go by smoothly and I am less likely to have crying children. Second, I find if they are bored, they are literally rolling on the floor, the seats, and touching everything. It's like you go in sick, and leave sicker. The key for the doctor's office is distraction. I am that mom who is constantly reminding the kids not to touch anything because of germs. My children seem to pick up illnesses more often than they pick up their favorite toy. If I could put them in a bubble, I would, but seriously, bringing along distractions is always a good thing.

One idea I came across is stuffing an old or inexpensive wallet with little colored papers, small pens, maybe even stickers. Your child can pretend it is their wallet and play make-believe or they can draw and place stickers on the little papers inside. Other neat quiet activities are dry erase books or sticker books. Any small toys which make sounds or light up are always good for the young ones.

Snacks and a drink are also good things to have just in case. I would keep these out of view, however, if your child is like mine. He sees snacks and won't stop until he gets to them and eats them all.

The Restaurant

Then there is the restaurant, a third stressful outing. Something makes parents feel we need to keep our kids quiet in a restaurant. Maybe it is society, what "they say," or from the media. Whatever it is, when my child starts crying or screaming in a restaurant, I immediately feel embarrassed. I feel like I need to rush them right out of there. But, why? They are kids. They are not going to act perfectly in a restaurant 100 percent of the time. Does this mean children shouldn't be allowed to eat at a restaurant, or that we should never leave the house? No. Maybe all of us should change our philosophy and realize if we are going to go out, we are likely going to face a screaming toddler, whether it is ours or someone else's. It is just the way it is. Maybe if we all simply accepted this as normal, trips out for parents would be a little less stressful. Well, we can't change the world, so what do we do?

To minimize the boredom and resulting tantrums, I found it beneficial to pack activities and snacks. Waiting for the food to come can be quite difficult for a toddler, so I pack a variety of small snacks to have on hand. I try to give them little by little until the food arrives, not enough to fill them up. For my son, I always had to bring along an entire meal because of his strange diet. I gave him his meal items first as we waited for our food and then I let him munch on snacks he loved while we ate our dinner in peace. My favorite waitresses bring the children's meals out with the appetizers. You can request this, so they can start eating as soon as possible.

We love to bring dry erase books or cards along with us to restaurants. I purchased a set of dry erase activity cards for my kids. It came in a pack of 100. I separated them into two sets, punched holes in the top corner, and put them together with a plastic or metal ring. This way, each of my children could have a set to flip through. Each card had a different activity, like matching, complete the picture, find the items, and so on. You can use either dry erase markers or dry erase crayons. I didn't even know dry erase crayons existed, but they do, and they make a lot less mess.

If you cannot find ready-made dry erase activity books or cards, you can always make your own. You can laminate activity cards. You can buy wipe-clean pockets, which are simply a little plastic pocket into which you can slide any regular-sized piece of paper. You can print any worksheet or even tear an activity page from a regular activity book and slip it inside the pocket. Then, your child can write and erase as much as they want. Of course an activity book will work just as well.

We also have this squishy silicon-like placemat which you can literally ball up and throw into the diaper bag. On it, there is a farm scene and the kids can color it with regular markers. Then, it wipes clean with water. This is really nice to have at a restaurant because the kids can color on them and then use them as a placemat when their food comes.

You can make your child their own activity box with a little metal lunchbox. I have seen people glue a Lego board to the top and put Legos inside for them to play with. You can put other things inside as well, like paper, pens, markers, and stickers, for example. You won't even need to bring it in as they will likely love to carry their little activity box.

There are tools out there which can make the restaurant experience a little easier as well. One tool is the sippy cup strap. There are plenty of straps you can hook around the sippy cup and then to the chair so it won't end up on the floor. My favorite item to take to a restaurant is this little box which holds a foldable silicon-like tray. There are little sections in the tray, just like a plate would have. The silicon material helps keep it on the table because it almost sticks. You can put your child's food here, and they won't be able to swipe their plate to the floor.

Finally, no matter where you go, it is always a good idea to pack antibacterial wipes or hand sanitizer. You can be sure toddlers will touch everything during an outing. If there is a germ out there, they will find it. At least this is one less thing I need to worry about.

Sometimes, people give me a hard time about the amount of things I bring with us when we leave the house. Maybe I go a little overboard, but in the end, the items I bring usually pay off. I will keep leaving the house prepared because it makes my life easier.

Meltdowns

Now, we are all going to have the experience when we are out somewhere and one or all of our children lose it. It's true; it is going to happen to all of us at one time or another. After all, we are raising terrible two-year-olds and trying three-year-olds.

On one such day, I decided to take my children to breakfast before running a few errands. I thought grabbing a quick breakfast out might be fun. Wrong! On this day, my son had a complete meltdown because he wanted to jump in the rain puddles in the middle of a busy parking lot and street. I was trying to calm him down and keep him from pushing the door open and running back out into the street. Both my and my daughter's umbrellas were still open and in our hands. For a few seconds, I just stood there wondering what to do next. I was at a loss. I needed to morph into an octopus in order to have enough hands to deal with what was occurring. Don't "they say" it is bad luck to have an umbrella open inside? It is likely, because I was already having the bad luck. I dropped my umbrella while I tried to pick my son up off the floor. As he wailed away, a lady who was on her phone came over, gave me a horrible look, and said, "Umm, her arm was stuck in this door," then returned to her phone conversation and then to her table. I was thinking, *Thanks so much for your obvious concern.* Apparently as all of this ensued, my daughter had gotten her arm stuck in the second set of double doors at the entrance to the restaurant, and I had no idea. The crying and whining continued as we ordered and ate. I felt like a complete failure. I would call this a failed outing, but in the end, everyone ate and survived and we finished all of our errands.

Sometimes we just have to take the good with the bad. If you dare to venture out, just know "the bad" is probably going to happen sometime or another and, more importantly, that it is okay when it does. Again I will say, not all outings end badly. A few rough ones beat being consistently stuck in the house. We have also all been there too.

I always hear about parents taking their child to the store and when the child has a tantrum, they run to the car and leave all of their groceries behind. I think if this is what works best for you, go for it. I think it is a perfectly reasonable plan; there have been plenty of carts left behind before you and there will be plenty thereafter. I personally cannot bear to leave behind all that work I just accomplished of collecting the groceries in the first place. What does this mean for others? It means they may have to deal with my screaming children. So, if your child is having a meltdown mid-shop, what should you do? I say, do what you feel is right.

One day, I took my children shopping for a variety of items. My son started screaming towards the end of our trip and would not stop. I did not leave my cart and run out of the store, even though I thought about it for a second. After all, we had made it this far. I finally just decided to pick him up and snuggle him tight until he calmed down. When we arrived home, I went to take off his shoes and realized my dad had accidentally put them on with the sneaker tongue stuck under his toes. I had let him walk some for a change of pace and his feet must have been hurting so badly. No wonder the poor boy was so fussy. I thought, *Thank goodness I decided to show him some love.*

Even if you feel you will be judged by missing out on an opportunity to teach your child, if you feel you should just snuggle them sometimes, do it. We sometimes feel we are supposed to ignore the behavior, or ask our child to stop, or run them out to the car so fast so no one else has to hear it, but the truth is, there is no manual for outings with children. There is no one thing you should do. You do what you feel is best in the moment, and who cares what other shoppers think? They have likely either been there before, or will be there eventually and they may get it. If not, then lucky them; at least they don't need to be the one responsible for handling it. I am sure it is not making them as uncomfortable as it is making you.

The bottom line is, don't let it embarrass you and really, what is wrong with just letting them scream? Okay, I know this sounds bad, but who says wherever we are, we have to run out as soon as our child has a fit? One time, I was shopping with my children in a clothing store and my son started screaming. He didn't want to be in his stroller another second. I remember saying out loud a few times to my son, loud enough for others to hear, "Sorry buddy, we have come too far to leave. We need clothes." I let him fuss. I felt like I owed everyone around us an explanation. It makes me sad we feel this way as moms, that we owe others an explanation. Tantrums are a part of being a toddler, and the more I think about it, I don't think we should feel guilty or feel the need to apologize for characteristic behavior.

If our kids lose it, it is not all bad. These situations can help teach our kids how to behave. There are plenty of strategies I have tried while out. Some strategies work on some days and then don't work at all on others. I use many of the strategies I shared in the discipline chapter (using empathy, distraction, ignoring the behavior, taking them to the car for a quick time-out). Never underestimate the quick snuggle as sometimes, just holding them tight helps...after all, you never know when their shoe might be causing them severe pain. Whatever you decide to do, remember tantrums are a part of life. Use them as learning experiences; don't let them get you down or keep you locked up in your house. Most of all, never forget you aren't alone; we have all been there.

TRAVELING

As if the outings around town aren't stressful enough, there will be times you will need to leave town with the children. My husband's parents lived at least eight hours away, so this meant extremely long road trips and plenty of flights. As you know, my husband is from Europe, so this also meant plenty of extremely long plane trips out of the country.

Now I can get myself ready to go out without the kids in no time. I have become so used to getting everyone ready that getting myself ready seems like a piece of cake. I guess this is a nice positive you acquire when you have children—the ability to get yourself ready at the speed of light. The getting ready is easy, it is the getting out of the door which is the tough part. One night, I was so stressed getting out the door, I walked out of the house for a ladies' night with bright blue socks under my dog-walking sandals. That would have really been something. I had to turn around when I was halfway to the restaurant to change into my boots.

Packing for a trip for just my husband and me is easy. Packing for a trip for the entire family, on the other hand, is more difficult than changing a baby in an airplane bathroom. The packing and the getting out the door are both the hard parts. You may find out soon enough how difficult it is to change a baby on an airplane changing station which is only slightly larger than a legal pad's size. I have no tips to help with this challenge. All I can say is good luck, but I can share some tips for traveling with children in general.

I have put together a list of items we might pack for a trip within the country. Looking at the list, it is a ton of items. When packing, it is hard to remember everything, and honestly, it is simply not fun trying to form a list while putting everything together. Hopefully this list will be helpful the next time you have to pack and will keep you from starting from scratch. First, be sure to delete anything on the list which you will already have waiting for you at your destination. No need to double up because trust me, it could end up being enough to fill a small trailer, or many even a large one.

Baby monitor
- Don't forget the cords which go along with it, and make sure you have both sides of the device.

Sound machine
- If you need one for your baby to sleep well, be sure to bring it. Note: I like to keep any electronics close to me, maybe in the diaper bag or a carry-on so they won't break. From experience, you may even want to seal them in a plastic bag in case something is spilled in your luggage. Trust me, this is not unlikely when traveling in a small space with young children.

Pajamas, wearable blanket, blanket, lovie, or stuffed animal
Portable crib (or place for your baby to sleep)
Sheets
Night light
Waterproof pad

This is helpful so you don't have to worry so much about a possible nighttime or naptime accident/leak. If my newly potty-trained toddler slept with us, we always brought along one of our large waterproof pads to put under the sheets just in case of a middle-

of-the-night accident, and of course to protect whoever's bed it was
we were using.

> *Diapers, disposable training pants, wipes*
> *Toothbrushes and toothpaste*
> *Lotion*
> *Ointments and medications*

This may depend on how long you will be gone and how easily
you can access medications at your destination. Some helpful "just
in case" medications to have on hand are Ibuprofen (they even
have chewable tablets you can more easily take on a plane; ask your
pediatrician about dosage if needed), Acetaminophen, Benadryl
(in case of an allergic reaction), saline nose spray or drops, and any
probiotic or vitamins your child takes regularly. Don't forget to bring
a medicine dropper if needed. If you have a medication which needs
to stay cold on a plane like we did, we were able to pack it with ice
packs. Be sure to contact your airline to make sure as there are plenty
of airlines out there and things change.

> *Thermometer*
> *Bath towels*
> *Bath soaps*
> *Wash cloths*
> *Hair dryer*
> *A bath sponge or tub cleaner*
> *Bows, hair ties*
> *Hair brush*
> *Snacks for the car or plane*

If you travel through a meal time, a quick peanut butter and jelly
sandwich is easy. The little fruit squeezable packets, fruit snacks, and
little bags of cereal or crackers always seem to be a hit.

Baby food
- Bring a few extra in case you don't have time to go straight to the store upon arrival. If you are flying, don't worry, you can fly with baby food. You just need to pull it out from the diaper bag to be reviewed when going through security.

Individual juices and/or water bottles
- Sealed baby juice can typically be taken through security; however, water bottles may need to be thrown out. You can purchase these after going through security.

Toddler travel potty and toilet paper for the car (just in case)
Travel high chair which hooks onto a chair or stands alone
Stroller

The last time we flew to Europe, we were required to check our stroller plane-side to the final destination, which meant we did not have access to our stroller during our entire layover. Our walk from gate to gate was over 20 minutes, then we had an hour to kill, and we were already exhausted. In case this happens to you, there may be places to rent a stroller at the airport. I recently came across a stroller which folds up completely and weighs less than 14 pounds. The purpose of it is to be handled like a carry-on and stored right on the plane with you as carry-on luggage. It would have been a life-saver on this trip!

Feeding utensils, bowls, sippy cups, bottles, bottle brush, detergent
Bibs
Diaper cloths
Teethers
Pump (if nursing)

Be sure to remember all the pump parts. When we traveled overseas with our four-month-old, I packed the pump and brought it along on the plane. It was not until we arrived when I realized I forgot to pack all the parts which are clearly needed to pump. This was baby brain at its finest. I couldn't pump the entire three-week trip.

> *Diaper bag or purse*
> *Shoes*
> *Clothes*

I will sound like my mother and mother-in-law now, but always bring some long sleeve shirts and pants, and a light jacket. Even in summertime, there can be chilly nights or lots of rain and clouds.

> *Socks*
> *Underwear (with plenty of extras)*
> *Laundry detergent (may want to buy there)*
> *Pillows (if you like your own)*
> *Phone and charger*
> *Passport, IDs, and tickets*

For the Car, Plane, or Train:

Plenty of wipes
- Trust me, there will be plenty of messes. Why is it that a colossal blowout always occurs on a long trip?

Travel pillow

Scented plastic bags for dirty diaper disposal
- Trust me again, you will not want to smell the poopy ones until you make it to the next trash can.

Toys and activities (more on this below)

Car seat
- If you are flying, you can bring your car seat. You can check it in. They have car seat storage bags or rollers which you can purchase ahead of time. Many rental car agencies will have a car seat available for rent if you plan to rent a car at your

destination. Be sure to ask in advance. I know at one rental agency in particular, these are certified new car seats which are used, then sent back to the factory for safety.

Baby carrier

- You never know when you will need to walk with a baby and still need your arms. This is especially so in an airport. When we were required to check our stroller plane side to our final destination in Europe, we were so lucky to have our carrier to use between flights and while waiting to get back into the country through customs. It literally saved us.

If you are going to the beach or if there will be any swimming, you may want to include:

Towels
Sunglasses
Bathing suits
Cover-ups
Sunscreen
Chairs
Pool or beach toys
Pool floaties
Goggles
Beach umbrella
Tent
Beach bag
Swim diapers

A helpful hint here, if you are going straight to a place to swim, no matter how convenient it may seem, don't put the swim diaper on in the car. I have noticed no matter the brand, these diapers leak immediately. You may think you are saving time, but in reality may just end up with a lot of extra mess to clean up. I usually keep my toddler in his regular diaper until just before we swim.

I count 75 different items, give or take. This is not even counting out each piece of clothing you have to include. Now, it is pretty clear why it is so difficult to pack for a family.

Toys and Activities

Toys and activities are important when traveling because of all the down time with nothing to do. It is very easy for children to become cranky and antsy which can almost certainly lead to crying and tantrums. But, what do you pack? There is not endless space for toys, especially on a plane. Here are some ideas.

For babies: Toys which make noise or light up (especially if it will be dark) and books are great.

For toddlers: Sticker books, magnets on a magnetic board (Note: be careful with magnets; especially for young children make sure they are large enough so they cannot be swallowed), books, children's magazines, paper, and markers are great. You can purchase the markers which are white in color and only show color on the special paper. This leads to less worry about making a mess or writing on something they shouldn't. We found something called a boogie board, which is similar to an etch-a-sketch, which is fun. If you have an electronic tablet, this can be beneficial (some of the apps can even be fun for an older baby to explore). Dry erase activity books or cards (which I mention in a previous section) are helpful. I found my children would spend a lot of time with these simply because they were new and different.

Snacks and Drinks

Bringing snacks and drinks along for a flight overwhelmed me at first. I wasn't sure what to bring, or what I was even allowed to bring aboard. We ended up purchasing a straw sippy cup which sealed closed, with a little snack cup screwed onto the bottom for each of my kids. These cups are really neat because there is a strap so the kids can wear them like a necklace while moving around or even while they are sitting on the plane. This was really effective because their drink and snack were in one place and easy to access. It was one less thing for Mommy or Daddy to have to carry. Sometimes, there is simply no room left in the diaper bag and two drinks and snack cups take up a lot of space.

Something else to consider is typically the flight attendants bring around a drink service and they should have juice. We had the flight attendant fill up the kids' individual cups and they were all set. They will even do half water, half juice if you like.

As the plane takes off and starts heading in to land, I feel like we all have some discomfort in our ears. What do we do as adults? Chew some gum, right? Well, obviously this may not be the best plan for a young child or baby. When we flew with young babies, nursing as the plane ascended and descended worked like a charm. Swallowing tends to help with that full feeling in the ears, so a bottle or a sippy cup of water or juice, or even providing the pacifier would also do.

Travel Logistics

By the way, if your worst flying nightmare comes true, and your children are crying or screaming the entire flight, I am here to tell you, don't worry about it. You and your children have just as much right to be there flying as anyone else on the plane. These are some of the travel challenges people must expect to face. It is not your fault and you do not need to feel guilty. It likely feels much worse for you than it does them because you are the one stressing over it and having to deal with it. They are welcome to use headphones and close their eyes if they so please. Unfortunately, you probably cannot. Yes, even on that overnight ten-hour flight. I have been there and I have survived. You can too.

If you are traveling outside of the country, bring any food you will need but that may be unavailable for purchase at your destination. You may want to ask around or do some research to make sure you will have access to whatever it is you may need. This is especially important for someone like me who has a child with dietary restrictions. For example, my son could not have dairy and they did not sell almond milk anywhere near our final destination overseas, which my son was used to drinking.

You always hear about or see those kids who fall asleep in the car. When picked up, they are out, draped over their parents' arms, their own arms dangling. Their parents put them right into bed and they remain fast asleep. This is not my children! We thought this would be the case when we left for the beach with my first child approaching bedtime. Well, she was up most of the trip and finally fell asleep as we neared our destination. When we stopped the car to check in, she was wide awake and it took us hours to get her to sleep in the new, strange place. Fortunately and finally, go to sleep she did, and the rest of the trip she went to sleep just fine. She was probably just getting used to her surroundings.

To help with sleep while traveling, bring along your child's favorite blanket or animal, sound machine, or whatever it is which might make your child feel comfortable in their temporary new environment. I will never forget the time we brought our sound machine overseas and when we got there, it was broken from being jolted in the suitcase. There was no sound machine like this we could purchase there. Our daughter loved the sound machine so much, she was waking all night without it. Finally, we put a radio on a channel with static all night long, believe it or not. I know, horrible, right? Well, it worked. She started sleeping through the night again. Our sleep wasn't so great, however.

Sometimes you may find yourself having to share a bed with your toddler while on vacation. I do believe some children sleep in the same spot most of the night. Our daughter, however, ends up at the end of the bed almost immediately and I do not think it would be possible for a person to move around more than she does. We will get kicked in the face or hit at least once each night if she sleeps in bed with us. Be prepared. If you do have a moving sleeper, you may want to at least get some extra pillows from the hotel and put them around the bed in case they happen to fall out. You never know! In case she does fall out, or in case something else happens on the trip, it is a good idea to check your health insurance policy to see how out of network care works. It never hurts to look for a few medical places in the area ahead of time. You don't want to spend time stressing over this should an emergency arise.

KEEPING IT ALL TOGETHER

"One day you'll wake up next to the love of your life in a pretty house with puppies and cute kids and all the hard things happening now will all be worth it." —Amaan Shaikh

When I first read this quote my sister posted on social media, I literally laughed out loud. I remember thinking it made my life sound so amazing. I would say instead that there are plenty of amazing moments now which make the hard work you continue to do as parents worth it. The quote makes it seem like such a simple life we have as parents, but maybe we should try to change our world view a bit and think of it that way. It seems so depressing when you think about things only becoming harder. I guess as a parent in reality, you get double the amazing things, but a different type of hard work comes with it, which includes anxiety, guilt, and frustration. We mustn't forget though, it also includes so much love. I showed this quote to my friend, who said, "It should say, 'All the hard things happening now will seem easy compared to the puppy that runs away and the cute kid who pees on your carpet.'" I love it. It is so true.

I remember recently when my sister told me how hard school was, I gave her advice to just keep going, continue working hard, and that the end is all worth it. I guess this is what I meant. The family, the children, the home—it really is worth the hard work overall. Sometimes, it is too easy to look at the small frustrations (which do add up pretty quickly) rather than looking at the big picture. There are days I find myself wondering, *What am I doing? Is anything I am doing working? Is anything I am doing benefiting anyone?* And even, *What do I have to show for all the things I am doing?* One night, when I was feeling pretty down on myself as a mom, my husband told me, "You are never truly rich until you have something money can't buy." In that moment, I stopped myself and thought about all of the things I do have—my family, my beautiful children, my husband. These are the things money can't buy and these are the things I value most. Over time I have learned that it is important not to focus on the frustrations and imperfections which come with being a parent, and instead, keep that beautiful big picture in the forefront of my mind.

I had recently told a friend about all of the things I needed to do to prepare for a beach trip. She texted me a few days later to ask if we wanted to play and said, "Or are you too crazy?" She quickly texted again and said, "I mean like too crazy with stuff to do. Haha. Not actually crazy."

I responded, "I liked the first question best because I sure am crazy." Who doesn't go crazy from time to time when you are taking care of young children?

I am pretty sure we are all crazy, at least sometimes. Parenting is so hard and there is a great deal of pressure coming at us from all directions. We see all the perfect posts on social media. We feel we need to be perfect too, but we forget there is so much more to the story than what people post for all to see. Someone's life may look super shiny, but on the inside, this may not be the case.

We feel we have to be the Pinterest mom and do it all—for example, the big birthday parties with tiered cakes and handmade decorations, or the Elf on the Shelf around Christmastime. Watch out if you forget to move the Elf, because this will make you feel bad too. I found out the hard way that if you really want to feel like crap, check social media on St. Patrick's Day. I saw all the things I was not doing for my children. Moms were baking cupcakes and cakes, or providing bags of treats for their kids and everyone else in their child's class. They even have these little sneaky leprechauns who play tricks and leave treats for the kids. I think my children will feel confused one day when they go to school and realize their friends have sneaky elves who sneak around on St. Patrick's Day and they don't. In fact, I was so busy this past year, I don't think I even mentioned St. Patrick's Day.

Maybe, if we stop putting so much pressure on ourselves, we will begin to enjoy the important times more and worry and stress less. Because really, are these things really that important? I say, feel good if you do it, but also feel good if you don't. Not doing all these special things doesn't make you any less of a mom. After all, it means more time to focus on enjoying your children and who could find fault with that?

Then, there is the internet. I have seen articles with titles along the lines of "The Best Parents Do These Five Things." After reading them, I think, *Oh great, and what if I'm not doing these five things? What does that make me?* Well the last time I checked, kids need a lot more than five things to grow into productive individuals. No two children are alike, so how could they all have the same needs? Then, I will come across another post or article the next day which discusses totally different strategies. Sometimes the abundance of ideas out there can make us feel like we are doing everything wrong. When I became a mom, there was really nothing else which mattered more than my children. There was nothing more fulfilling or more important than them. Many might even think of having children as the main purpose of their life, but think of how much pressure this places on us as parents. This doesn't even include the pressures I mentioned from friends or the media. So again, how could we not be crazy at times?

I will admit throughout my parenting journey, I have had some pretty crazy moments. I will never forget one day when I was so overwhelmed with my baby and my toddler and life in general and my husband decided not to respond to my requests for help. He remained quiet. I am sure he did not mean to ignore me; it just happened, but my patience was thin. I will admit what I did next was not pretty. I threw the apple juice down onto the kitchen island...very hard. It was so hard, in fact, the juice exploded all over the entire kitchen. Well, throwing the juice did not make me feel better at all. I just realized that now I would have to spend an eternity cleaning up the sticky juice which was literally everywhere and I burst into tears. After this occurrence, I really thought, *Man, I need to keep it together!* Well, as a mom, especially one with young children, I am not sure if it is even possible, but maybe we can work on keeping it together most of the time. So, the million dollar question is, how do we keep it all together?

Perfection is Impossible

After the slamming of the juice situation, I felt especially horrible. I thought, *What kind of mom would do this, to get so angry that she actually throws her child's juice?* I thought I was the worst of the worst and that there was no excuse for my behavior. I felt horrible for quite some time, then it hit me: we are not perfect, and we are not supposed to be.

When I feel I have messed up, I try to remind myself not to worry, that tomorrow is a new day. I try to think of each day as a fresh start, although, it is way more difficult than it seems. Sometimes, I am feeling good in the morning, but then I just seem to mess up again. For example, one day, my one-and-a-half-year-old son was sitting in a padded chair coloring with my daughter, and I looked away for a second. He fell to the ground and somehow sliced the little piece of skin between his top front teeth and his top lip. I have no idea how this even happened. I freaked out, and for most of the day, felt like the worst parent ever for even looking away. The next morning, I remember thinking, *Okay this is a fresh start,* until as we were snuggling and watching a TV show, my son somehow managed to slide over my daughter and fall off of my bed head first by 7:30 a.m. I tried to catch him, but I was too slow. Once again, I felt like a failure and the day hadn't even started.

Still, each day is truly a fresh start. We can't feel bad about each and every mistake we make. If we are continuously focusing on all of our past mistakes, how will we ever be in a good mood? If we aren't in a good mood, how will we ever have a good day? If we are feeling so negative, we are bound to make more mistakes. We can't let our mistakes pile up on our minds until we are teeter-tottering around about to crash to the ground ourselves. We have to try to let our negative feelings go, realize that it is okay, and start fresh, as hard as that may be. We have to realize we are not our mistakes and we are not perfect either. We are the middle ground. Mistakes are thus expected. If we realize this, the inevitable mistakes may not throw us off quite so much. Being perfect is simply an unrealistic expectation.

If you look up the definition of mother in the dictionary, you are not going to find the word perfect in there. The definition of mom is not to be perfect. It is "a female parent" or "a term of address for a female parent or a woman having or regarded as having the status, function, or authority of a female parent (www.dictionary.com)." As moms I feel like we think some pinnacle of perfection exists, but it just doesn't. Our goal should not be perfection, but to raise our kids and do the best we can. Along the way, there are most definitely going to be road blocks, bumps, and bruises and that is life. We have to cut ourselves some slack. How boring would the world be if we were all perfect all the time anyways?

I feel like as a mom, or a parent, we are always trying to make everyone happy. We feel we need to make sure our children, our spouse or partner, and even our friends and family are happy. One day, I was talking to my neighbor and he made the comment, "I believe if you try to make everyone happy, you will make no one happy. You cannot make everyone happy and it is not our job to." This is such an interesting thought and it rang true. Sometimes we give so much of ourselves that we hardly have anything left to give. When we get to this point, how are we going to be successful at making anyone happy? We must first take care of ourselves and ensure we are happy, so we can be effective parents. Having an expectation to be perfect is not going to make anyone happy, I promise.

Sometimes I feel like I keep trying over and over again to be perfect, and then there are other times when I just feel like giving up all together. I have learned being a good mom doesn't mean we must treasure every moment. That would be impossible. There are days of almost constant whining. There are days when I literally have to force myself to continue moving forward. There are days when no one listens to a word I say. I cook a nice meal, for what? No one eats it.

On one particular morning, we already had one new outfit by 8:00, food was covering the floor along with all of the coloring books and children's magazines, and two hours and three different prepared meals later, I had yet to even eat breakfast myself. My son can't ever eat enough, so I am always trying to find more food, and I might as well not prepare meals at all for my daughter because she likely won't eat them. I had asked my daughter if she wanted some of my son's pear. Her response was no. After my son devoured it, I heard my daughter whine, "I want a pear."

I replied, "Well, it's gone." Of course, I was out of pears.

After breakfast, my son got into the spice cabinet, again. He dumped chili powder all over the stone fireplace. This was another mess and our second outfit change of the day. I had even inadvertently insulted my three-year-old. In the craziness, I became frustrated because no matter how many times we talk about it, she still thinks dinner is the first meal of the day. We had started using a schedule to help with this, and I asked her what meal we were eating. When she responded that she didn't know, I thought I was saying the right thing when I said, "You know it. You are smart. Think about it."

When she still didn't know, she told me, "I guess I'm not smart," and my heart literally ached. The mommy guilt came on strong. This day was one of the rough ones, but at least my daughter burped and then said, "Excuse me." Here was a positive and I would need it. Later that day, during naptime, I received a call from my husband. He had been in an accident and totaled his car. At first, I thought, *Of course this happened to us.* It was one more thing to deal with.

I just wanted to give up after the day I had and it wasn't even 2:00 yet. But, you know what, Winston Churchill once wisely said, "When you're going through hell, keep on going." Man, he had a way with words for parents. We can't give up. We must keep going. If we keep moving, things must turn up eventually.

The more I thought about the accident, I came to realize it was miraculous my husband and the other driver were both completely unharmed. This was a pretty big reality check for me. I realized, rather than feeling angry, I should have been feeling thankful that everyone was okay. Was it really awful, or was it amazing that Daddy was safe? Sometimes, it is all in how we look at life.

All my life, I have wanted to be a mom. I had looked forward to it. I felt like it was my one true calling, like it would be the thing I would excel at most in my life. It's hard because now that I am a mom, and a stay-at-home mom at that, there are days I find myself believing I actually suck at it. There are days when I don't even like it. Sometimes, I feel like I just can't cut it in any area in my life. There are days when I feel like I am constantly yelling at or getting frustrated with my kids, am constantly yelling at my husband or giving him a hard time, and I feel like I can't even manage to be a good daughter, sister, or friend either. There have been times when I felt like a complete failure in all areas in my life. I think becoming a mom has been the most challenging thing I have ever faced in my life so far. It has stretched me in far more ways than I could ever have imagined.

It's just hard being a parent. It's not only the constant whining, mealtime wars, messes, and recurrent frustrations. It is thrown food and sippy cups. It's taming lions—oops, I mean toddlers. It's major freak out moments, like when you somehow get locked out of a room, your house, or maybe even your car with your child still inside. Maybe they were the one to lock you out in the first place. It is constantly cleaning up one mess after another. Who has time to clean up your home when you are already spending your entire day cleaning up mess after mess, and still nothing looks clean? But you know, if parenting is so difficult—if parenting is one of the hardest things we will have to do in our lives so far, if it tests our patience more than we ever thought possible—then just think how much we will learn from being a parent. Just think how much we will grow.

Before becoming a mom, I felt I was doing just fine, but becoming a mom has brought out many issues in me and put them right at the forefront for me and everyone else to notice. For example, I never thought of myself as having a lack of patience until I became a mom. The thing is though, now that I can see these issues, now that I know I have them, I am learning, growing, becoming more polished, more calm, patient, accepting, and understanding than I ever have been before. I feel I owe this in its entirety to being a mom. To be honest, I have realized it takes the rough days for me to really grow and learn the most.

We can't forget, along with those tough days which challenge us beyond belief, there are those amazing days and moments which are better than anything I have ever experienced in my entire life. It is so hard to believe being a parent can be so trying, yet so amazing, so much so you cannot even put it into words. I have learned that we have to expect to be challenged, expect we will have areas to grow, but know we will indeed grow.

During these years when our children are young, we are dealing with one or more babies or toddlers and let's face it, this is challenging on its own. We are also dealing with our own raging hormones. We go from being pregnant, to nursing, to adjusting to regular life with periods, and then maybe back to being pregnant again. I don't think our body ever gets the chance to really settle down. I mean, I felt like a raging lunatic during these times...and still do, by the way. One moment, I would feel like the luckiest person on earth, that I had the most amazing kids in the world. The very next moment, I felt I was about to turn into the raging hulk and I thought, *Who are these little people in my house? They cannot possibly be my children!* And "baby brain"—forgetfulness, or having trouble remembering things when pregnant—is a real thing and it does not go away once the baby comes. Maybe it only gets worse. At times, I feel like my brain is so full, it cannot possibly hold another thing, and I don't even work. With all of these things going on, we are bound to "lose it" at times, but again, there is no way one can be perfect.

The first key to keeping it all together, I think, is to realize and accept this. We are not perfect; we never will be, and it's okay. My husband always tells me, and he even told me this in the juice-throwing situation, "Give yourself more credit." Yes, we all need to give ourselves more credit as the great moms we are, mistakes and all. The fact of the matter is, what our children need most is love. They don't need us to be perfect. In their eyes we already are perfect.

Find the Positives

Second, as I learned from my bad day which ended in my husband's accident, I think we need to look for the positive in each situation. Today, I am cooking dinner. The baby needs a bottle. I hear, "I need to go potty." I think I hear those words more than I use the word no. I tell myself the bottle and dinner prep will wait. I take my daughter to the potty and then begin cutting the meat. I smell a stinky smell. *Is that the raw chicken?* I smell the chicken. *Nope, that's the baby.* I can smell the stinky diaper all the way in the kitchen from the family room. "Okay, I will be there in a second," I say as the baby cries. "Just wait, Mommy has raw chicken all over her hands."

As I wash my hands, my toddler says, "Mommy, I want to go play with Daddy."

"Wait sweetie, he is on a work call," I respond as I continue working on dinner.

I'm finally finished with dinner preparation. I go change the baby and think to myself, *Oh dear, this will be the third clothes change today.* Everywhere is a mess. Aren't diapers supposed to hold everything in?

Oh no. I look up with dirty hands and see my bridesmaid dress for my friend's upcoming wedding in a ball on the floor. I yell out, "Lili!" My toddler must have pulled it off the hanger. I secure the baby and before the dog ruins the dress, I pick it up by the hanger strings as gently as possible, as I am sure I have some residual poop on my hands from the epic diaper change. I throw it on the bed, grab some new clothes for the baby, and we are all set. Whew, what a night!

Well, dinner ended up being delicious, my bridesmaid dress didn't end up ruined, and then my son slept so calmly on my chest as I rocked him to sleep, the best feeling in the whole world, so in the end my day was perfect! It is so nice when the sweet moments make the rough points of the day fade away. What would you call a day like this? I will call it my beautiful mess. See, it is all in the way you look at it. If you look hard enough, you can find positives in almost everything.

There will be days which are extra tough. These days may make it really hard to focus on those positives, but try, because the positives are what make all the difference. It was one of those extra tough days. My son had a difficult night for the third night in a row as we were trying to wean him from his reflux medication. I was going on way less sleep than usual and was up for an hour and a half trying to get my son to go back down, praying and praying until he finally fell asleep and didn't wake back up as soon as I laid him down. The next thing I know, I wake up to my three-year-old having an accident. She has been well potty trained, even at night for some time. She has not had an accident for months. Of course, it must be on one of the nights when my son keeps me up. It also happens to be the day after company leaves, so I add this laundry to the other eight piles in line for the wash.

I put the comforter in the washing machine and head down to feed the children breakfast. Of course, when I pull out the comforter, it has collected some brown goo which tends to happen repeatedly with my washing machine. I never had this issue with my old washing machine, but it seems this is more common with the high efficiency machines. Sometimes I wish companies would stop trying to improve things which already work just fine. I am scraping the goo off of the comforter and decide to wash it again, but not before I clean out the center compartment in the machine to make sure it doesn't happen again. As usual, my children are getting into everything while I do double the work with the laundry. I think, *Why does everything have to take twice as long? I don't have time to do it the first time!*

Finally, I get my daughter into the bathtub. My son has all of a sudden learned how to unroll the toilet paper and flush the toilet. He is having a ball, although, I am not. He grabs the hair dryer from the cabinet and holds it over the tub. That seems quite dangerous. Thank goodness it isn't plugged in and my daughter is not yet in the tub. I put it away. Finally, I give my daughter her bath. All finished. We all make our way to my bathroom so I can dry her hair with my good "quick" hair dryer. I hear her yell, "Mommy, CJ is heading towards the toilet."

"Fantastic," I say to myself as I realize his hands are splashing around inside of it and I now have another outfit to change. I grab another outfit and my son is now chewing on a tampon, a wrapped and clean one thank goodness. I swear I couldn't make this stuff up.

Once everyone is good and dry, we move on. We are all dancing and my daughter is singing a song from *The Little Mermaid*. I think we have gotten through the tough morning, but we are not out of the woods yet. As my daughter spins around, she seems to have made herself dizzy. I hear a boom. She has slammed her head into the door jam. I go grab an ice pack and make her bed while she holds it there. I look over and my son is sitting against the wall, purposely banging his head against it. All I can think is, *Is this really happening?* One thing is for sure, there will never be a dull moment in this household. I have one child who bangs her head by accident and screams and another who bangs his head on purpose and screams. What a fun day! To top it all off, I feed my son lunch and give my daughter a pack of fruit snacks to eat to keep her entertained while I make hers. When I check on her, I see a nice squished fruit snack completely stuck in her freshly washed and combed hair.

After I handle that mess, I go put my son to sleep. He feels so soft and warm lying on me as we rock. He curls his arms into my chest and sleeps on my shoulder, then hugs my neck. He is such a snuggle bug. Then, I let my daughter's nap wait a bit and do a one-on-one art activity with her. She loves it and is so happy.

These two things recharge my heart and I feel much better. Make sure you take time to recharge your heart. You may recharge it by spending time with your children like this or by spending time by yourself, or a little bit of both. Just make sure to find that time to recharge and it will make your daily life seem a little easier and joyful once again.

It is not always easy to be positive. I use the term "of course" in my head quite a lot. This could be a good or bad thing. "Of course, this would happen" can make you feel better if you are using it in a way to laugh at what is happening, but we need to be careful not to get into the negative thinking where we assume everything will always go wrong. Without fail, this thinking will put us into a pretty sour mood. There are always going to be days I feel like I might lose my mind, like this one. There are just so many ups and downs, but the inevitable ups also mean the bad always gets better. When my day gets really messy and it seems like I might lose it, I have to stop myself and remember the positives will come eventually. Life never stays negative. Just wait for the positive. This time, it was my son's loving and my daughter's smile.

Here is another example. My son hits the food bowl, which made me drop it to the floor. Who knew cereal could fly six feet in the air? At least it's mostly on me...instead of the floor. Oatmeal cereal is all over my face. Oatmeal is supposed to be good for your skin, right? Now the knife I am using to cut up veggies falls off the table. How does that happen all by itself? No one even touched it. It's always something. But, there were two positives here: I didn't need to use the floor cleaner, and I got a facial out of the experience.

The next day, my son hits his bowl again. This time the bowl somehow does a complete 360, turning completely back over onto its bottom and somehow does not spill a drop. It was pretty cool. Then, he hits his spoon and the cereal lands perfectly on his bib, not on him or his sleeve. I am thankful for this small thing because the food didn't spill all over him. The moral of the story is to be positive. Some days test my patience and I could easily become really angry, but I have learned to laugh it off, take the good with the bad, and remember there is always good.

Laugh It Off

Sometimes laughing it off can be just what the doctor ordered. My day had been particularly trying and long filled with my dog taking the world's smelliest poo ever on the floor, which I had to clean up while trying not to vomit. This was followed by a long afternoon where my daughter barely left time-out due to her behavior. My husband was going to be arriving home late, after the kids were already asleep.

For my husband's upcoming birthday, I had ordered a special cookies and cream chocolate bar that he had fallen in love with when we were in Europe. I convinced myself I needed to find him one because one of my family members opened the single bar he had brought back all the way from Europe, leaving it open to become stale. For what reason, you might wonder? Oh, just to give my daughter a treat after dinner, which she surely did not even need. I thought for a minute before ordering that there was no possible way it was going to arrive in solid form, but figured why would they offer to mail chocolate if they didn't have a good way to do it? Well, the chocolate arrived after my rough day in the mailbox with a hot, melted ice pack inside. It was 90 degrees that day. Needless to say, it was completely liquefied. Might I add the chocolate bar cost nine dollars?

I was unreasonably upset and called the company. I explained how I ordered my chocolate bar (all the way from Germany) and it was melted. I mean, I am sure I had done dumber things before. The guy on the other end looked at my account and asked if my last purchase had arrived well, which was a devotional for moms, but the devotion book had a humorous title which included the name of a drug. As I told him yes, I was thinking, *This guy sure thinks I am a manic drug dealer. I am calling upset and surprised the chocolate bar I ordered all the way from Germany was melted and the last thing I ordered was a book about drugs.* I mean really though, it was a daily devotion for moms which included Bible verses and all. It was a very nice book. Well, no matter what he thought, I had a good laugh and my day turned around a bit. At least it got me through to bedtime.

Patience Takes Practice

A big part of keeping it all together involves patience. Don't be surprised if one day your three-year-old tells you, "You're too tense." This happened to me. I asked her where she learned the word "tense."

She responded, "From the Aladdin genie."

There are probably some of you out there to which patience comes naturally. If so, you amaze me. For me, and I would guess for most, patience is learned. You see, I don't believe patience is an instinct; usually, it must be learned or practiced. I have had patience for many things throughout my life, but with parenting comes a new type of essential patience. It took trial and error—yes, definitely plenty of errors—for me to increase my patience. My patience is tested daily.

Patience is a virtue, so "they" often say. The definition of virtue is "moral excellence" or "conformity of one's life and conduct to moral and ethical principles, uprightness, rectitude. (www.dictionary.com)" That to me is not something which happens overnight. To conform to something consistently usually takes practice (I don't think it just happens in an instant), and so does patience. Virtue also means "goodness." You are a good person and a good mom, which means, you can also be patient.

To increase patience, I try thinking about the things I have been blessed with often. As the Berenstain Bears would say, "Count your blessings." The more I focus on my blessings and the great moments, the easier it is for me to exercise patience. If I write down all my blessings and review them frequently, my patience increases even more. It is simply easier to remain calm when you are continually reminded of the things which make you feel happy and blessed.

Sometimes our patience changes. For example, my husband would say his patience has changed in the grocery store. He used to have all the patience in the world at the store, but now he has none. Why? Maybe because it is stressful to go to the grocery store with children, but he even loses patience when he is there alone. Maybe it is because we seem to have so many more things to do these days, so those lost minutes at the grocery store are much more significant than they ever used to be. For me, when my baby became a toddler, I realized I needed to have enough patience to be able to stop and think and choose my battles. Not only does patience need to be practiced and learned, but it is ever changing. No wonder it is so hard to be consistently patient.

When talking to my dad about this topic, he asked me, "Is there such a thing as having too much patience?" At first, I thought no, but the more I thought about it, it is not out of the question. My dad said he thinks action is more important than patience. I can understand this too. If it means you are losing patience when you scream, "Stop it now" as your child is doing something dangerous (like running around the pool when they can't swim), maybe failing to exercise patience at that time isn't such a bad thing. In this situation, action is quite valuable. So, if you believe you are lacking in the patience area and are feeling mommy guilt over it, don't. You will get there. I realized, as with many things, we cannot keep doing the same thing and expect our results to be different. We have to stop and evaluate whether what we are doing is working for us, and then go from there.

Don't Stack Issues

Sometimes, a lack of patience can lead to anger. Any moms out there find themselves fuming over minor and ridiculous things, things which simply shouldn't matter at all? One day, my son grabbed a newly washed baby spoon and put it on the floor, so I picked it up and washed it. I sat it on the counter to dry and somehow I managed to knock it back onto the floor. I became furious and thought, *Of course I drop it on the floor again after I just washed it.* Sounds crazy, right—that I got so mad over such a minor detail? It had been one of those days where it seemed one negative thing was happening right after the last. All those little details were adding up and I finally found myself irate. It made sense in the context of my entire day why I became so angry, but the truth is, no matter what had occurred, it is silly along with all of the other things which occurred that day. This wasn't the first time something like this had happened, so I started thinking about how I could handle situations like this in the future.

First, I figured the reason I was so mad in the first place is because of all the piled up frustrations during the day. I learned to stop stacking the issues which happen over time. If something frustrating happens in the morning, I have to try to let it go and start fresh again. If not, all these minor frustrations add up in my mind and I end up blowing up at one point or another. It's like a mental landslide, or like shaking a soda can. Each time something happens, you shake the soda can more and more, until eventually it is bound to explode. I found if I try to put each minor incident out of my mind completely as it happens, each future event is much less frustrating on its own. If I don't let it all pile up in my mind, I can more easily remain calm. It isn't easy to erase things out of our memory. It takes practice, but the key is self-talk. I have to watch the self-talk I use after the event. I could tell myself, "It's no big deal, let it go." Stay away from statements like, "Oh great, of course that would happen to me, wonder what will happen next?" Maybe you can even literally tell yourself, "Don't shake the soda can" when something annoying happens. Maybe it could at least make you laugh?

Next, I realized we can use avoidance when possible. Thus, in this situation, I could have put the spoon somewhere else. I could have simply put the spoon away when it fell on the floor the first time. I mean, who cares if it touched the floor for a second? It's pretty clean and there is the five second rule, right? I figure I need to stop worrying or stressing over every little thing.

Lastly, I realized I needed to recognize my anger coming on at the start. There are usually some tell-tale signs we are getting "fired up." Our blood pressure starts to rise. We get hot. We might feel tense or stiff. Our breathing rate probably starts to change. Now, I try to recognize these signs right away and I try to stop and think, *This is silly, let it go.* I can try taking deep breaths to calm my breathing rate and increased blood pressure, or I might even pray. Then I try to move on, blocking it out and not letting it be there to "stack" upon later. Now, this is way easier said than done, but as with many things, practice makes perfect.

Mindfulness

I have found deep breathing and mindfulness can play a huge role in remaining calm and keeping it all together. When we find ourselves in a moment of anger, we can take a deep breath. We can use mindfulness by moving our focus from the situation to our breathing. I try to imagine where I feel each breath in my body as I breathe in and out. When I feel I am about to lose it, stepping away and focusing on my breathing for a minute rather than reacting usually makes for a better outcome.

I also find this exercise helpful at night when I wake up and I am thinking of the million things I need to do. I stop those thoughts and instead think about every breath and where I feel it in my body. You can imagine your breath going to your lungs, then imagine it relaxing your arms, your hands, your legs, and so on, until you get all the way to your feet. I find this relaxes me and helps put me back to sleep. Another way you can do this exercise is to tighten each muscle, one by one, in your body for a few seconds, then relax in the same way until you have relaxed each muscle in your body. What makes the difference here, is your mind leaves whatever it is you are stressing over and focuses on relaxation.

Sometimes, when things get tough (and especially when we focus on the negatives), we will find ourselves feeling down. As parents, there will be plenty of times we are simply in a bad mood. In order to keep it all together, I find it important to remember good moods and bad moods are just that—moods. Moods are only there for a short while, and then they change. A mood is simply a frame of mind in that moment. It doesn't last forever. When I am in a bad mood, I try to remember that this too shall pass. Soon these moments will be in the past, so hang in there.

Worry

Try not to worry. This is a loaded statement which is definitely easier said than done for most of us. I feel like worry comes with the job of being a parent. We all do it. I cannot even count the number of times my husband tells me I am always looking for something to worry about. Well, I assure you, there is no need to look. As a mom, it is all right there for me to worry over.

I have worried mostly about my children's health, especially all of the issues my son was having due to his reflux. I worried probably every single night since my youngest toddler was four months old until he was in his twos about the strange gasping sounds he made. The doctors all told me it was likely normal. They told me as long as he wasn't turning blue and he continued to breath, it was fine. Well, that comment was not so comforting for me. I was not sure I wanted to wait and see if my son ever turned blue in the middle of the night. So, of course, I still worried nightly. It is so difficult, but we have to try to control our worries by letting them go. Otherwise, I swear it can break us down.

Ever since I can remember, I have been a worrier. I worried as a child and I continue to worry as an adult. When I was young, I remember a quote my mom always shared with me. "Worrying is like rocking in a rocking chair. It gives you something to do, but doesn't get you anywhere." Another favorite is, "Worrying doesn't stop the bad; it only stops you from enjoying the good." I truly believe both of these statements and try to think about them anytime I am feeling worried. I have realized all of the time spent worrying about my son's reflux and strange breathing did nothing to make it better. Does worrying really solve anything? No, it does not. You can worry and worry and worry, but the worrisome thoughts are never going to make anything change or improve. If anything, they will only make the situation worse.

One afternoon, I was leaving the grocery store with my son strapped to my chest in his carrier and my daughter in the basket. When I was almost finished loading the car, a young lady said, "I was just about to offer to help you load your car, but it seems this isn't your first rodeo."

I thanked her kindly.

My daughter said, "She was a pretty and very nice lady."

I was thinking, *Yes, this lady is my new best friend.* She couldn't have made me feel any better that day. I felt accomplished and like I was doing something right. I learned two things here. First, we need to hold on to those feelings of accomplishment and remember those nice comments we receive. We could use them on a tougher day, but I also realized just how much of a difference we can make in another person's life just by saying a few words—maybe even to the mom who looks completely frazzled at the store. We have all been there. Just stopping and telling her, "You are a great mom" could make her day more than we know. It feels good to make others feel good. I realized maybe I needed to focus a little more on what I could do to help others feel better. Maybe those great feelings which come to us from helping others can keep me from some of the unnecessary worries I have and the questioning I do about my own self as a mom.

Another such moment occurred when I was feeling a little down one day. Maybe feeling a little down was an understatement. I had kept myself up worrying over my son the night before. It had been a long, hard day. I felt I had been through the ringer and I was just trying to hold myself together. I had both of my children at the store. Both were crying and whining. I had already bribed them both with a toy to hold so they would quiet down and I could have at least a minute or two of something resembling peace. Two older women stopped me and said, "Wow, aren't you lucky?"

I had to kind of snap myself back to reality and I somehow found the words, "I am."

I am not sure if the words came out more like a statement or a question, but one lady responded, "You have both a little girl and a little boy. They are beautiful, and you are looking great too after having two children."

I tried not to cry those happy tears which would have made me look crazy, and said, "Thank you so much. I really am blessed."

In fact, my response couldn't have been truer. When we let go of all the worries and frustrations, a beautiful thing is left.

Faith

I would be remiss not to mention faith in this section. Faith has pulled me through so much as I have been challenged as a mom and as I have grown. My experiences remind me never to forget the power of prayer. When things feel like they are falling down, I have such comfort in knowing I should simply put my problems at His feet and trust. I love the verse which speaks about leaning not on your own understanding. I can be so wrapped up with anxiety and worry in my own head as I try to figure out why something is happening or when trying to figure out how to fix things. I find comfort in realizing sometimes, we cannot lean on our own understanding. We won't make sense of it. We just have to trust that everything will end up working out as it should.

Faith is what got me through my son's reflux and gasping as there was no understanding it or figuring it out on my own. I had to understand and actually start believing it is okay if we don't know all of the answers and that being a good mom didn't mean having everything figured out perfectly. I began to realize I had to let go of the silly things I was obsessing over and keeping in my mind and instead start enjoying life. I realized things don't have to be "just so." I realized I had to start being silly instead; to start flying by the seat of my pants a little bit, and to start having fun. Otherwise, we will surely miss out on some pretty great moments.

Surround Yourself with Support

Surround yourself with a strong support system. Hang out with friends who don't judge or compare, with those who understand and can empathize with what you're going through. One day, I had one of my best friends and her two children over. She has a toddler and a young baby too, so she certainly understands it all. As they were about to leave, my friend kindly said, "Umm, she has a knife" as my daughter was scraping it across the window. Luckily it was only a butter knife, but I was not even sure where she found it. Then, I couldn't even walk them out because my son had stuck his hand, which was covered in baby food, in his eye and then flung his spoon across the floor. I had more baby food to clean up...I mean, who knows how much old food and sticky mess is between those hardwood floor boards. As I wiped it up, I couldn't even say goodbye to my friend, but it was okay.

She completely got it. I didn't even need to apologize.

Hang out with friends who are there for you. One day, I felt like a complete failure. Well, there are plenty days when I feel like a failure, but today, I felt particularly strongly about it. I remember my son fought me during a bath before naptime. He was all of a sudden scared of the bathtub, and of the towel trying to dry him off, and of the clothes going on him. My daughter absolutely refused to eat anything which was put in front of her. I went to lay my son down for nap, and he refused to lie down. He screamed and cried if I left the room, and when I came back in, he refused to lie down and laughed when I told him that no, it was time for sleep. I needed my son to sleep, because I knew at this point, I was going to have to wake him up for his sister's dance class in less than an hour and I would have a horrible time controlling him there without a good nap. After coming in and out of the room multiple times, I yelled, "Lay down" very loudly. Then, I left the room and proceeded to cry. I felt like nothing I had done was right that day, and even in the recent days. I felt like the worst mother ever because I raised my voice at my children, my son who was still just a little guy and my daughter, who was unsuspectingly coming down with strep. Frankly, I just felt like poo.

We went to dance where my daughter refused to listen to the teacher. I even had to beg her to go, even though dance class was something she usually seemed to enjoy. I was given a flyer as we left. On it was a photo of a mom and her daughter and a quote which said, "If you ever feel like giving up, just remember there is a little girl watching who wants to be just like you...don't disappoint her." On one hand, it made me feel like complete crap because I was thinking, *Well, I am sure I have disappointed her.*

The thing which ended up resonating with me was, "If you ever feel like giving up." I believe we all feel like this from time to time. We might say, "What's the point? I give up. I can't seem to do anything right." I really needed to hear this at the time, because I honestly did feel like giving up. It made me feel better to know I was likely not alone.

I shared my feelings with two of my best friends. They were there for me. They told me, "You have two toddlers. You are not the first mom of two who has felt this way," and "We are all entitled to bad days. You love your kids and they know it." What amazing things to hear.

One of my best friends has two children and all of our kids are one year apart. Altogether, our kids were almost one, two, three, and four years of age at the time. When I brought up the sleep regression, she told me not to worry because she remembers having the same conversation with me exactly one year earlier about her son. She told me it would pass. Thinking back, I remembered telling my friend exactly that. I told her to hang in there; it would probably pass. The thing is, sometimes, it is so hard to accept our own advice. I listened to my friend and trusted her advice, but I wouldn't trust my own.

There were two things I learned in this situation. One is to heed your own advice. Ask yourself what you would tell a friend if they were in the same situation and trust that advice. The second is to have a friend to whom you can vent. If you cannot take your own advice, it is likely much easier to take it from a friend who you care about and who you trust.

Surround yourself with friends who build you up and support you. Surround yourself with those friends who make you feel better and not worse. Surround yourself with friends who accept you for who you are. These are the people who will help you keep it together when you feel you aren't. They will help you see that it is okay; that it happens to the best of us. Find that friend who meets you where you are, and who can help you pick up the pieces, either emotionally (when we can't take one more second of frustration), or literally (when the kids break something or make a huge mess). My neighbor came to visit after my second child was born. I fed my daughter lunch, and when she seemed finished, even though I didn't know my new neighbor very well yet, she just got up, walked my daughter to the bathroom, and washed her hands for me. I mean, that simple act meant the world to me, more than the cookies she brought (well, yes, that was a close second), and more than her gift. I cannot tell you how much effort it would have taken me to put the newborn down, get him comfortable, pick up my daughter, walk her to the bathroom, and then hoist her over the sink for a couple of minutes, while I struggled to wash her hands. Surround yourself with people like this, true friends. Never hesitate to ask them for help or guidance. Then, be that kind of friend to others in return.

MY LOWEST LOW

Recognize and anticipate that there will be times when you feel like you are at your lowest low and know that no matter what, you will come back out again. I find it interesting how our lowest lows in life can somehow change us the most for the better. It happened to me. If we can figure out how to find happiness in the midst of troubles, we are on the road to a happy life.

There was a time when I truthfully felt I had hit rock bottom. I mentioned the day we went to get an X-ray for my son to find the level of constipation he was experiencing. That was a Thursday; it was another rough day, but I hadn't hit my low quite yet. That weekend was tough. My son progressively became fussier throughout the weekend, and we would soon find it wasn't just the bruised gums from teething causing him pain.

Saturday night was upon us. As I rushed to leave the house to have dinner out with family, I accidentally left a full bag of grapes on the kitchen table. You might be thinking, *Oh no worries, worst case she will need to throw them out.* That on its own might have been rough, if you only knew how much my son loves grapes; however, I would have been thankful to simply throw them out.

Unfortunately, when we returned home we found the bag of grapes on the ground. My dog had eaten almost the entire bag, including most of the stems. We called the emergency vet, because I had heard grapes can be poisonous for dogs. I wasn't sure if this was a real thing. We found out soon enough—grapes can be very toxic for dogs. There is no way of knowing how toxic they are as it all depends on the dog. So, my husband left to rush her to the emergency vet.

In the meantime, I headed upstairs to put my son to sleep. He was fussy to the max at this point. He kept grabbing at his stomach, was arching, and seemed to be in so much pain. I had a feeling the pain was due to constipation. He had been pooping daily, but he went back and forth from regular poop to hard poops consistently. I trusted my gut and gave my son a glycerin suppository as the doctor had recommended in the past. The suppository helped get some poop out and calm him down enough for him to fall asleep. My son's strange night gasping came back worse than ever before shortly after I laid him down for sleep. The gasping went on and on while I cried, messaged a friend, and spoke to my sister-in-law about what was going on with both my son and my dog. Thank goodness for them, because I don't know how I would have kept it together as much as I did otherwise.

My husband messaged me about how the veterinarian wanted to charge us almost $2,000 to run tests on the dog, induce vomiting, then stop vomiting, give her carbon, and then keep her for three days on an IV. I wanted to scream. With everything going on at once, I thought I might literally lose my mind. We decided to do everything except for have our dog stay at the hospital for three days. They let her come back home with us. After all the tests, she seemed okay. We would now have to wait and see. We would need to take her back to our veterinarian on Monday for another blood test to check her levels.

We got through the following day. It was a great day. My daughter had her first dance recital. She did so well. She just about did all the right moves. There is nothing better than the feeling you have when you see your child succeed at something. I cried happy tears of pride for my daughter.

Family commented about how happy and content my son looked. It was hard to believe he was experiencing any issues, reflux included based on his sweet personality. Sorry for TMI here, but my son pooped six times. I thought, *Maybe this is it. We are in the clear.* Well, never speak too soon. The next morning, I received a call from the GI doctor's office. I was told I needed to take my son to the hospital, that he was completely full of stool. I explained he had pooped so much in the last day and asked if maybe he would be okay. The nurse explained he had so much stool in his system on Thursday's X-ray he did not even have room for food, and with this much stool, it was unlikely he had cleared out. She explained the hospital would need to clean him out with the use of a feeding tube and medication. She asked what time that day I wanted to go to the hospital and I asked to go right away. I wondered, *Why hadn't someone told me Friday when my son was in so much pain?* We had a family vacation lined up. We were supposed to leave the following morning. I mean, yes, that was the least of my worries. My priority is my son, always, but when she mentioned this would only take 24 hours, I thought maybe the beach would be a nice positive the entire family could look forward to.

I ran around the house, called my husband and parents, got coverage for my daughter, packed bags, and gathered toys. I couldn't stop crying but all the while was trying to remain calm and explain to my daughter that everything was fine. We rushed to the hospital to make it in time for our registration scheduled for 10:30. Then, we waited and waited. It became almost time for my son to eat lunch. He was extremely fussy. The hospital had no record of the visit and could not get in touch with the doctor because he was performing surgeries. I became more and more worried, frustrated, and upset and ended up in the bathroom as always with stomach issues. Sorry, TMI again, I am sure.

Thankfully my husband made it to the hospital or I may have had a panic attack. We were in our room by noon only for more waiting. My poor little guy couldn't eat, and he could only have clear fluids. We spoke with the hospital doctor, who thank goodness, we loved. I explained my son had pooped quite a bit. She asked to do another X-ray to ensure he was still full of stool. She said she only wanted to do the clean out if it was absolutely essential because it is invasive. I agreed and we waited for the X-ray results.

Now, of course, I was even more nervous. I knew if he had to have this procedure done, there would be risk. I prayed the X-ray results would be clear. I couldn't imagine having to decide if my child should have to go through this or not, or risk having to come back and do this all again should he continue to have issues. The X-ray results showed he was still full. The doctor said that, thanks to the suppository, the bottom area had started to break up, but he was still really impacted at the top and there was still no room for much else in his system. She and the GI doctor agreed we needed to go through with the clean out.

I told my group of good friends that my son was literally full of shit and that we were at the hospital. I know, it's a horrible thing to say, but a little bit of humor can go a long way when you are down in the dumps. No pun intended. I have an ongoing group text from a group of friends from high school. I always hear it isn't likely you will remain friends with those you went to high school with, but somehow we remained friends. I guess this is one more thing that I should keep on my list of blessings. That list of positives can come in handy at times like this.

Fortunately, a best friend who happens to be a wonderful nurse was in town. Check, another blessing. She came to the hospital to sit with me as I went through what would be the toughest part of the hospital stay. My husband had waited as long as he could, but it was Monday and he had to leave to take my dog to the vet for her blood test. The vet said even though our son was in the hospital, our dog would need to come today because if her toxicity levels were high, treatment would need to begin right away. Thank goodness for my friend. I explained everything to her. She made me feel better and assured me that everything we were doing was normal based on her experience. She waited in our hospital room and listened to my son scream and scream for what seemed like an eternity as we got him ready for his procedure across the hall. The screams were loud enough to hear clearly through two closed doors and across the hallway.

My poor baby had to be put into a papoose, which is like a board with cloth wrapped around him to hold down his arms. They tried to put an IV in the hand he used less. Somehow, it clotted and we had to try the other arm. They finally got the IV in his good arm and then they moved onto the feeding tube which needed to be inserted through his nose and down to his stomach. All the while this was happening, my son screamed and cried, "Mama, Mama, Mama." The worst part was when the nurses (who really were wonderful) had to hold down his head and insert the tube. I just saw his little eyes moving back and forth searching for me while he continued to cry out my name. I had the option to stay out of the room. I chose to go into the room. I felt that maybe as his mommy, I could provide at least a little bit of comfort by being in there with him. The nurses told me he would never remember this, but that I would. At least he will not remember this, because I could never forget it.

"They" always say it could be worse. I guess they are right. It could always be worse, but there is really nothing worse than seeing your child in pain. I don't care if it's a paper cut, a shot at a wellness visit, or something pretty major. It is the most difficult thing in the world to see your child in pain. I am not even talking about just physical pain here. I am talking emotional pain too. I cannot even imagine when my children get their heart broken one day.

When you see your child in pain, you have a right to be upset. You have a right to cry. You have a right to seek comfort. Never feel like you don't have a reason to cry or hurt because "it could be worse." Of course, it doesn't hurt to heed this advice and remind yourself it could be worse, but it is okay to show and experience emotion. Tears can heal too. Then after you cry, and cry some more, those words can come in handy: "it could always be worse." Then, you can find some comfort in those words too.

I barely kept it together as everything was happening in that room, but when it was all done, the second my son wrapped his little soft arms tightly around my neck, I lost it and cried. They were ugly tears, the kind with the sobs and awkward loud noises. I don't even want to know what my face looks like when this happens. I am sure it is embarrassing to say the least. I walked back to our room and again, thank goodness for my friend. She gave me a hug. It was just what I needed. I pulled myself together.

My husband returned just after this. My friend and I went down to the cafeteria and had a bite to eat. Thank goodness I ate. I didn't even realize I hadn't eaten all day. The food helped me feel a little better. We finally saw the doctor and she told us they would be running medicine into his stomach from the feeding tube to loosen up the stool. We asked how long he would be hooked up to the feeding tube with the medicine. She answered she didn't usually like to guess because it varies from child to child; but then said it would be at least 48 hours. In my brain, my mouth dropped and I became quite anxious, but outwardly I think I looked relatively calm.

Once our son was situated and all hooked up to his IV tube and feeding tube, we started talking about the upcoming vacation. We didn't have much else to do. After all, our 15-month-old would need to stay within two feet of this IV contraption for at least the next 48 hours. Based on the timeline, it looked like we would be missing the vacation.

My husband went home to pack up my daughter's things, because at least she should go and have a nice time with her Mimi and Papa. Of course I wasn't fully packed. These things never happen for me in advance. The packing is always finished at the last possible second. The funny thing is—well it was not funny at the time, it was more infuriating—my son was completely packed and I had not even started packing for my daughter.

Another really great friend came to keep me company soon after my husband left so I wouldn't be alone. I didn't think I would do well alone with my thoughts at this point. I needed moral support. Truthfully, I was more emotional than I had ever been in my life. My friend walked in with a bag full of snacks (really yummy ones too), drinks (including energy drinks), and another full bag of her child's toys. She said she thought my son could use some fresh and different toys to play with while stuck at the hospital in one place. I cannot put into words how much this meant to me.

She stuck with me while I called my husband and explained where all of my daughter's clothes were and what to pack. Yes, you did read that correctly—I did need to remind my husband where all of my daughter's clothes were stored. I remember reading an article once about how there is one primary parent who typically being a primary parent who keeps track of those kinds of things. That parent is definitely me, but I am okay with it. I feel lucky to have a husband who works as hard as he does and would do anything for the family. Anyways, as I am talking to my husband over the phone and trying to explain where everything is, my son is losing it and does not want to sit still for another second. My friend is squatting down showing my son toys and reading him books without even giving it a second thought. She stuck with me until my husband returned even though she has two children of her own at home, one of them a breastfeeding three-month-old.

Once my son fell asleep, I just sat there and cried. I cried tears of joy this time because I had such good friends who dropped everything to take care of me. If you can say you have even one friend like this in your life who is there for you, you really are set. I cried tears of joy over the support I received, from my friends and from the helpful nursing staff and hospital doctor.

The following day, we had a chance to meet with the hospital nutritionist. He asked us what our son's feeding schedule looked like and we filled him in. This entire time I had been wondering if it was something I had done, or not done, for my child which caused all of this. To even think that I was the reason he was going through all of this pain was agonizing. I asked the nutritionist if it was my fault, if it was something I did to cause this. He actually seemed to get a bit emotional himself as he said it wasn't my fault. He said, even if you are doing everything perfect, there is a second being here who gets to decide if and what he wants to eat. It is extremely difficult. He also said based on our schedule, it seemed we were doing everything right. He offered a few suggestions to help us provide additional fiber and liquids, which I found very helpful.

The meeting took some weight off of my shoulders when I learned it likely wasn't my fault, but I still felt horrible for what my son was going through. As parents, we are charged with a huge responsibility. We aren't perfect. We are bound to make mistakes. Accidents are bound to happen. We will face very difficult times and low lows, but we need to remember never to blame ourselves. We are doing the best we can. Through it all, we are providing our children so much joy, happiness, and love. I believe this is what matters most.

We had to stay at the hospital for 72 hours total. It was an excruciating 72 hours of my rambunctious toddler remaining two feet from an IV post. We survived with all of our toys and the toys from our friend. We survived multiple X-rays and blood draws, pricks, and sticks. I survived sleeping on the hospital recliner. I spent one night worrying if his stomach was too distended (the thing the doctor told me to watch for) and therefore, worrying the "risk" of the procedure would occur. We survived more than 80 diaper changes, and a horribly red bottom. I heard tears over and over again from my son. It was hard—it was the hardest thing I had had to go through thus far in my life.

Every time my son needed an X-ray or a prick, or to have his diaper changed, we would say, "I know, I know," as he cried. This happened so often that sadly, when we left my baby had learned to say "I know" so clearly every time he got upset. We did get through it though. My son did get cleared out. Before we left, I told the doctor I was so worried this would happen again because we saw no major signs this time. My son had been healthy and happy. He only had issues at night and he was even pooping daily. The doctor told me she hated to say it, but she thought it was because he had gotten so used to feeling this way that it felt normal for him. Poor little guy. This broke my heart. We left with worries, but at least we finally made it home.

We missed the beach trip, but we were able to spend some quality time with my son. He received all of the attention for a couple of days from both Mommy and Daddy. This was so great after all he had been through. He was very happy. I cried more and more tears behind the scenes each time I received a photo from my parents and sister. Tears of happiness for my daughter, but to be honest, there were also tears of sadness because I had to miss out on all of these experiences my daughter was having without us. It was the first year she would truly be able to enjoy the beach. She experienced many firsts. I was emotional, but more than anything, I was happy she was able to have such a great time rather than sitting at home worrying about us being at the hospital. There are two ways of looking at everything. I decided to choose joy.

When It Rains, It Pours

I thought, *We must be out of the woods now.* Well, my parents made it home with my daughter from the beach. Everyone was healthy and happy. We had let my parents borrow our new van for their trip. Upon their arrival, they filled us in on how they hit a pole in the parking garage. Fantastic, now we had one more thing to handle. Well, I guess we weren't out of the woods yet.

At this point, I wasn't sure I could handle this setback, and especially not any more setbacks, but still more came. It seemed we kept getting hit with tough things. I refilled my son's reflux prescription. When I got it home, I could not open the bottle. My husband wasn't home yet and I tried everything, even a rubber gripper. Nothing would work. I thought, *I seriously cannot drive 30 minutes to and from a pharmacy right now.* Thankfully, my husband opened it when he returned home. However, two days later, it was stuck again. I called the pharmacy who said I would need to come in and they would help me open it. I probably became angrier than I should have and said, "My son just got out of the hospital. I honestly cannot drive 30 minutes to your store to have the bottle inspected." The pharmacist understood and sent a new bottle with a regular top to me through my mother who works near the pharmacy. I asked the pharmacist if this has happened to other customers. Her response was, "Not really." Great, of course it was just me.

I experience vertigo from time to time and it chose the perfect time to reappear. Maybe it was stress-related, but it was back. Not only did I feel emotionally exhausted, but I also felt dizzy and sick. I started to feel better when my son started sleeping again, but this only lasted a couple of nights. Then, the night waking returned and his strange gasping came back. I remember one night in particular when my son woke up twice screaming in pain and remained screaming for quite some time. On this particular night, the second time my son woke, I gave him to my husband because honestly, I couldn't hold him anymore. My arms were like jelly and emotionally, I couldn't do it.

As I headed to the bathroom, I tripped over a cord which was in the way because my son had grabbed it earlier in the day and dropped it there. The cord wrapped around my ankle somehow and tripped me up. It hurt. I grabbed the cord and went to throw it across the room in anger and the cord went over my shoulder and literally whipped my back. This hurt even worse. I started to cry and literally collapsed to the floor. I yelled at God asking him why he wouldn't help us. I had definitely hit a new low. I felt horrible for yelling at God and I felt horrible that I had to pass my son off to my husband. I thought, *What kind of mother am I to not even be able to handle comforting my child after all he has been through?*

Looking back I realized, however, it was actually a good thing I recognized I needed a moment and took time for myself. It did not bother my son that his father held him and comforted him for a little while. I realized it was okay to feel the way I did. I had been through a lot too. It isn't easy to comfort another human being when you feel completely lost yourself.

It turned out that my son was constipated again almost immediately following his discharge. I couldn't believe this kid was pooping hard balls of stool immediately after what he had been through at the hospital. We called the GI doctor who was near impossible to get a hold of, who finally just doubled all of the laxative types of medications he was taking. The GI doctor also informed us he would like to do another X-ray, this time using a barium enema so he could see the intestines. He wanted to evaluate him for something called Hirschsprung's disease. I was so sad my son would need to go through yet another procedure. At this time, I had not even seen our GI doctor or even heard from him about what he thought might be going on with my son. I am so thankful for our pediatrician who talked with us about his thoughts on the situation, and who told me this was the right plan to find out what was causing the chronic constipation.

We had the X-ray done. It was so sad to watch my son cry more tears while we held him down taking X-ray after X-ray. Hadn't this little guy been through enough? Finally, we heard from the GI doctor's nurse. She told us the results were normal, but the doctor wanted to do a rectal biopsy next to make sure it was not Hirschsprung's. I asked if anything was even slightly off for the doctor to want to do another procedure. She said no, that this is what they do for babies who are having chronic constipation. I received no other explanation. I only got a, "Talk to your husband and see if this is something you would like to do and let us know. If so, the doctor himself will speak with the surgeon who will set up a meeting with you to discuss the procedure."

We didn't know what to do. It seems like in the medical world, everything is trial and error. I feel like there isn't ever one clear cut answer to any question. All we can do is seek out the answers, trust our doctors, and above all, give our babies all the love we can give.

In the months prior to my son's hospitalization he had already been through so much. There were times when things seemed to start getting better, so we would start weaning him off of his medication and then all hell would break loose again. There was a time when his strange night gasping stopped. This lasted at least a month and a half, and then *bam*, it was back again and so were my worries. I had felt I might go insane. At one point, the GI doctor noticed my son had lost weight. He told us it was a failure to thrive. It actually broke my heart to hear this term over and over, *failure to thrive*. It may be one of the toughest things I had personally heard up to this point about my children. I was pretty sure my son was a thriving, happy little boy, but apparently he wasn't doing so well in medical terms. I choose not to dwell on the medical language and to continue to believe my child was my perfect little boy, but at that point, we needed to know what was going on and we wanted to fix it. We didn't want him to be in pain anymore. So, he had an upper endoscopy. It confirmed he had reflux, but it only gave us more questions about his constipation and his gasping. Eventually, I realized I personally could not control my son's reflux and the more I tried to control it or understand it, the worse and more stressed I felt.

Now we had to decide if we should do a second endoscopy. We spoke to the pediatrician at our follow-up visit a couple of days after speaking to the GI doctor, who recommended we go through with the second endoscopy and biopsy. He explained why he felt it was helpful in less than a minute. He explained that the X-ray does a good job of telling you if you definitely have the disease, but it does not do a great job of telling you 100 percent that you don't. He also said the clean out could have affected the X-ray's results. This made perfect sense, so we went ahead and set up our appointment with the surgeon.

As we were working through all of this, my son became sick with a fever of over 102 degrees Fahrenheit. The fever began right before bed. I ended up sleeping on his floor and holding him every hour—at one point I let him sleep on my chest while he cried and moaned. I remember crying with him. I felt so sad he had to go through yet one more thing. Once again I asked, *Hasn't this boy been through enough?* He was given an antibiotic (after two days of seeing how things went). I thought, *Great, maybe we will get back to normal.* Well, then the antibiotic seemed to cause him even more pain than the illness did. He was screaming for hours. It seemed the antibiotic was making his reflux worse.

The following morning, the nurse called me back to let me know we would be hearing from the surgeon. She also asked if I would cancel our appointment with the doctor and wait until we obtain the results from the biopsy to meet. I explained my husband and I had actually been looking forward to talking with him about what he thought could be going on with our son thus far. She said, "Fine, keep the appointment." I was shocked the doctor had not called himself if he felt we needed to cancel the appointment, just to make sure we didn't have any questions or concerns. I mean, we hadn't even spoken to him since our last appointment well before my son's hospital stay.

While I had her on the phone, I asked her if she thought he could be having a reaction to the antibiotic or if it could be increasing his reflux. She said possibly, then firmly told me I would need to speak to the prescribing doctor. She said if her office had prescribed it, she would 100 percent be able to answer my questions, but since they hadn't, I would need to speak to the other doctor. I thought, *Okay, so it seems you know an answer but don't want to give it to me?* But, I just said I already had a call into the pediatrician.

I asked her if she would tell me the surgeon's name. She responded in a very rude voice with "I have some advice for you parent to parent. I already told you the surgeon's name. You need to start writing down everything we say. I know it is hard to remember because you have kids. Write it all down, so you don't need to call us and ask 100 different questions." I about lost it, but I kept it together and responded, "I have pages and pages of notes. I apologize as I must have forgotten this one thing." If there is one thing I am good at, it is writing things down. I decided I wasn't going to let this nurse who does not understand the term empathy take the one thing away from me I was sure I was good at, note-taking! I mean a nurse without empathy, who ever heard of such a thing? Isn't that an oxymoron? I told the nurse goodbye and she said, "You will be here tomorrow. You can ask all of your questions then."

I hung up and proceeded to bawl hysterically. I had been through enough. My baby was sick again. I was at my lowest low. I could not believe she would have said something so rude to me. I felt so alone, like even the doctor did not care to meet with us when so much had happened to my son. It seemed the only person who really cared about him was my husband and me. I called my friend and my husband to vent, and once again they helped me through my continuing moments of weakness.

We got through the dreadful five days on his antibiotics. During these five exhausting days, we had our appointment with the GI doctor. The first thing the doctor said when we walked in was, "So, why are you here? We tried to cancel this appointment." My husband and I calmly explained we had not heard from him since before our son went to the hospital and we were hoping to talk to him about what he thought was going on. The doctor responded with "Well, this is why I want to do the rectal biopsy, to find out."

Through the rest of the appointment, rather than make us feel better about what was going on, he only succeeded at making us feel worse. Then, he finished the appointment by saying, "I will meet with you two or three months after the surgery." I was thinking, *Are you kidding me? He wanted to cancel this appointment and not even speak with us until three months following his next surgery?* I couldn't believe my ears.

My husband and I decided never to go back to this doctor again. No matter how tough things had gotten, or how alone we felt, we knew we just needed to keep moving forward. Just when I thought things were settling down again, I went to get ready for bed feeling okay about everything. As I walked upstairs, it was way too hot. I checked the thermostat and our air conditioning was clearly broken. Great, perfect timing. It broke right when it started hitting 90 degrees outside. My son was still sick. We needed the air conditioning on so he could get better. My husband went to take a look at the unit as I cried. He came back to bed and told me he thought he could fix it in the morning. I quietly cried myself to sleep. It was one more thing on this plate of mine that I felt was already overflowing and my plate was about to crash into the ground and shatter.

The Spark

We celebrated Memorial Day with family and friends. My son seemed to be getting better. My husband and I went on a date to celebrate our fourth wedding anniversary. When we left, rather than being excited about celebrating four amazing years together, I broke down and cried yet again. I told my husband how horrible I felt the night the air conditioning broke. I said, "I keep praying every night for God to help me be a better mom, a better wife, a better sister, and a better daughter, but I feel like it isn't working." At this difficult time in my life, I felt I just couldn't be a good person no matter how hard I tried. I was thinking that night, *Maybe my family would be better off without me. Maybe I am the problem.* I felt horrible because my bad moods had led to me snapping at people. I was crying often. There were times when I yelled and really felt like I was going to lose it. I know now the people who cared about us had only been trying to help, but some of the advice and comments "they" shared only made me feel like I was doing everything wrong. I felt like maybe I was the one who was causing all of the issues. Maybe I was making the wrong decisions for our family and for our kids.

My husband listened and was quite upset by what I was saying. It hurt him that I was hurting so badly. He didn't realize I was feeling that way. He said, "What I want you to do is stop praying about trying to be a better mom, wife, and person because you already are all of those things. Pray instead for God to help you stop being so hard on yourself. You are the greatest mom and wife and person already. I could never imagine anyone better." He also told me to stop caring what other people think and say, because I was a great mom and I did not need anyone else's approval. I was so thankful in that moment to have my husband. Looking back I realize I was not a horrible person, mom, wife, or anything. I was just going through a tough time and holding myself to way too high standards. Looking back, this conversation was the spark which would change my "self-talk" and give me a new outlook on life.

Overall, my son was doing better...that is until the night when he got a new fever of over 102 degrees. He was up throughout the night with a fever as high as 102.9. My poor little guy had been through enough. Luckily, it was just a virus. So, he had a hospital stay, X-rays, and two illnesses now, all within three weeks. I say luckily, but I actually felt we were pretty down on our luck.

When we got home from the doctor, my son kept grunting to show me he wanted to play with my daughter's snow globe. I sat him right in my arms at the kitchen table as my daughter was eating her dinner and flipped it over to show him how it snowed. He was loving it. I let go of it and let him hold it for one second. He was still right in my arms, and he dropped it less than two inches onto the kitchen table. The snow globe shattered. I immediately checked to make sure no glass was touching my son. Thank God no one was cut. I looked at the glass and it was as thin as a piece of toilet paper. I mean, really? Who makes a *Frozen*-themed snow globe, clearly meant for children, with glass this thin? It was bound to break. I had to put the sick, screaming baby down so that I could wipe and pick up the glass and vacuum, all while he screamed and while my daughter cried and repeated over and over how much she loved that snow globe.

On its own, this incident probably wouldn't be a big deal, but it was just one more thing. At this point, I thought emotionally, I couldn't go any lower in this low month. I had had it. I was keeping it together, barely, but I knew if one more thing happened, I would hit my breaking point. I don't know what would have happened if I did, because I had truly never felt this low before in my life. All I knew is it probably wouldn't be pretty...at all...and it may have involved me going to a mental hospital.

The bad luck continued and more things did happen. My son wasn't getting any better. We went back to the doctor and turned out he had an ear infection. Then, my daughter became sick again with a very high fever and cough. She had to start on an antibiotic for the second time. She starting having bronchospasms—enough to make her throw up, and enough to stain my carpet in our somewhat new home. The stain was so bad even the professional cleaners with the extremely loud machine—which woke up both of my sick children—could not get it out. My husband then backed into a coworker at work. Next, we lost our electricity the night before my son's surgery to rule out Hirschsprung's disease. We had no lights for over 48 hours. We had to throw out all of our food in the fridge and freezer and start fresh. Things just kept on going wrong, but somehow even though I felt so low before, I kept it together. I didn't end up checked into a mental hospital, at least not yet.

Choose Joy

I had felt we were destined for clouds, clouds ahead indefinitely, but for some reason I was okay. I knew that the sun would come out soon. It cannot possibly remain cloudy forever. I also realized while I sat around focusing on all the negative happening around me, I was missing out on happy and precious moments and experiences.

Right there in that low, I suddenly recognized I had taken a year off of work and the school year was basically done. Thank goodness I had decided to take another year off because if I had to go back at the end of the summer, I would have totally regretted all of the time spent frustrated and worried rather than enjoying this special time with my children.

In actuality, our worst-case scenario gave my husband and I wonderful one-on-one time with our son while we were in the hospital; one-on-one time where we literally could not be more than a couple feet away from him. As I thought about it, I started to see the good in this and I started to look at the hospital stay differently. For my son's whole life, he had to share time with his sister. This was really the first length of time he got 100 percent attention from us.

It wasn't just the time spent worrying during this difficult time I would have regretted. Since my son was born, I spent a lot of time dreading getting out of the house, worrying naps would be missed and the children's routine would be ruined, that I probably missed out on a lot of great moments. I decided from then on, I would start to enjoy the moment. I realized you cannot let your current situation—no matter how bad it seems, no matter how down you may feel—keep you from enjoying the good. I realized I needed to choose joy. I decided to stop waiting for things to get better and to stop saying, "When things start to get better, or when [insert event here] finally happens, I will be happier and begin enjoying life again." I knew if I kept this up, I would spend my whole life waiting for things to improve rather than looking for the good in the "now." I blinked and my daughter was three. I will blink again and she will be in kindergarten. This time is precious and it is time I will never get back.

Once I had this realization, things started to improve. Moving forward, I would expect tough things to happen, but I wouldn't allow those tough things to get in the way of enjoying life. So, if you find yourself at your ultimate low, know the sun will come out. In life, things can go from rough to great, but things can also go from good to bad or even from bad to worse. Always remember, life is not stagnant. Good will come soon. It would be impossible for it not to. In the meantime, try to enjoy life where you are. You don't want to miss out on precious time as you wait around for things to change.

The Turning Point

The sun did come out eventually. It may have started when I was staring at a pager waiting for my son to come out of his biopsy surgery. When they took our son back for the surgery, we were told we would be paged when they were finished. They told us to relax until it went off. I remember thinking, *Yeah, like that will happen. Relax, really?*

My husband and I took the pager and went to grab a coffee at the hospital Starbucks. As we were sitting there, it was so strange. Rather than the anxiety I was expecting, we both felt a calm come over us. We both just knew everything was going to be okay, and we were right. The surgery went well and our son woke up a happy boy. No tears at all, even after the anesthesia. It was unreal and an unexpected relief.

Soon after, our electricity came back, and we found out our son did not have Hirschsprung's disease. We would just need to continue to monitor his constipation and continue with constipation medications. We were so thankful our son did not have to go through more surgeries. Then, we were invited to a family member's beach house for the weekend. Of course, there were the typical challenges a family with children would have, like packing the entire house, traveling on five-hour car trips with children, giving multiple baths a day trying to clean off all of the sand, all four family members sleeping in the same room, being kicked in the face by your daughter and trying to be so quiet as not to wake up your son in the portable crib next to you, but all in all it was a delightful trip.

On the way home, after stopping at a restaurant and having a successful dinner (even with two tired, antsy children), both kids started screaming as loud as they could back and forth. Then, they laughed and laughed at each other. You may think it sounds horrible, all the screaming, but it was hilarious and adorable. We all ended up laughing together. My husband said, "You know, there aren't many moments in life when you feel so completely fulfilled, but this is one of those moments." It was so true. Everything simply felt better.

I honestly don't know if things really did start getting better, or if it was that I finally started to learn how to handle the downs better. I still had plenty of rough days. The everyday struggles continued, like a couple of days later, I had spent a large portion of the day getting the house back in order after the power outage. My level of frustration was pretty high after trying to manage this and take care of two toddlers at the same time. I started to mix up my ingredients for my pot pie and realized I didn't have the can of vegetables I needed. I scrounged some vegetables together. Something which was supposed to take no time at all starting taking forever. I noticed my son had a poopy diaper. As I changed him, he grabbed the diaper from under him and slung it across the room, poop and all. At the same time, my daughter yelled, "Mommy, I have to go potty." Of course. Fortunately, I had taught her how to move the stool and add the potty seat. I talked her through that process while cleaning up the mess. After we ate and I cleaned the kitchen, I went up to the playroom to find my children playing with their dad. My daughter was straddling his feet like he was a pony and yelling out, "Ride 'em toes" and my son, at only 16 months old, was straddling my husband's stomach and giggling so hard. It was one of those sweet moments you want stamped in your memory forever, and suddenly the day didn't seem so horrible. It seemed great. I am not sure if things truly started to improve, or just that I started being able to find joy in the midst of it all, but either way, it felt good.

That being said, the tough medical struggles continued. Soon after my son had his surgery, we switched to a new GI doctor. We loved our new doctor as we could tell he truly cared about our son and the issues he was experiencing. He explained everything to us in detail, which really helped ease our minds and eliminate a lot of worry. He referred us to a pulmonologist because he wasn't sure if the gasping was caused by the reflux in its entirety. He and the pulmonologist recommended a sleep study to make sure there were no major issues going on during his sleep. I don't think anything could have fully prepared us for a sleep study, especially for an 18-month-old.

As we walked into the office, we were met by a sleep technician. He was funny and great with my son. I filled out lots of paperwork including many questionnaires about my son's sleep habits. Then it was time to get him all hooked up. I swear there were thousands of cords. When the technician was all through, my son looked like the terminator. We actually helped our son get through it by telling him he was a super hero. The technician was shocked how well he handled the whole thing, especially at his age. There were stickers with so many cords coming out all over his back and stomach. He had stickers all over his head which were attached to wires. Then, his head was all wrapped up with gauze so he wouldn't touch the cords. It looked just like a helmet. He had monitors on his feet under his socks. He had belts around his stomach monitoring his breathing in and out. The worst part for him was the little tube going into his nostrils which monitored air flow in and out. He had to sleep all night with cords everywhere. I am not sure how, but for the most part, he seemed to sleep. Little did I know, he had actually woken at least 27 times that night. Although the experience was quite difficult, we found joy as we made it through with flying colors and we were so proud of our son. He was so tough and seemed to be able to handle anything.

After I had waited about a week and half following the sleep study, the results arrived in my mailbox. I started reading them and the words on the page made me terrified. It said my son was diagnosed with obstructive sleep apnea and periodic limb movement disorder (PLMD). Of course, the results arrived somehow before any doctor or medical professional had spoken with me about them. I remember waiting on pens and needles as I called the doctors multiple times and hoped to hear back. Finally, a nice positive, the results were favorable. The pulmonologist and ENT agreed the strange breathing was likely not an issue. The obstructive sleep apnea was mild and could be caused by something as simple as his adenoids being very large. The PLMD was nothing to worry about, but was likely caused by what we found to be low iron stores. He ended up taking an iron supplement for about six weeks. This seemed to cause more constipation, but we made it through and his iron stores went back up enough to stop for good.

It's All About Perspective

How did I make it through this tough month? I talked to a friend. I talked to my husband. I admitted how I was feeling and received comfort. I found my joy. I realized I needed to stop expecting things to run smoothly all of the time. Let's face it—things are just not going to be smooth when you have two toddlers running around. I learned there are always going to be rough patches. There are always going to be bumps. What matters is how we deal with them. Every time we get through a rough patch, we grow. I remember being really scared when I read the results of the sleep study, and thinking, *What if this is dangerous? What if this is serious? What if I had lost my son?* This made me rethink the way I was looking at things quite a bit. I realized I needed to appreciate the time I had with my children because no matter how scary this sounds, this time is not guaranteed. I try to remind myself that when I am having a bad day or during those inevitable moments when I feel like I might go off the deep end, that these moments are still a gift. We can't take them for granted.

My son had been through so much during his first two years. He had been to two GI doctors, an allergist, an ENT, a pulmonologist, and a pediatric surgeon. He had huge amounts of blood drawn from his arm five times. He had three surgeries including scopes with biopsies and ear tubes. He had a sleep study. He had been on more medication than I could even count. He had so many diet restrictions. He was stuck in a hospital for 72 hours on a feeding tube of medication for constipation. He had five X-rays including one with a barium enema. That is a lot for a little guy under two years old to handle.

Then after all of this, there it was again…the joy. We never did find out the exact cause behind my son's strange night gasping. It could have been because of his reflux, his adenoids being so large, his soy and milk intolerance, or it could have simply been his way of breathing. I think the sleep apnea, intolerance, constipation, and reflux were all intertwined and simply exacerbated each other. After all, we had our best nights when they were all in check. Fortunately, shortly after he turned two, these things significantly improved. Our prayers had been answered. He seemed to be growing out of it all, except for the constipation, but we win some and we lose some. We couldn't be more thankful. It was like a huge weight was lifted off of our shoulders. Everything was just better, and it was the best feeling in the world. It was like the joy of all joys.

Once again, I was shown how important it is to look for the positives in a situation. There were so many positives which came out of this time of anguish. I learned about my son's strength. The doctors kept saying how strong he was throughout everything he had been through. Because we went to the hospital, I was able to speak with a great doctor with similar personal experiences to us who gave us hope. I even ended up finding the best diaper rash ointment ever. I realized I had some true friends in my life who I knew I could always count on and a husband who stood by me even at my worst.

Somewhere in the middle of this difficult time, my husband and I put the kids down for a nap and had just sat down to relax a bit, maybe even watch a show or movie. I remember my daughter called out "Mama, Mama" from her room. I went up to lay with her for a few minutes until she was comfortable, then headed back downstairs. Not one minute later, my son called out "Mama" over and over again from his crib. My husband laughed and said, "Well, don't you feel loved?"

I laughed and responded, "Well, that is one way of looking at it."

It would have been easy in the moment to become frustrated because I didn't have even a moment to myself that day, but on the other hand, I sure am loved and that sure does mean a lot.

Steer Clear of Irrational Thinking

I learned we need to focus less on how we can be a better mom, wife, sister, daughter, person, and so on, and more on how not to be so hard on ourselves. I learned the only thing making me less of a good mom was allowing myself to question my abilities instead of feeling good about the mom I am. Nothing can bring a person down faster than feeling like they are a bad mom, or person, and it's just not true. It is irrational thinking. Thinking we are a bad mom or a bad wife, or whatever, is an irrational thought.

As a school counselor, I used to ask my middle school students to challenge their irrational thinking. I would give the example of, if you woke up today and said things like, "Oh, today is just going to be horrible. It's rainy, it's dreary, I know I will do horrible at school today" and you continue this type of thinking all day, how do you think your day will be? One hundred percent of students told me they would have a bad day. The opposite was also true. I would say, if you woke up today and said things like, "Today is going to be a great day. I am going to do my best, good things are going to happen to me today, I am going to work hard, and I'm going to try to enjoy myself" and continue this thinking all day, how do you think your day would be? One hundred percent told me it would be great. From this example, think how powerful our words can be. Our words can truly make our day great or do just the opposite.

I believe our thoughts affect our feelings which in turn affect our actions. So, if we are thinking negative thoughts, it will make us feel bad, and then we act according to those feelings. If we are using the irrational thought, "I am a horrible mom," we are going to feel sad, down, and maybe even angry. Then, when we are feeling sad and angry, we will be more likely to yell, overreact, or become easily frustrated. Our mood can actually impact our interactions with our children. This in turn reinforces our irrational thinking even more. Nothing can make us into a bad mom faster than believing we are a bad mom. It is a self-fulfilling prophecy, a never-ending circle. If we can continue to focus on the positive things we are doing instead of the negative, then we will continue to be the great moms and people we truly are.

The fact is we are not horrible moms. As parents, there are times we will feel guilty. We are going to mess up. We are going to make mistakes. We are going to have to make tough decisions, and we may not always make the right ones. The bottom line is, we are human. This is normal. This is okay. I bet we do way more things right than we do wrong. If we wrote down every single thing we did in a day, there would be so many more smiles than frowns, and so many more laughs than cries. There would be so many more positive things spoken than bad. There would be so much more fun than boredom, and most importantly, there would be lots and lots of love.

The more you practice picking out the positive, the more natural it will become. Someone once told me if you do something for 21 days, it will become a habit. I like to think about this when I am trying to make a change or do something challenging. If I can stick with it for 21 days, it will probably become second nature, like a habit. Go ahead, give it a try. Try to stay positive and block the negative "stinking thinking" for 21 days. See if it starts to become second nature for you.

Mistakes Are a Part of Life

If we truly believe there is something which would make us a better parent, we can't allow ourselves to feel bad about it. We just work on making a change. Maybe it is more self-control or patience, for example. I am sure we could all use more of that from time to time. We can work on ourselves without feeling down on ourselves. We should feel good about the fact we are trying to make things better.

I will never forget my second Mother's Day. I had a great day, that included my husband surprising me with donuts, some beautiful chalk drawings he did with the kids, and an amazing dinner, and we decided to watch a movie. It was one of those comedies about being a mom, but I remember I started bawling tears of joy at the end of the movie. One character told the mother—who had been really questioning herself as a parent—that she was blessed with those children for a reason. Basically, he was saying God knew what kind of parents we were going to be when we were blessed with children.

The mom in the movie seemed like a hot mess the whole time and she never felt she lived up to what the other great moms were doing, but the truth is, she was great in her own way and she really loved her children. It helped me see that we need to stop questioning ourselves and feeling so guilty each time we make a mistake. We need to stop comparing ourselves to other people. We need to appreciate the mom we are and what we have to offer, and just go on loving our kids with all our hearts. Believe it or not, our kids also learn when we make mistakes. They can learn how we deal with the mistakes and how we work through them. They can learn to apologize. They can learn how not to be so hard on themselves. They can learn persistence as we work on changing things for the better. These are all huge strengths. The bottom line is, I believe God would not bless us with children without equipping us with what we need to be their parents.

Tough Times Build Resilience
Not only did I learn a great deal from these tough times, but it

also helped me appreciate when times are good so much more than I had before. Sometimes, when everything is going well, we start to get comfortable. We might begin to take the good times for granted. Towards the end of this rough month, I started to focus less on the bad things which kept coming our way and started to focus more on—and fully appreciate—the moments which were great. Sometimes it takes the tough situations to change us the most for the better.

As a school counselor, I used to speak to my students a lot about resilience, the ability to bounce back. Not everyone has or will develop this quality. It takes tough times and challenges to build resilience. It is not a quality we are simply born with. Times like these can be really difficult, but they can also teach us how to bounce back if we handle them appropriately. This resilience can help us work through tough situations which are sure to occur in the future. No matter how tough things seem to get, trials and tribulations can help shape us into the people we are supposed to be.

And when we think we are finally getting this parenting thing down, don't forget that still doesn't mean we are perfect. There will still be tough times. We will still make mistakes and this is okay. When these setbacks occur, we need to pick ourselves up and try again. We have to focus on the progress we make rather than the steps we take back. We are not perfect. We never will be. The more we put ourselves down, the harder it is going to be to pick ourselves back up and be the person we are hoping to be in the first place.

Live in the Present

I found it helps me not to dwell on what happened yesterday or worry about what is coming. The more I remain in the present, the easier things seem and the more I enjoy those regular day-to-day moments. I remember reading a quote in my daily devotion one day, "You can't change yesterday. Tomorrow's not here yet. All you have is today (*Daughters of the King Daily Devotionals 2.0*)." All you have is today. It is a powerful, but true statement. Now, each day that I have, I try to choose joy. It really is our choice. We can choose to remain joyful no matter what comes our way. We can try to let our mistakes and the tough things go, or we can choose to hold onto those things and let them define us. Sometimes when I make a mistake, it's like I can't let myself off the hook. It's as if I need someone else to do it, someone else to tell me I'm still a good mother. Usually, it ends up being my husband as I vent to him. The truth is, we don't need to have someone let us off the hook. We are great parents— not perfect though, but no one is. If we find ourselves stuck in yesterday, worrying about tomorrow, or simply in a bad mood, sometimes we just need to stop, let it go, take a moment, and remind ourselves we can choose joy.

When in doubt, show your kids love. Love is what matters most. One day I was asking myself as I was tickling and kissing my daughter and son all over and they were laughing and laughing, *Is there such a thing as kissing and hugging and telling your kids you love them too much?* No, I don't think so. Live each day like it is your last and place as many hugs and kisses upon your kids as you can. Nothing made this clearer for me than when my dear friend and fellow mother passed away suddenly. This friend loved her child so much and everyone could see it. I learned how important it is to make sure that at the end of each day, before my kids go to sleep, I tell them how much I love them. If one thing is for certain, my children will go to sleep knowing how loved they are. At the end of the day, no matter how bad it is, if you have loved and loved on your child, then you are winning, I promise. So, keep up the great work! Remember, as Mother Teresa would say, "If you want to change the world, go home and love your family."

ABOUT THE AUTHOR

Lauren Jumrukovski is a licensed pre-k through 12 school counselor turned stay-at-home mom and author. She holds a B.S. in psychology (which she earned along with a minor in sociology), and a master's degree in counselor education. She truly believes parents are the experts at raising their own children. She has built her brand around challenging what "they say," and believes in the power of intuitive parenting. She motivates parents to stop questioning themselves, to realize there is no one right way to parent, and to go with their gut. After all, parents know best.

Lauren's favorite things include writing, baking, getting creative, traveling, and soaking up the sweet moments with her kids. Lauren resides in central Virginia with her husband, three children, and dog, Daisy. For more information and to check out her parenting blog, visit www.theysayparenting.com.

ACKNOWLEDGMENTS

Thank you to my wonderful team at Mascot Books. I will be forever grateful for your help in making my dream a reality.

Thank you to my first readers, who gave me confidence: Maria, Mom, Ilija.

To my children, I am so thankful that I get to be your mommy. You make every day an adventure. Loving you gives me more happiness than anything else.

Thank you to my sweet friends who told me I wasn't crazy when I said I wanted to write a book, and who provided me encouragement every time I questioned myself.

Thank you to my husband. Honestly, I could not ask for a better supporter. Thank you for all the extra me-time you made sure I had in order to write, for believing in me, and for always supporting my dream. Thank you for being okay with me putting our whole life on paper in order to make a difference in someone else's life.

Thank you to my family for your unconditional love. Thank you to my parents who somehow and somewhere along the way planted this seed of motivation and determination. You have guided me into who I have become. To my sisters, thank you for putting up with me, for your praise, and for cheering me on.

Thank you to my mother-in-law, father-in-law, and sister-in-law for your constant encouragement, unwavering support, for continuously believing in me, and for helping me believe I could do this.

Thank you all for being my biggest fans! Together, you guys have helped make my dream come true!